Latter★day
Patriots

Latter★day Patriots

Nine Mormon Families and Their
Revolutionary War Heritage

Gene Allred Sessions

Published by Deseret Book Company
in cooperation with the Historical
Department of The Church of Jesus
Christ of Latter-day Saints
Salt Lake City, Utah
1975

*To
my children,
Ami and Reed*

Illustrations

Maps

Foreword

When thinking of their heritage, Latter-day Saints appropriately dwell on the stirring scenes of Mormon history—western
New York in the 1820s, Ohio and Missouri in the 1830s, Nauvoo and
the trek across the Plains in the 1840s, and the Great Basin in the last
half of the nineteenth century. But Latter-day Saints in the United
States are partakers of a much larger inheritance that has its roots
deep in the soil of early America. The Prophet Joseph Smith, for
example, had ancestors who came on the *Mayflower;* both of his
grandfathers and his paternal great-grandfather served as soldiers in
the American Revolution. Thus, many members of The Church of
Jesus Christ of Latter-day Saints have a distinct and extensive Revolutionary War heritage—a heritage sometimes obscured by the important events accompanying the establishment of the Church in
western New York State in 1830. This volume, through the medium
of nine individual histories of colorful Latter-day Saints and their
ancestors, illuminates some of the breadth of our American heritage
while telling the story of Mormonism as it affected the lives of a few
descendants of participants in the Revolution.

It is important that American Latter-day Saints realize that in
recent years the Church has become an international organization
with worldwide goals. While chauvinism has no place among
Latter-day Saints, real patriotism has always been a keystone to the

faithful. President J. Reuben Clark, Jr., liked to explain his success as a diplomat by referring to his attitude that "the other fellow thinks just as much of his country as you do of yours." But while recognizing that the Church is not nationalistic, we can still appreciate the United States as a cradle of the Restoration. As the following sketches demonstrate, affection for this land and a recollection of sacrifice in the war for independence were part of the teachings embraced by several persons prominent in the Latter-day Saint movement.

There is still another purpose for a book such as this. Men and women are to a large degree what their families have made them. Despite the objections of some critics, there is validity to a view of history that looks to the structure of kinship as a determinant in the course of events. It is clear that the experiences of the home, for good or ill, have had a major impact upon the life of every human being. The stories and traditions transmitted around the hearth for generations have a profound effect upon the family member, giving him a self-concept that cannot be quantified. How much Joseph Smith gained from his grandfathers' tales of the revolutionary epoch will never be known, but by his own words we may know that he remembered, and remembering, believed things about himself and his people that influenced the course of Latter-day Saint history.

As we planned this book, we were pleased to have on our staff in the Historical Department of the Church Gene Allred Sessions, a historian well read in the American Revolution, who himself comes from families having origins deep in both American and Mormon history. Using the abundant records in the Church Archives, Dr. Sessions has produced a series of essays that, while they make no claim to being original scholarly contributions to the literature about the Revolution or about Latter-day Saints, still manage to convey a great deal about both American and Mormon history. A worthy reminder of the congruence of American ideals and Mormon ideals, this series of essays enlightens while it entertains.

Leonard J. Arrington

Preface

As perhaps no other event in history, the American Revolution has stirred the hearts of the American people. Its ideals and its heroes have become inseparable parts of the image Americans have of the United States as it is and as it ought to be. American members of The Church of Jesus Christ of Latter-day Saints have characteristically participated in a century and a half of Fourth of July celebrations and other patriotic pageantry with considerable enthusiasm. Even during periods of stress between the Mormon people and the government in Washington, Latter day Saints have cheered the symbols of the Revolution, condemning in their troubles not the system it projected but the occasional corrupters of that system.

The reasons for this persevering patriotism have eluded persistent searchers and probably will continue to do so. This volume suggests a partial explanation and yet an obvious one: Mormons are no less partakers of the heritage from the revolutionary years than are other Americans. They, like most Americans, are prone to nebulous idealism or on occasion to drawing selectively from the rich but ambiguous revolutionary legacy. But in one specific respect the Mormon leaders sought to magnify this heritage through a glass of doctrine—that is, in their repeated efforts to inspire a profound allegiance to the Declaration of Independence and the Constitution of the United States as inspired documents.

Beyond these thoughts, this book presents no thesis. The author pretends no scholarly dissertation upon the nuances of Latter-day Saints' patriotism. This book is designed rather to teach some history in an interesting setting, to provide Latter-day Saints with a broader understanding of what kind of people they have become, and why.

Each chapter covers basically the same period of time—from the Revolutionary War to the present—and tells in each instance a different part of the story of the war and of the Mormon experience in the succeeding years. The individuals were selected for the study on the bases of their ancestors' experiences in the war and of their own part in the growth and development of the Church. The nine cases, therefore, involve many of the significant topics of both revolutionary and Mormon history loosely woven together into a fabric of people, their kinship, and their time. But the main consideration in preparing this volume was that it should be an enjoyable experience for the reader, and at the same time an educational one.

In addition to thanking the several family members who provided assistance in the preparation of the various essays in the book, the author wishes to express his gratitude for the help of numerous others. Of particular value were the careful readings of the manuscript and valuable suggestions of his colleagues in the Historical Department, K. Haybron Adams, James B. Allen, Leonard J. Arrington, Maureen Ursenbach Beecher, Davis Bitton, and Ronald G. Watt. Jill Mulvay, Dean L. May, Bruce D. Blumell, and William G. Hartley also made useful comments on portions of the book that fell within the purview of their scholarly interests. Christine Croft Waters did some groundbreaking research on the project, while Debbie Lilenquist and Valerie Christensen Searle lent their considerable talents to the final preparation of the typescript. The author is especially indebted to the wisdom and advice of Dean C. Jessee and Glen M. Leonard with regard to editing and final publication procedures, and to Shari Anderson, Linda Jones, William G. Hartley, and K. Haybron Adams for their work in procuring illustrations for the volume. As usual, Keith Montague and his associates handled the design and graphics with excellence.

The author, of course, assumes total responsibility for the contents of this book, praiseworthy or otherwise.

I love that Flag.—When in my childish glee,
A prattling girl upon my Grandsire's knee,
I heard him tell strange tales, with valor rife—
How that same Flag was bought with blood and life;
And his tall form seemed taller, when he said,
"My child, for that, your Grandpa fought and bled."
My young heart felt, that every scar he wore,
Caused him to love that banner more and more.

I caught the fire, and, as in years I grew,
I loved that Flag—I loved my country too:
My bosom swell'd with pride, to think my birth
Was on this highly favor'd spot of earth.

There came a time, I shall remember well—
Beneath the "Stars and Stripes" we could not dwell:
We had to flee: but in our hasty flight,
We grasped the Flag, with more than mortal might;
Resolved, that, though our foes should us bereave
Of home and wealth, our Flag, we would not leave.
We took the Flag, and journeying to the West,
We wore its motto graven on each breast.

(From "My Own—My Country's Flag,"
by Eliza R. Snow, 1861.)

Joseph Smith, Jr.:
An American Prophet

On December 16, 1833, the young American prophet, Joseph Smith, Jr., recorded a lengthy revelation from the Lord which, among other things, declared that "it is not right that any man should be in bondage one to another. And for this purpose have I established the Constitution of this land, by the hands of wise men whom I raised up unto this very purpose, and redeemed the land by the shedding of blood."[1] Canonized as latter-day scripture, this passage and related others have taught Mormons that the birth of American independence and the subsequent establishment of the United States under the maxims of the Constitution were wrought by divine power, that God himself had presided over the revolutionary struggle and had ordained the American system.[2] The Book of Mormon proclaimed further that the very land of the American continent had been blessed for the growth of liberty, and that God had preserved it as the promised land of freedom, where the kingdom of God could take root and receive nourishment as a free institution in a world otherwise fraught with tyranny and intolerance.[3] Thus for members of The Church of Jesus Christ of Latter-day Saints the socio-political ideals of the American Revolution became inseparably connected with their spiritual creed.

Throughout the nineteenth century, and in spite of the abuse they suffered first by the neglect of the federal government and then

1

directly at its hands, the Mormons clung to their belief in the divine foundation of American laws and traditions. Indeed, they saw their religion and their way of life in much the same way the Patriots of 1776 had looked upon their course. They were preserving and expanding upon the best principles of the revolutionary ideal just as the rebellious colonists believed they were retaining the beneficial aspects of the British system. The Mormons blamed the corruption and unrighteousness of the officials within the American system for the persecutions and indignities they were suffering within it. Thus the concerted persecutions of the nineteenth century did not prevent them from thinking of themselves as dedicated upholders of the Constitution and the principles of the American Revolution—equality, liberty, and human rights.

During their all too brief tutelage at the feet of the Prophet in the 1830s and 1840s, Mormons had imbibed richly of Joseph's own sense of place in the American pageant. Yet if they could separate him from his mantle in any way, it was in the realm of daily politics. "I am above the kingdoms of the world," he once said. ". . . The Lord has not given me a revelation concerning politics. I have not asked Him for one."[4] But he did not deny inspiration in the realm of political ideals and expounded broadly on the Constitution and upon justice. In current affairs, he was never loathe to make his political views known, though emphasizing the worldly origins of these views.

As secular scholars have categorized Mormonism in its temporal setting of frontier religion, so they have explained Joseph Smith as a product of the New England Yankee setting.[5] In the purely political sense, Joseph may have agreed: "It is a love of liberty which inspires my soul—civil and religious liberty to the whole of the human race. Love of liberty was diffused into my soul by my grandfathers while they dandled me on their knees. . . ."[6] The inheritance of the spirit of '76 was very real to the Prophet—as real as his grandfathers' knees.

The roots of Joseph's family tree plunged deeply into the primordial soil of America. Seven of his progenitors arrived on the *Mayflower;* three signed the famous Compact, a significant step in the growth of the American concept of government. One of these, John Howland, ancestor of Joseph's mother, Lucy Mack Smith, was the last survivor of the *Mayflower* voyage at the time of his death. The first of the Prophet's Smith family to arrive, however, came to

2

Boston in 1638 from Willoughby, Lincolnshire, England, at the age of twelve. Robert Smith grew to manhood in Boston but eventually acquired a 200-acre farm in nearby Boxford, which overlapped into the township of Topsfield. There his son Samuel built a home, and there the next three generations of Smiths were born.[7] It was Robert's grandson Samuel Smith, Jr., who held the greatest official prominence among the Prophet's progenitors, holding at various times nearly a dozen different elective and appointive offices in Topsfield, ranging from grand juryman and road supervisor to town clerk and delegate to the provincial congress.[8] "He was one of the most prominent citizens of Topsfield. The greater part of his life was spent in the service of the people."[9]

With the approach of the Revolution, Samuel numbered himself among the most ardent patriots in the Massachusetts colony. He served on virtually every local committee that supported resistance and then rebellion in the decade prior to 1776. Most dramatically, he became chairman of the Topsfield Tea Committee formed to bolster a similar Boston group in its revolt against the inflammatory Tea Act and its resultant Tea Party of December 16, 1773. But Samuel was not content with only a civilian role in the Great Adventure, and in July 1780, at the age of sixty-six, he joined a regiment raised in Essex County to reinforce the Continental Army. As long-time captain of militia, Samuel Smith served as an officer for some three and a half months. He died five years later, eulogized as a "sincere friend to the liberties of the country," having participated fully in the birth of the Republic.[10]

The Prophet's paternal grandfather, Asael (Asahel) Smith, was born March 7, 1744, in Topsfield. He later moved to a place near Windham, New Hampshire, married, and established a reputation as a religious nonconformist espousing the Universalist views of John Murphy.[11] By the time of the Revolution, Asael was also known for his physical prowess, supposedly able to handle "with ease two ordinary men."[12] In line with this strength and independence of character, and with the activities of his father, Samuel, he was among the first Americans to enlist in the patriot cause at arms. With three of his wife's brothers,[13] he joined a New Hampshire regiment mustered to fortify the northern frontier in the summer of 1776. Historians have compared with Valley Forge the campaign in which Asael participated through the next fall and winter. Few died in combat, but more than five thousand American

Samuel Smith was chairman of the Topsfield Tea Committee formed to support a similar Boston group which was responsible for the "Boston Tea Party" (Painting by Harold Von Schmidt, The John Hancock Mutual Life Insurance Company)

perished of "pestilence, want, and exposure."[14] Asael himself never fully recovered from the rigors of his service to the Revolution.[15]

Following his discharge, Asael continued to live in New Hampshire, where his family eventually grew to include eleven children, the second son of which was Joseph Smith, Sr. But in 1785, on the death of his father, Asael returned to the family estate at Topsfield to live out his days.[16] As his famous grandson later noted, he never forgot the revolutionary experience and its meaning. He believed that the blow for American independence had struck Daniel's "stone cut out of a mountain without hands" that would smash the image representing "monarchical and ecclesiastical tyranny." God, he wrote further in 1793, "conducted us through a glorious Revolution and has brought us into the promised land of peace and liberty; and I believe that He is about to bring all the world in the same beatitude in His own time and way; which, although His way appear never so inconsistant to our blind reason, yet may be perfectly consistant to our signs."[17] In 1799, he again revealed his regard for the fruits of the revolutionary age in his will:

"Bless God that you live in a land of liberty, and bear yourselves dutifully and consciably towards the authority under which you live. See God's providence in the appointment of the Federal Constitution, and hold union and order precious jewels."[18] Although lacking in sound documentation and possibly the product of family lore, one final comment of Asael Smith may be pertinent to our discussion: "It has been borne in upon my soul that one of my descendants will promulgate a work to revolutionize the world of religious faith."[19]

Ironically enough, Asael Smith died in 1830, the year his grandson, Joseph, officially proclaimed the restoration of the gospel of Jesus Christ with the organization of His church again on the earth. It was said that Asael, though never baptized, accepted the mission of his descendant and thrilled in the fulfillment of his earlier prediction.[20]

The other "grandfather's knee" belonged to Solomon Mack, father of Joseph's mother, Lucy. Born at Lyme, Connecticut, on September 15, 1732, he was the son of a Congregational minister. Solomon's heritage as a patriot extended not only to the Revolution but through the French and Indian War (1754-63). It was actually in the earlier conflict, which the historian George Bancroft called the first phase of the Revolution, that Solomon experienced some of his most harrowing service. In all he served for six years. He narrowly escaped death several times, once as he participated in a fierce struggle near Fort Ticonderoga on Lake Champlain in 1754.[21] Between wars, he married and pioneered in the "back country" of Connecticut,[22] and in 1773 moved finally to New Hampshire.[23] At the outbreak of the Revolution, Solomon manufactured saltpeter for the Patriot army prior to his enlistment in the militia. After duty as a freighter and brief service in an artillery company, he was injured severely while felling trees, but he soon recovered and, with his two sons, Jason and Stephen, shipped aboard an American privateer.[24]

After the war, Solomon made a few commercial voyages and then returned to his family in the township of Gilsum, New Hampshire. Stephen Mack had settled in Tunbridge, Vermont, and there, while visiting her brother, Lucy Mack met Joseph Smith, Sr.[25] The parentage of the American Prophet thus came together, both from the loins of patriots of 1776 who would "dandle" their grandchildren on their knees to instill in them the "love of liberty."[26] But the Revolution had more than philosophical and folkloric effect

5

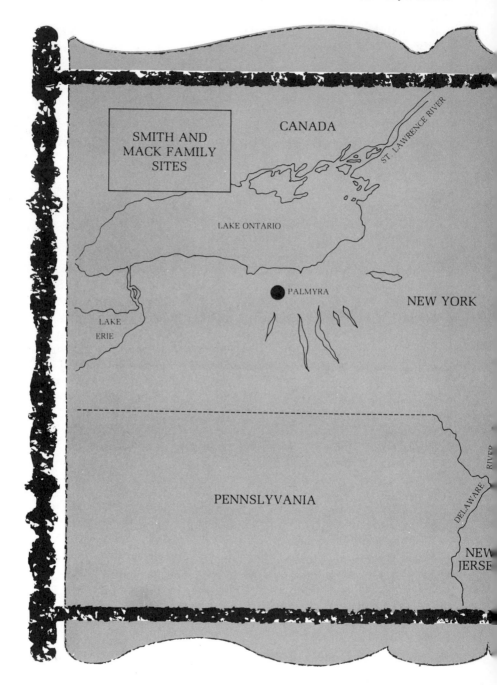

SMITH AND
MACK FAMILY
SITES

CANADA

ST. LAWRENCE RIVER

LAKE ONTARIO

PALMYRA

NEW YORK

LAKE
ERIE

PENNSLYVANIA

DELAWARE RIVER

NEW
JERSE

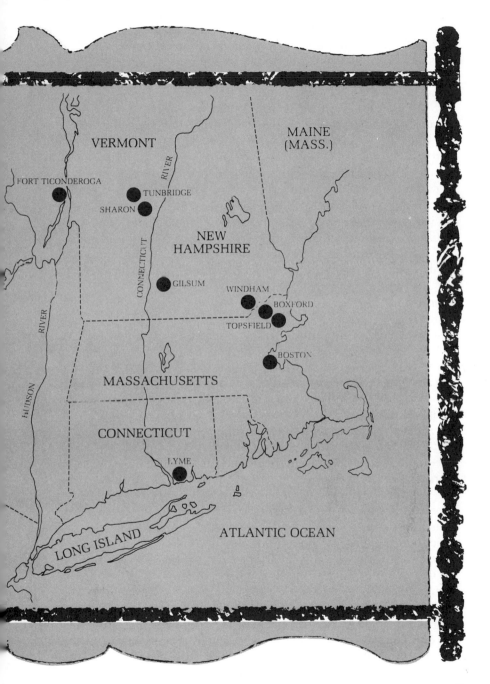

upon the course of the Restoration, for Joseph and Lucy soon partook of the new nation's bumptious spirit of expansion.[27] They consequently took their young family into the Genesee country of western New York where the first events of the Restoration took place through the instrumentality of their son Joseph.

It is not the purpose of this chapter to produce a biography of the enigmatic Mormon Prophet. His life of less than four decades has been an immense challenge to biographers for a hundred and thirty years. Indeed, to date and despite notably ambitious efforts, no man knows his history.[28] Moreover, it is not within our purview to analyze extensively Joseph's political philosophy,[29] nor do we wish to overemphasize the "Americanness" of Mormonism, neglecting its worldwide goals and activities. But the United States was the fertile ground into which Mormonism sank its roots; the Revolution and the Constitution were necessary harrows in the hand of the Lord to cultivate that ground for the sowing of the Restoration.

In fulfilling his turbulent ecclesiastical mission, Joseph Smith often found himself, by desire or otherwise, in situations that required him to search deeply for his own foundations of political and legal philosophy. In addition to his constantly changing role as de facto ruler of a dynamic people, he was placed on trial numerous times, often for his life, and at other times he was denied due process and suffered consequent punishment at the hands of mobs and even of those who were sworn to uphold the enlightened system of laws born during the revolutionary epoch.

His own unhappy ordeal was only precursory to that which his people would undergo for several decades after his murder in 1844. Persecution in the United States continually threatened to deprive Mormons in the nineteenth century of each of the Enlightenment's three natural rights—life, liberty, and property. Indeed, Joseph himself suffered ultimately the loss of all three despite conscientious and persistent appeals for protection under the Constitution, which had supposedly codified those rights into an inviolable and sacred compact. As a result, the Prophet found himself in the distracting role of political philosopher more often than he may have wished.

Joseph believed firmly in the concept of natural law. The primary article of that natural law in Joseph's mind was also the keystone of Mormon theology—free agency. For example, incensed at the expulsion of the Missouri Saints from their homes in the

8

winter of 1833-34, Joseph wrote: "We are not disposed, had we the power, to deprive any one of exercising that free independence of mind which heaven has so graciously bestowed upon the human family as one of its choicest gifts."[30] Further, he believed that all worthy law was designed to uphold that great principle, for God "has taught man that law is necessary in order to govern and regulate his own immediate interest and welfare; for this reason, that law is beneficial to promote peace and happiness among men."[31]

The Lord, reasoned Joseph, had established all good, including good law. "If law is good, then law, or the principle of it emanated from God. . . . Consequently, then, he was the first Author of law, or the principle of it, to mankind."[32] The language of this letter indicated a hesitancy to deny the possibility of bad laws emerging under the auspices of a good system. It was this idea that would sustain the Saints through another seventy or eighty years of difficulty with government in the United States: that the Constitution was certainly inspired, but that fact did not prevent corrupt men from distorting its good principles in the course of making and enforcing law to the benefit of their evil designs. No matter how perfect and divine the system, persecution such as the Saints were suffering would always be possible as long as those administering the system refused to receive guidance from its "God-sent" provisions, or those assuring man's natural rights.

"It is one of the first principles of my life," Joseph said nearly ten years later, "and one that I have cultivated from my childhood, having been taught it by my father, to allow every one the liberty of conscience."[33] The Prophet was concerned that the Constitution did not seem to protect the right to that liberty of conscience for a weak or unpopular minority. He would seek an expansion of the document's interpretation to prevent a people such as the Mormons from suffering revocation of its natural rights at the hands of a local majority. In short, the concept of the protection of minority rights by the federal government such as gained fruition a century later was within the long vision of the Prophet:

I am the greatest advocate of the Constitution of the United States there is on earth. In my feelings I am always ready to die for the protection of the weak and oppressed in their just rights. The only fault I find with the Constitution is, it is not broad enough to cover the whole ground.

Although it provides that all men shall enjoy religious

freedom, yet it does not provide the manner by which that freedom can be preserved, nor for the punishment of Government officers who refuse to protect the people in their religious rights, or punish those mobs, states, or communities who interfere with the rights of the people on account of their religion. Its sentiments are good, but it provides no means of enforcing them. It has but this one fault. Under its provision, a man or a people who are able to protect themselves can get along well enough; but those who have the misfortune to be weak or unpopular are left to the merciless rage of popular fury.[34]

On the other hand, Joseph Smith had always believed that the American system, created with blood and the hand of God, ought to be an effective guarantor of human rights, despite its apparent failure to protect the Saints and other minorities. The climactic event of the Mormon experience in Missouri during the 1830s was the surrender at Far West of Joseph and several other leaders of the Church following an actual attack on the Saints by the militia forces of the state. Governor Lilburn W. Boggs had consistently sided with the "old settlers" in their representations against the Latter-day Saints. By the end of October 1838, Missouri troops, acting under the governor's order that the Mormons be either driven from the state or exterminated, had pushed the disciples of Joseph into defensive positions at Far West. Skirmishes in the countryside had killed several, including David W. Patten, president of the Quorum of the Twelve. Then, on Tuesday, October 30, a mob-militia unit descended upon the Mormon settlement at Haun's Mill and murdered seventeen people. News of this event shocked the young American Prophet. His people were being slaughtered within the nation whose capstone had been dedicated to liberty and the protection of the innocent. With a heavy heart, he agreed the next day, October 31, to place himself in the hands of the militia in order to prevent a more devastating massacre at the refugee-swollen village of Far West.[35]

The Prophet Joseph, Sidney Rigdon, Lyman Wight, Parley P. Pratt, and George W. Robinson were marched to the enemy encampment, where they were placed under heavy guard and required to lie in the open air through the night while being subjected to continual abuse from their captors and the downpour of a cold rain. The next morning they were joined by Hyrum Smith and Amasa Lyman, who had also been captured. The Mormons had

10

grounded their weapons at Far West and were now suffering rapine pillage at the hands of the Missourians.

During the night of November 1, the Prophet and his fellow prisoners were tried by court-martial, convicted of some unknown crime, and sentenced to be shot the next morning as an example to their people. Consequently, General Samuel D. Lucas, commander of the militia at Far West, ordered his subordinate, Brigadier General Alexander W. Doniphan, to "take Joseph Smith and the other prisoners into the public square of Far West, and shoot them at 9 o'clock tomorrow morning." Doniphan, incensed at the total lack of justice in the affair, immediately replied, "It is cold-blooded murder. I will not obey your order. My brigade shall march for Liberty tomorrow morning, at 8 o'clock; and if you execute these men, I will hold you responsible before an earthly tribunal, so help me God." In the midst of shameful evasion of the American ideal, a courageous man, a true patriot, prevailed, and the lives of the brethren were preserved. Lucas, realizing that his order had been issued on shaky grounds, heeded Doniphan's warning and sent Joseph and the others in chains to Independence. They were then jailed at Richmond to await trial. Following their convictions for "treason," they were taken to Liberty, where they were imprisoned for an indefinite term. Back in Far West, militia General John B. Clark had told the Saints that they would never see the faces of their leaders again, "for their fate is fixed—their die is cast—their doom is sealed."[36]

Through the winter of 1838-39, the American Prophet, having been denied the justice prescribed under the maxims of the American ideal, suffered the agonies of imprisonment in the dank jailhouse at Liberty, Missouri. But as life returned to the countryside with spring, so did new energy and vibrance to the indomitable young Prophet. Among his first thoughts as his spirits began to rise were meditations upon the nature of the American system, which, in spite of all he and his followers had suffered under it, he continued to believe was founded "in the wisdom of God." Writing to the Saints, now settling in Illinois, he proclaimed that "the Constitution of the United States is a glorious standard. . . . It is a heavenly banner; it is to all those who are privileged with the sweets of its liberty, like the cooling shades and refreshing waters of a great rock in a thirsty and weary land. It is like a great tree under whose branches men from every clime can be shielded from the burning rays of the sun."[37]

This profound and consistent allegiance to the ideals of the American Revolution is one of the most remarkable elements in the life of Joseph Smith. So great was his sense of patriotism that even his disciples who were born and raised abroad quickly adopted the loyalty of the Prophet to his heritage. John Taylor, a British immigrant, looked "back to the time when this nation was under the iron rule of Great Britain, and groaned under the power, tyranny, and oppression of that powerful nation. We trace with delight the name of a Washington, a Jefferson, a LaFayette, and an Adams, in whose bosoms burned the spark of liberty."[38] In the face of the indignities they suffered, and at the inspiration of their prophet-leader, the Saints also prayed "that the spirit that burned in the bosoms of the patriots of '76 may fire the souls of their descendants. . . ."[39] And when the need arose, Joseph himself could appeal to the "spirit of '76" as when he told the people to let it "burn in their bosoms, and when the occasion requires, say little, but act; and when the mob comes, mow a hole through them."[40]

In April 1839 the Prophet and his companions were taken from Liberty Jail ostensibly for transfer to another prison, but on the evening of April 15 the guards accompanying them became intoxicated and the Mormon leaders escaped. It is possible that they were allowed to slip away on purpose so that the Missourians would no longer have to deal with the problem of their presence under such shameful legal proceedings.[41] Joseph, in explaining his reasons for the escape, cited a desire to "again take our stand among a people in whose bosoms dwell those feelings of republicanism and liberty which gave rise to our nation."[42] Seven days later, after traveling on the back ways mostly by night, Joseph Smith arrived at Quincy, Illinois, for a joyful reunion with his family and friends.

For the next six months the Prophet directed the building of a new settlement for the Saints on a bend of the Mississippi River in Hancock County, Illinois. Under his direct leadership the Church quickly recovered from the nearly devastating Missouri experience, and by the end of the summer of 1839 it had regained its momentum. True to his conviction that the United States government would be anxious to redress the grievances of the Latter-day Saints against the Missourians who had denied them their basic rights, Joseph Smith determined to go himself to Washington, D.C., in an attempt to lay before Congress the plight of his afflicted people.[43]

12

On October 29, 1839, almost a year after the surrender at Far West, the Prophet and three companions left for the East. As they crossed the Appalachian Mountains on their way into Washington, the driver of the coach stopped at a tavern for a drink and the horses bolted, running down a hill at full speed. A woman passenger immediately stood and attempted to throw her infant from the coach, but Joseph restrained her and further attempted to calm the other travelers. Opening the door, he managed to climb into the coachman's seat and to rein up the horses. When the excitement had passed, the passengers, among them some Congressmen, thanked Joseph profusely, praising him for his "daring and heroic deed." They began to discuss the possibility of mentioning the incident in Congress. Possibly, Joseph thought, "they would reward such conduct by some public act," which could accrue to the benefit of his mission, "but on inquiring my name, to mention the author of their safety, and finding it to be Joseph Smith the 'Mormon Prophet,' as they called me, I heard no more of their praise, gratitude, or reward."[44] With that adventure as a portentous prologue, Joseph arrived in Washington on the morning of November 28, 1839, to begin his work in the forums of the American government.[45]

On the morning following their arrival, Joseph Smith and Elias Higbee went to the White House to see President Martin Van Buren. Upon hearing their story, the President looked at them "with a kind of half frown," and indicated that he could do nothing for them without incurring the wrath of the entire state of Missouri. The two continued to press him, however, and before they left Van Buren had agreed to reconsider their problem and indicated his sympathy for the Latter-day Saints. The Prophet also took the opportunity to tell the President about the Restoration. "Suffice it to say," the Mormons reported to Nauvoo, "he has got our testimony."[46]

They managed to gain the sponsorship of the Illinois delegation and thereafter presented their petition and memorial to several members of both houses of Congress who seemed favorably disposed. After writing to Nauvoo for affidavits to back Mormon claims, Brothers Smith and Higbee departed for Philadelphia on December 21. They spent Christmas there among some Saints, stayed about a week, and then returned to Washington. On February 5, 1840, the Prophet preached a sermon that was attended by a newspaperman from New York, Mathew S. Davis, who subsequently wrote of his impressions of Joseph Smith to his wife,

Mary. Davis reported the sermon in detail, hoping to satisfy his wife's curiosity. "Joe Smith," he reported, "is a plain, sensible, strong minded man. Everything he says, is said in a manner to leave an impression that he is sincere. There is no levity, no fanaticism, no want of dignity in his deportment. He is . . . above the middle stature, and what you ladies would call a very good looking man." Davis was moved by what he saw and heard. "I have changed my opinion of the Mormons," he wrote. "They are an injured and much-abused people."[47]

Unfortunately, most persons of influence in Washington had little time to notice the Prophet in their midst. The President and the Vice President, John C. Calhoun, granted him interviews but made it clear that they valued the vote of Missouri more than the "just cause" of the Latter-day Saints. "I became satisfied," said Joseph, "there was little use for me to tarry, to press the just claims of the Saints on the consideration of the President or Congress."[48] Early in February, he returned to the West.

The history of the Prophet over the next four years brought to Joseph Smith the same stature in temporal affairs that his calling as prophet had brought to his spiritual attainment. He became mayor of the largest city in the state of Illinois, which his people raised from the soaked ground of the river bank on the power of faith and determination. He organized a capable military force, the Nauvoo Legion, under the powers granted him by the legislature of the state, and became its commanding officer with the brevet of lieutenant general. The Church that he had founded a decade before and that had endured the severest persecution across half a continent thrived under his leadership. By the early days of 1844, the thirty-eight-year-old religious leader was ready for a more heady adventure. He decided to run for President of the United States in order to give his views on government and the positions of the Saints a chance to be heard.

Although Joseph may not have entertained a hope of victory in the presidential election of 1844, he demonstrated during the course of his short-lived campaign two important elements of his latter-day patriotism. First, no matter how serious the difficulties he and the Mormons had had with the government, he was determined to carry forth his mission within the confines of the American system. He had no desire to rebel or to eschew the allegiance to the United States of America he had learned while sitting upon the knees of his

Patriot grandfathers. In addition, Joseph Smith had a clearly defined set of principles in his mind with which he believed the inequities of the government could be corrected. His platform, officially titled "Views of the Powers and Policy of the Government of the United States," which he signed February 7, 1844, certainly reflected his political ideology and is truly a remarkable document.[49]

Joseph Smith based his political thought upon the ideal of equal rights as outlined in the Constitution. For him and his true disciples there could be no room for either bigotry or introverted self-interest. "Unity is power," he believed, and without the protection of equal rights, unity, hence the stability of government, was impossible: "Great Britain surely lacked the laudable humanity and fostering clemency to grant . . . a just plan of union; but the sentiment remains, like the land that honored its birth, as a pattern for wise men *to study the convenience of the people more than the comfort of the cabinet.*"[50] The British failure to guarantee this principle of the state existing in unity for the benefit of all men, according to the Mormon candidate, brought divine intervention and the Revolution. Joseph perceived a golden age that was fading rapidly because of the lack of a national pride founded in "innocence, information, and benevolence."[51] The failure of immoral power politics demanded a rededication to the divine ideals of the revolutionary age. "Open, frank, candid decorum to all men, in this boasted land of liberty, would beget esteem, confidence, union, and love."[52] In brief, the Prophet wanted to see the United States governed in the same way that he governed the Latter-day Saints—on the principles of truth and righteousness.

In the United States the people are the government, and their united voice is the only sovereign that should rule, the only power that should be obeyed, and the only gentlemen that should be honored at home and abroad, and on the land and on the sea. Wherefore, were I the president of the United States, by the voice of a virtuous people, I would honor the old paths of the venerated fathers of freedom; I would walk in the tracks of the illustrious patriots who carried the ark of the Government upon their shoulders with an eye single to the glory of the people.[53]

As spring warmed toward summer in 1844, tensions between the Mormons and the "old settlers" of Illinois had risen to the danger point just as they had in Ohio and Missouri before. It seemed

15

that the same results of persecution and expulsion were in the offing, but Joseph Smith determined to protect the position of the Saints. Afflicted by apostates within his camp and by vicious anti-Mormons from without, the Prophet by the first of June had to turn his attentions completely from the campaign and related matters to take care of things close at hand. Tragic as they were, the events of June 1844 captured the Prophet Joseph Smith in some of his greatest moments—moments that earned for him in every way the epithet of "Latter-day Patriot."

Enemies of the Church established in Nauvoo a newspaper, the first issue of which appeared on June 7, 1844, with the avowed object of forcing the repeal of the Nauvoo City charter and with the certain purpose of breaking the back of the Saints' influence over their own affairs in western Illinois. The city council therefore directed the abatement of this *Expositor* as a public nuisance. Joseph had no intention of allowing the anti-Mormon forces to gain the upper hand as they had in Missouri. Whether the action against the *Expositor* was thoroughly defensible or not was an insignificant question next to the considerations of defense that motivated the Latter-day Saints, now extremely wary of attack after their history of continual persecution and the common deprivation of their rights as citizens. The subsequent destruction of the press by the city marshal on June 10 rang the death knoll of the Prophet and his brother, Hyrum. Those persons anxious for the destruction of Joseph's power seized upon the incident as an opportunity to prosecute the Mormon leaders for "riot." Complaints were brought before a justice of the peace in nearby Carthage, and the stage was set for the final drama in the saga of the American Prophet.[54]

By June 18 the situation in and about Nauvoo had become so volatile that Joseph Smith and other officers of the city decided to place the community under martial law. Mobs had reportedly assembled "in Carthage and other places" for the avowed purpose of attacking Nauvoo. At two P.M. the Nauvoo Legion drew up into ranks near the Mansion House, and General Joseph Smith mounted a platform in full uniform to address the troops. Seldom in the history of the United States had patriotism, or the love of one for his country and his people, been more abundantly and magnificently displayed as it was on that hot summer afternoon. His light hair framing his face in a golden hue, the Prophet appealed for calm and confidence. He proclaimed the righteousness of what the leaders of

16

Joseph Smith's Last Public Address (Drawing by John Hafen, Archives of
The Church of Jesus Christ of Latter-day Saints)

the city and of the Church had done to protect their charges from the gathering enemy, and he assured the Legion that it was not merely his blood after which the mob thirsted, but the blood of every believer in the Restoration. "We are American citizens," he declared. "We live upon a soil for the liberties of which our fathers periled their lives and spilt their blood upon the battlefield." The Latter-day Saints had the distinct responsibility to see that those rights were not destroyed. The American Prophet had raised the title of liberty. "Will you stand by me to the death, and sustain at the peril of your lives, the laws of our country, and the liberties and privileges which our fathers have transmitted unto us, sealed with their sacred blood?" At that point the "thousands" listening shouted "Aye!"[55] Joseph then called upon all Americans, "from the Rocky Mountains to the ocean," to assist the Saints in their battle to preserve their freedom.[56]

In perhaps the most dramatic moment of his career as a leader of men, Joseph Smith then drew his sword and raised it high into the air. "I call God and angels," he said soberly, "to witness that I have unsheathed my sword with a firm and unalterable determination that this people shall have their legal rights, and be protected from mob violence, or my blood shall be spilt upon the ground like water, and my body consigned to the silent tomb."[57] As a cool breeze may provoke a chill on a hot day, so did the words of the Mormon leader. There was something portentous and ominous in the scene, and more so in retrospect. A latter-day patriot was about to give his life for his people.

I do not regard my own life. I am ready to be offered a sacrifice for this people; for what can our enemies do? Only kill the body, and their power is then at an end. Stand firm, my friends; never flinch. Do not seek to save your lives, for he that is afraid to die for the truth, will lose eternal life. Hold out to the end. . . .

God has tried you. You are a good people; therefore I love you with all my heart. Greater love hath no man than that he should lay down his life for his friends. You have stood by me in the hour of trouble, and I am willing to sacrifice my life for your preservation.

May the Lord God of Israel bless you forever and ever. . . .[58]

Nine days later, in Carthage Jail, the American Prophet kept his word and laid down his life for his people and in the name of truth.

18

Joseph's fatal and submissive trip to Carthage was a graphic symbol both of his patriotism—his love for the Latter-day Saints— and of his belief in the ideals of the American Revolution. Although he was about to be deprived of his ultimate natural right to life, he placed himself in the hands of the system out of reverence for the protection of his rights under the *magnae chartae* of American liberty, the Declaration of Independence and the Constitution of the United States. But his strong grasp of the enlightened meaning of those documents and his love of liberty have instilled in generations of followers a Revolutionary War heritage beyond the scope of national boundaries, and even beyond the realm of natural phenomena; for the same principles that called for the birth of the United States, said a nephew and successor to Joseph seventy years later, had brought forth the laws that God wrote upon the tablets of stone.[59] "In other words," said still another kinsman and successor, "if we fail to sustain the constitutional law of the land we have transgressed the will of our Heavenly Father."[60] No people can claim a greater inheritance of the Spirit of 1776 than the Latter-day Saints, and Joseph Smith would have had it no other way.

John Young:
Soldier of the Revolution

From the earliest settlement of Europeans on the North American continent, fierce struggles for possession of its vast lands marked its history. The great powers—English, French, Spanish, and Dutch—raced each other for territory that would provide a key to unlocking the treasure chest of resources sequestered within this "new" world. By the end of the seventeenth century, this rivalry for empire had deepened to the point of serious military confrontation, particularly between Great Britain and France, who would fight a series of colonial wars in which the French would lose all of their North American possessions to their cross-channel enemy (1763).

A more continual though less spectacular conflict also ensued between the Europeans and the Indians. Uprisings were frequent along the expanding frontier; constant and brutal "Indian Wars" became part of the way of life in virgin America. Because the colonial governments were hard-pressed to provide regular troops to fight these recurring and pestering wars, there developed in the thirteen colonies a system of militia defense by citizen-soldiers who could change their peacetime tools for muskets at the sound of a war whoop. But during protracted service even such amateur troops had to be paid, and in America the most valuable and readily available medium for payment was land—thousands of acres of it in a seem-

21

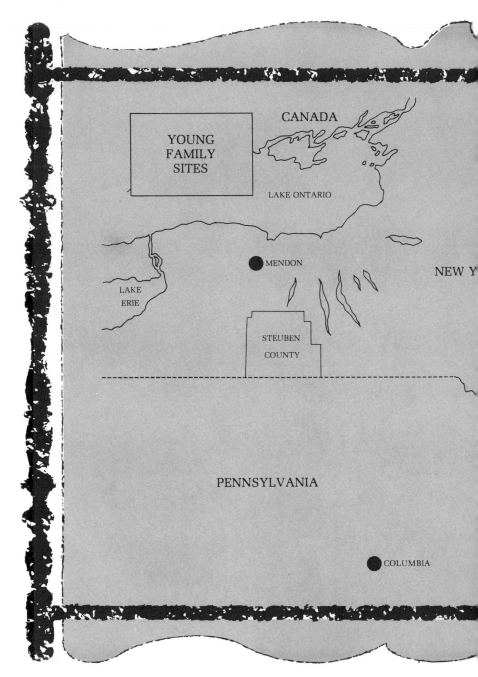

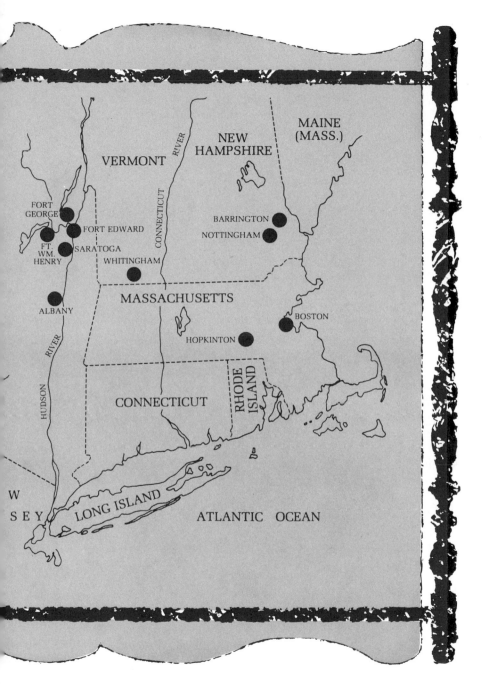

ingly endless treasury.

Emerging with a record of "faithfulness and bravery" from one of these Indian wars was a young shoemaker named William Young. In 1721 he received as a reward for his service a number of freeholds in the townships of Nottingham and Barrington, New Hampshire, several miles into the interior west of Portsmouth. Before moving some years later to Boston and eventually to Hopkinton in Middlesex County, Massachusetts, William increased his holdings in New Hampshire, and by the time of his death in 1747 had accumulated a comfortable estate. His will of that year left some $10,000 (a very large sum in that time) to his widow, daughter, and minor son.[1]

The son, Joseph, born February 12, 1729, was but eighteen at the death of his father. To illustrate the rise in the family's status from that of a cobbler, or "cordwainer," Joseph was engaged in the study of medicine, a difficult but prestigious profession acquired at the time through apprenticeship. He practiced in Hopkinton, where he also farmed, and then served as a surgeon in the British-American army during the French and Indian War (1754-63),[2] the imperial conflict that finally settled the Franco-British rivalry in North America by the expulsion of France from Canada and the trans-Appalachian region. This clear victory set in motion many of the forces that led to the American Revolution just over a decade later.

On at least one occasion, Dr. Young himself nearly became one of the many casualties of the bloody conflict. In August of 1757 he was at Fort William Henry[3] on the upper Hudson River when French and Indian forces under the Marquis de Montcalm laid siege following the capture and destruction of nearby Forts Oswego and George. Hopelessly outnumbered, the British commander agreed to surrender, only to have his men treacherously set upon by the Indians. Joseph Young was among 1400 British-American survivors of that betrayal who fought their way out and eventually to safety at Fort Edward.[4] Outlasting the war, Joseph returned to Hopkinton, where he was killed in 1769 when struck by a falling pole.[5]

Joseph Young had married in Hopkinton a widow with four children, to which they added two daughters and four sons. They named their third child and second son John. He was born March 6, 1763, the year of the end of the last war for empire and the beginning of a dozen years of revolutionary ferment. Growing up in the midst of it all, John Young inevitably became a part of the great movement—so much a part that in 1776, at the age of only thirteen, he became, like Andrew Jackson, a teenage soldier in the American Revolution.[6]

One of John Young's sons remembered that his father "served under General Washington,"[7] which would indicate that he was a regular soldier in the Continental Army. Indeed, John served several stints in that army.[8] In September 1777, he was scarcely in his fifteenth year, but nevertheless a man among seven thousand others under General Horatio Gates near a place on the upper Hudson called Saratoga,[9] and near a time that was crucial. Little more than a year had passed since the Great Declaration, and the Patriots had already brushed up against total defeat several times. But for British bungling, the incipient American cause could easily have suffered a crushing blow in the first few months of war for independence. Washington's army was in striking need of a clear victory. The French, still angered over their recent humiliation at the hands of the British, were waiting in the wings for evidence of Patriot determination and strength before committing themselves to a military alliance with the Americans. A victory would also have other less tangible effects upon the Patriot effort. It would be difficult to go into another winter encampment with a record of only hardship and defeat. In short, the tremendous wartime factor of morale was at stake. Gates and the troopers under him, John Young of Hopkinton among them, knew this, and they were prepared to give their best.

A large army under British General John Burgoyne was moving down the Hudson Valley from Canada to take Albany. On September 13 and 14, he moved his men and equipment across the river to the west bank, cutting his chance of retreat and thereby committing his troops to victory or decisive defeat. Gates, having established fortifications at a place on the river called Bemis Heights, awaited the British attack. Finally, on September 19, the tension exploded as a contingent of Patriots fought a fierce engagement with part of Burgoyne's army at a nearby farm; and though indecisive, it forced the British to dig in three miles north of Bemis Heights. The Patriots waited, and as the suspense grew, so did the American army. Continentals like John Young cheered at the daily arrival of hundreds of New York and New England militiamen who were pouring into the Patriot camp. Conversely, Burgoyne's situation worsened. He was running low on supplies and morale was low. On

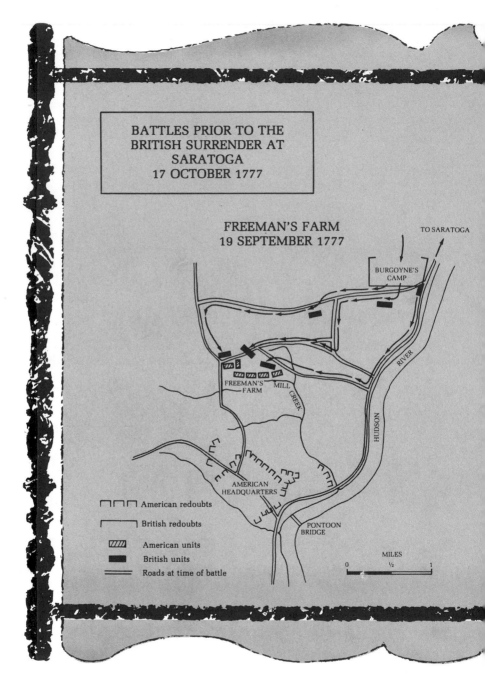

BATTLES PRIOR TO THE
BRITISH SURRENDER AT
SARATOGA
17 OCTOBER 1777

FREEMAN'S FARM
19 SEPTEMBER 1777

TO SARATOGA

BURGOYNE'S
CAMP

RIVER

FREEMAN'S
FARM

MILL CREEK

HUDSON

AMERICAN
HEADQUARTERS

PONTOON
BRIDGE

⊓⊓⊓ American redoubts

⊓ British redoubts

▨ American units

■ British units

═══ Roads at time of battle

MILES

0   ½   1

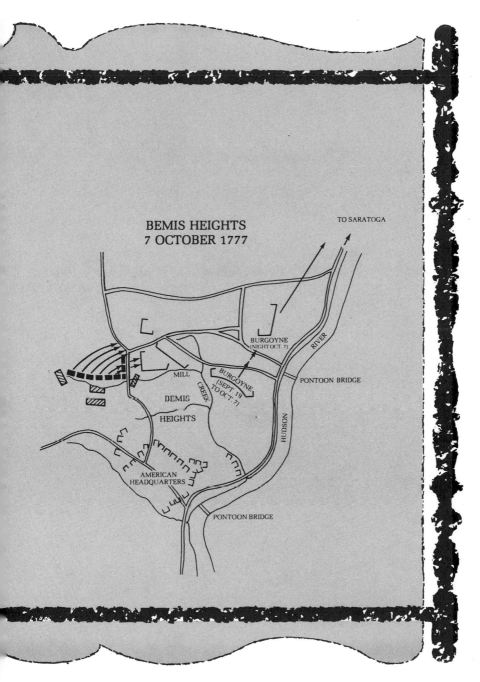

BEMIS HEIGHTS
7 OCTOBER 1777

TO SARATOGA

RIVER

BURGOYNE
(NIGHT OCT. 7)

MILL

BURGOYNE
(SEPT. 19
TO OCT. 7)

CREEK

PONTOON BRIDGE

BEMIS

HEIGHTS

HUDSON

AMERICAN
HEADQUARTERS

PONTOON BRIDGE

September 24, for example; heavy rains exposed the bodies of the dead buried near the British camp, which in no way encouraged the already demoralized redcoats.

Burgoyne decided to attack while he still could on October 7. He split his force and led half of it against the American left wing, but the Patriots, sensing a startling victory, attacked both parts of the British army. As the day ended, the jubilant Americans counted only 150 casualties, while the royal army had lost some 700 killed, wounded, and captured; Burgoyne was in full but useless retreat. On October 13, Gates completely surrounded him at Saratoga and demanded unconditional surrender. Four days later, Burgoyne's once splendid army, now numbering less than five thousand worn and ragged men, laid down its weapons. The American Revolution had turned the corner, and John Young was there.[10]

Following the thrilling and significant victory at Saratoga, John returned home for a time, carrying as a reminder of his momentous experience a cannon ball. But the exultation was only temporary; the war had just begun, and John was in it for the duration, participating in at least three other campaigns in Massachusetts and New Jersey.[11] When it was finally over in 1783 and the cause of liberty secured, John Young was only twenty years old. He had spent a third of his young life in the service of his country. Now he could begin to enjoy the fruits of his labor—life in a free land.

Burgoyne surrenders to General Gates at Saratoga, 1777 (Painting by Howard Smith, The Continental Insurance Companies)

In 1785 John married a nineteen-year-old Hopkinton girl named Nabby (Abigail) Howe. The Howes had been Loyalists during the war, but unlike many of their fellows who took the British side during the Revolutionary War, they chose to remain in the United States, despite their disagreement with the course of independence.[12] In January of 1801, John and Nabby moved with their eight children to Windham County, Vermont. Nabby was expecting again as they traveled, and on June 1 in Whitingham she gave birth to a boy whom they named Brigham—Brigham Young—a name that would have more meaning to the growth of America than his parents could ever have dreamed.[13]

Fourteen years after Brigham's birth, Nabby Young died from the rigors of frontier life. Brokenhearted, John moved west into Steuben County, New York, and in 1827 to the town of Mendon in Monroe County. There in 1831 he heard two preachers telling about a modern prophet named Joseph Smith and of the restoration of the gospel of Jesus Christ. He had to know more about this strange word that rustled his soul like the wind through a great oak. Consequently he traveled the next spring to Columbia, Pennsylvania, to investigate the principles of the new church, and there on April 5, 1832, Revolutionary War veteran and pensioner John Young was baptized into the restored church of Christ.[14] Brigham, who had first heard of the Prophet and his work in 1830, followed his father into the Church nine days later, being baptized in Mendon on April 14, 1832, by Eleazer Miller.[15]

In the fall of 1832, John Young, now remarried, moved with his family to join the body of the Saints in Kirtland, Ohio. There, in 1834, he fell extremely ill. Happy to have seen and participated in the birth of a free nation and in the advent of Christ's church again to the earth, he prepared to die, calling his children about him for his blessing. But Brigham was unsure about the propriety of such a blessing and went to the Prophet for direction. Joseph said that Father Young's request was righteous and within his prerogative, and that he would ordain him a patriarch so that he could bless others in the Church. Following the ordination, John quickly recovered and served as one of the first ordained patriarchs in the last dispensation.[16]

On one occasion, John Young's status as a revolutionary soldier probably saved the lives of his daughter and grandson and family. In the fall of 1838, they left Kirtland for Missouri, but upon their arrival in Columbia they encountered a militia unit under General Gaines preparing to march west to destroy the Mormons. John's grandson, Evan M. Greene, went to the general and obtained a pass for safe conduct into Illinois by saying that his grandfather had been a soldier in the Revolution. In granting the request, however, Gaines divested the family of its wagon and goods. The party thus escaped, although the old veteran suffered greatly from the hardship and exposure of the journey. He never recovered, and he died at Quincy, Illinois, on October 12, 1839.[17] The Prophet Joseph Smith noted his passing with the following:

This day President Brigham Young's father, John Young, Sen., died at Quincy, Adams County, Illinois. He was in his seventy-seventh year, and a soldier of the Revolution. He was also a firm believer in the everlasting Gospel of Jesus Christ; and fell asleep under the influence of that faith that buoyed up his soul, in the pangs of death, to a glorious hope of immortality; fully testifying to all, that the religion he enjoyed in life was able to support him in death. He was driven from Missouri with the Saints the latter part of last year. He died a martyr to the religion of Jesus, for his death was caused by his sufferings in the cruel persecution.[18]

John Young lived to see his son Brigham become president of the Council of Twelve Apostles,[19] and had he lived a decade longer, he would have seen him succeed Joseph Smith as President and Prophet of the Church. He would have witnessed further the continuing persecution of the Saints in the very nation for which he had fought so hard to bring liberty and freedom of conscience, but he no doubt would have thrilled at how his son and his people, in the face of great suffering, were to maintain their patriotism and their loyalty to the principles for which the veteran had staked his "life, liberty, and sacred honor" during the Revolution.

From all of this, Brigham Young's awareness of a Revolutionary War heritage, like that of the Prophet Joseph, was very concrete. He had heard from his own father the stories of Saratoga, of Patriot fervor, and of hard-won liberty. Brigham Young believed in America and in its institutions, and he was always loyal to them, but he believed first in The Church of Jesus Christ of Latter-day Saints, and he was loyal above all to its people. His life was the essence of conflict between these great loyalties, yet he was convinced that given righteousness, there should be no friction between true religion and politics. "Government belongs to God," he once said. "No man can draw the dividing line between the government of God and the government of the children of men. You can't touch the Gospel without infringing upon the common avocations of men."[20]

That conceptualization of government never changed in Brigham Young's mind, for he believed in the ideology of "true theocracy," or more specifically in the regulation of men in all things by God. A theocratic government, Brigham said, was "one in which all laws are enacted and executed in righteousness, and whose officers possess that power which proceedeth from the Almighty. That is the kind of government I allude to when I speak of a theocratic government, of the kingdom of God upon the earth."[21] These ideas are not at all in variance to Brigham's allegiance to the Declaration and Constitution, for he saw that God had sketched the pattern for his true theocracy on those same documents during the revolutionary epoch. "Even now," he asserted in 1859, "the form of the Government of the United States differs but little from that of the kingdom of God."[22] Only the requisite righteousness of its administrators might be lacking.

To serve God, and keep His commandments, are first and foremost with me. If this is higher law, so be it. As it is with me, so should it be with every department of the Government; for this doctrine is based upon the principles of virtue and integrity; with it the Government, her Constitution, and free institutions are safe; without it no power can avert their speedy destruction. It is the life-giving power to the government; it is the vital element on which she exists and prospers; in its absence she sinks to rise no more.[23]

For Brother Brigham, as for his predecessor, Joseph Smith, sinfulness on the part of the government officials was the great problem in politics; yet, again like the Prophet, he reiterated fervently the doctrine concerning divine control in the course of the American experiment.

The General Constitution of our country is good . . . for it was dictated by the invisible operations of the Almighty; he moved upon Columbus to launch forth upon the trackless deep to discover the American Continent; he moved upon Washington to fight and conquer, in the same way he moved upon ancient and modern Prophets, each being inspired to accomplish the particular work he was called to perform in the times, seasons and dispensations of the Almighty.[24]

[The Government] *was instituted in the beginning by the Almighty. He operated upon the hearts of the Revolutionary Fathers to rebel against the English King and his Parliament, as he does upon me to preach "Mormonism." Both are inspired by him....*[25]

Still further we believe that the Lord has been preparing that, when He should bring forth his work, that, when the set time should fully come, there might be a place upon his footstool where sufficient liberty of conscience should exist, that His Saints might dwell in peace under the broad panoply of constitutional law and equal rights. In this view we consider that the men in the Revolution were inspired, by the Almighty, to throw off the shackles of the mother government, with her established religion. For this cause were Adams, Jefferson, Franklin, Washington, and a host of others inspired to deeds of resistance to the acts of the King of Great Britain, who might have been led to those aggressive acts for aught we know, to bring to pass the purposes of God, in thus establishing a new government upon a principle of greater freedom, a basis of self-government allowing the free exercise of religious worship.

It was the voice of the Lord inspiring all those worthy men who bore influence on those trying times, not only to go forth in battle, but to exercise wisdom in council, fortitude, courage, and endurance in the tented field, as well as subsequently to form and adopt those wise and efficient measures which secured to themselves and succeeding generations, the blessings of a free and independent government.[26]

Yet he believed, again as did Joseph, that the Constitution was changeable, that its inspiration did not dictate perfection.

Can the Constitution be altered? It can.... The signers of the Declaration of Independence and the framers of the Constitution were inspired from on high to do that work. But was that which was given to them perfect, not admitting of any addition whatever? No; for if men know anything, they must know that the Almighty has never yet found a man in mortality that was capable, at the first intimation, at the first impulse, to receive anything in a state of entire perfection. They laid the foundation, and it was for after generations to rear the superstructure upon it. It is a progressive— gradual work.[27]

32

In President Young's mind, the best way to accomplish that "gradual work" was hand-in-hand with God. This belief in a theocratic arrangement led his followers into serious difficulties with the federal government, as the strong American doctrine of separation of church and state reacted against the Mormon assumption that men were to be ruled in all things by God and his agents on earth. In part at least, the longevity of the Mormon leadership's activity in politics traces to the attitudes of Brigham Young, as does the strange sort of ambivalence with which the Saints regarded the United States government well into the twentieth century. Said Governor Young in 1855:

The relation between us and the Government may be likened to a man having twelve sons, and all the elder sons pitch upon the younger one, as Joseph's brethren of old did upon him. They persecuted him and lied to their father about him, and tried to alienate the feelings of the man from him, and succeeded in a measure in estranging the feelings of the father from the young child. So it is with the General Government and us. We have plead [sic] time and time again, and will plead, saying, "Spare us, love us; we mean to be one of the best boys you have got; be kind to us, and if you chasten us, it may be said that we have kissed the rod and reverenced the hand that gave it, and tried again: but be merciful to us, for do you not see that we are a dutiful child?" But no, Tom, Dick, Bill, Harry, and the rest of the boys are eternally running to the old man with lies in their mouths, and he will chasten little Joseph . . . until he is driven into Egypt for succor. Well, if this is not Egypt enough where will you find it?[28]

And again in the same sermon—

Our whole interest is in [our Government]; we cling to it as a sucking child to its mother's breast, and we will hang to it until they beat us off, until we can hang no longer, and this will never happen, unless they drive us from it under the pretext of what "Mormonism" is agoing to do. What is the Kingdom of God going to accomplish on the earth? It will revolutionize not only the United States, but the whole world, and will go forth from the morning to the evening, from the rising of the sun to the going down of the same, so shall be the ushering forth of the Gospel until the whole earth is deluged with it, and the righteous are gathered.[29]

Before Brigham Young died two decades later (and well beyond his death), attempts to beat the Mormons away from their loyalty to the United States were more frequent and concerted than the "modern-day Moses" could previously have supposed. Perhaps the greatest effort to unhook the Saints from the United States came during the trying months of 1857 and 1858 when an army carrying the Stars and Stripes moved upon Utah to subdue Brigham and his reportedly rebellious followers. By the fortunate coolness of responsible leadership on both sides and the interposition of an old friend of the Saints, the so-called Utah War ended without bloodshed, but the coming of Johnston's Army painted in stark relief the curious relationship between the Saints and the American government.[30] President Young was henceforth even more anxious to clarify the position of the Church with regard to the foundations of the government of the United States. Had not Joseph called them inspired? And was not Brigham the son of a Revolutionary War veteran? The Mormons rebelled only against unrighteousness.[31]

Ironically, only a few years after the Utah War but far removed from its scene, real disloyalty to the institutions of the United States became a rampant disease as eleven southern states seceded from the Union. During the Civil War, Albert Sidney Johnston himself raised his sword against the very government that had sent him to smash the "Mormon rebellion" in 1857. In a sermon in the Tabernacle in March 1863, Brigham Young commented upon the place of the Saints in the Civil War, and in the course of his words he remembered an earlier evidence of his people's loyalty, the march of the Mormon Battalion in 1846.

We were accused of disloyalty, alienation, and apostacy from the Constitution of our country. We were accused of being secessionists. I am, so help me God, and ever expect to be a secessionist from their wickedness, unrighteousness, dishonesty and unhallowed principles in a religious point of view; but am I or this people secessionists with regard to the glorious Constitution of our country? No. Were we secessionists when we so promptly responded to the call of the General Government, when we were houseless and friendless on the wild prairies of Pottawattamie? I think not. We there told the brethren to enlist and they obeyed without a murmur.[32]

In forming that battalion of five hundred men, brother [Heber C.] Kimball and myself rode day and night, until we had raised the full number of men the Government called for. Captain Allen said *to me, using his own words, "I have fallen in love with your people. I love them as I never loved a people before." He was a friend to the uttermost.*[33]

This plea of loyalty was an integral part of Brigham Young's message to his people. He had no desire to foment discord in the United States or to support anything that would weaken its institutions. Only righteousness and the freedom to pursue it were important in the context of political strife. To secure that latter principle, his own father had spent his teenage years in the peril of his life, and Brigham's followers would be true to that sacrifice.[34]

In the course of his public utterances, Brigham Young succinctly demonstrated his full possession of an inheritance from the revolutionary age. The Mormons were certainly his heirs in this regard, but so were his own children. Willard, for example, born April 30, 1852, to Brigham and Clarissa Ogden Chase Young, was the first native-born Utahn and the first Mormon to enroll in the United States Military Academy. Willard's appointment to and subsequent arrival at West Point caused something of a national stir, because general sentiment ran high in 1871 against the Latter-day Saints and their polygamous leader. Due to their institutions, Mormons were supposed to be alien to America, inherently disloyal. By the end of his four years Willard Young had dispelled that myth for all who knew him or his record. He was commissioned into the Corps of Engineers in June 1875, having graduated fourth in a class of forty-three. Finishing fifth in engineering, fifteenth in law, eighth in geology and mineralogy, sixth in ordnance and gunnery, and second in discipline, Willard lived up to the heritage of his father and grandfather and denied by his accomplishment any suggestion that his people were disloyal or inferior.[35]

Following his commission, Willard Young continued to demonstrate a remarkable capacity and dedication. After serving two years at Willet's Point (later Fort Totten) on Long Island, he participated in the Wheeler Expedition, which surveyed west of the hundredth meridian, including a careful survey of the Great Salt Lake. He then returned to West Point as an assistant professor of civil and military engineering in 1879. Four years later, he went west again to supervise the construction of the Cascade Locks on the Columbia River, forty miles east of Portland, where he also directed harbor improvements. In 1891 he resigned his commission to become president of Young University in Salt Lake City, but he soon returned to military service, first as a brigadier general in the Utah National Guard in 1896 and then as an army colonel in 1898. During the Spanish-American War he served in Cuba, and following victory engaged in more engineering work in the East. From 1906 to 1915 he was again in Utah as president of Latter-day Saints University in Salt Lake City, but with the outbreak of war in Europe, he again entered the service of his country as United States agent in charge of the Kansas City district of Army Engineers. The armistice brought him home once more in 1919, whereupon he took charge of the Church construction program. He died July 25, 1936, completing a life of dedication to his country and his religion in a manner befitting the grandson of a Revolutionary War veteran and the son of a prophet.[36]

Richard W. Young, a grandson of Brigham Young, followed in the footsteps of his uncle, also pursuing with notable success a career in the U.S. Army. A son of Margaret Whitehead and Joseph Angell Young, Richard was commissioned at West Point in 1882 after graduating from the academy fifteenth in a class of thirty-seven. Two years later he received a law degree from Columbia College and entered the Judge Advocate General Corps. Following duty on the east coast and at Fort Douglas, Utah, Richard resigned his commission in 1889 to practice law in Salt Lake City, where he also held the rank of brigadier general commanding the Utah National Guard. In 1898 he reentered the army for service in the Spanish-American War and was discharged a year later, having completed an impressive tour of duty in the Philippines. Again in Utah, he held numerous civic positions and in 1904 became president of the newly formed Ensign Stake. But with the entry of the United States into World War I, he took the command of a division artillery. He died on December 27, 1919, a year after his return from France.[37]

Still another of Brigham's numerous children, this time a daughter, demonstrated the Spirit of 1776. This grandchild of John Young, Susa Amelia, impressed some people as being more like her father than any other of Brigham Young's children.[38] Born the daughter of Lucy Bigelow Young on March 18, 1856, in the southeast corner room of the Lion House in Salt Lake City, Susa exhibited at an early age a keen mind and "a passion for music and books."[39] She became editor of the literary magazine at Deseret University at the age of fourteen. After a mission to Hawaii with her husband Jacob

Willard Young (Archives of The Church of Jesus Christ of Latter-day Saints)

Richard Whitehead Young
(Archives of The Church of Jesus Christ
of Latter-day Saints)

Susa Amelia Young Gates
(Archives of The Church of Jesus Christ
of Latter-day Saints)

F. Gates in the 1880s, she founded the *Young Woman's Journal,* with which she associated for the next forty years, much of the time as its editor. She wrote prolifically, leaving at her death in 1933 a bibliography of published works twenty-two pages long and shelves of unpublished manuscripts.[40] Her works included several novels, an invaluable genealogical tool entitled *Surname Book and Racial History* (1918), and a well-received *Life Story of Brigham Young* (1930).

The broad scope of Susa's participation as a prime mover in the national woman's movement before and after the turn of the century is beyond the limited realm of this essay,[41] but in the course of this remarkable activity she displayed proudly her heritage both as Latter-day Saint and as an American whose lines ran through the revolutionary age and beyond. For Susa Young Gates, as for her father, Mormonism and basic patriotism were inseparably connected. "My religion means to me patriotism to my country: it gives me a reverence and affection for the Constitution of the United

States, with an unshakable fealty to the Government founded thereon."[42]

In Susa's mind, the greatest blessings of the American system were the guarantees of agency and equality, and again Mormonism was for her the strongest exponent of those principles. "Socially," she wrote in 1918, "my religion proves to me the divine equality of sexes and of various peoples. The only inequality is that of the individual, the personal ego which differs necessarily with age, environment and obedience to law."[43] Her crusade for woman's suffrage echoed the cardinal theme of the gospel. "The right of the individual to exercise his agency in full," argued Mrs. Gates, "belongs to both sexes alike. And that right should be cherished and studied as carefully by women as by men. The right of choice, of full franchise, the free agency of man, demands the highest powers of man's intelligence for its exercise and right use."[44]

Susa never missed an opportunity to illustrate in her tart style an awareness of a heritage both as Mormon and American. She remembered, for example, her visit to London in 1899 as a delegate to the International Council of Women:

> We had promised ourselves that we would not let "the eagle scream," on this important visit, but we could not help that thrill of pride which swept over us when we silently compared our many beautiful and elegant American women with their high-born sisters and friends. Not a whit behind were they in grace, in costume, nor in intellect.[45]

She had in her appearance and demeanor that intangible quality of heritable dignity that impressed deeply those she met through the years. One acquaintance noted her passing in 1933 with particular sadness. "She reminded me so much of my own New England ancestry," he lamented, "I hate to see it all passing on Beyond."[46] Susa would have been pleased: "Now, I am exceedingly proud of my Puritan ancestry and strict Puritan training," she said thirty years earlier; "therefore I boast, in the bosom of my family, you know, of my New England integrity."[47]

This brief illustrative sketch alone would earn for the family of veteran John Young a place in this volume, but one more event in the life of Susa Young Gates erected an important monument to the Revolutionary War heritage among the Latter-day Saints. On December 3, 1897, Susa convened in the Lion House a meeting of

Mormon women to organize a Utah branch of the Daughters of the Revolution. Also attending the meeting were Elder Heber J. Grant, an apostle of the Church, and President George Q. Cannon of the First Presidency.[48] President Cannon recorded the experience in his journal as follows:

> *I attended a meeting to-day, by request, in the Lion House, of a number of sisters who are desirous to organize a chapter of the society known as the Daughters of the Revolution. Sister Susa Y. Gates has had letters from the east upon this subject, and I have been spoken to before about it, and I urged them to take the matter up. They wished me to address them, which I did briefly, setting forth the reasons that I thought ought to prevail with them in forming this organization. . . . I thought the organization of this society would have the effect to develop patriotism, and would furnish advantages for those who wished to learn about their genealogy, and would have the effect on the nation to show that we were not a horde of foreigners, as a great many of our maligners have industriously circulated in the past. There are many young women who can join this society, and I feel it would be attended with good effects.[49]*

As a result of this meeting, the first Utah chapter of the Daughters of the Revolution came into existence at the hands of Susa Young Gates and the leadership of the Church.[50] For Susa, it was doubly satisfying. As she wrote a year and a half later, Mormon women in making this move had taken a large step toward the realization, at least in symbolic terms, of her vision of them in their rightful places among their American sisters:

> *Another gracious testimony that God is with His daughters comes to us in the report of the convention held on April 26th [1899] in Philadelphia, by the Daughters of the Revolution. The four young girls who went out as the representatives of the Utah Society were met with the most cordial welcome. . . . The Convention was so surprised to see four young, intelligent and lovely girls from "out West"; the President spoke of them as "four lillies sent from Utah's vales." How proud we are of our noble and gifted girls! And how grateful we feel to the gracious Eastern women who saw with such clear vision past the fogs and mists of prejudice right into the sweet innocent hearts of our precious girls. "By their fruits ye shall know them," and we may safely yet humbly and modestly challenge the*

*world to produce purer, lovelier, or more intelligent girls than our
own "sego lillies!"*[51]

Thus from the key battle at Saratoga to the settlement of the
American West, the family of John Young contributed significantly
to the bicentenary history of the United States. Though Mormonism
would soon take upon itself the worldwide goals of a truly international religion, the Youngs stood eloquently as witnesses to the
loyalty of the American Saints to the land that gave birth to the restoration of the gospel and to the revolution that made it possible.

Daniel Wood:
Conscience More Than Comfort

In considering the American Revolution, it is easy to forget in the midst of patriotic fervor that not every person in the thirteen colonies believed that violent separation from Great Britain was the best course for his country to follow. "I discern the goddess, but on the other side of the river," one American wrote of independence late in 1776. "Most men are for plunging into it to embrace her. I am for going over to her in a boat, distrusting my power to swim across the stream."[1] Indeed, of the 2.5 million inhabitants of the colonies at the dawn of the revolutionary period, an estimated 500,000 people chose the conservative path by remaining loyal to the King and Parliament.[2] Thousands of such colonists served in more than forty Loyalist provincial corps during the course of the war for independence. In several campaigns these Tories, or kingmen, bore the burden of battle for the British army; and though never developed fully as a fighting force, they were on the whole integral participants in the Revolution. Perhaps most significant in this participation were the thousands of civilians who supported the British cause due to beliefs derived from whatever motive—abhorrence of violence, parochialism, economic expediency, or simple and profound adherence to the institutions of the mother country.[3] As a consequence of their convictions, they suffered vile persecutions at the hands of an insistent majority. The

Daniel Wood (Archives of The Church of Jesus Christ
of Latter-day Saints)

American Revolution was therefore a special kind of civil war with all of the divisiveness and tragedy attendant upon such internecine conflicts.[4]

Loyalism was expectedly stronger and more fully developed in some areas than others because of the composition, history, and economy of the local population. It was particularly vibrant in the South, resulting primarily from the dominance of the Anglican Church in that region and growing out of antagonisms between the poor farmers of the inland and the pro-Revolution planters of the coastal areas. Pennsylvania also contained a healthy Tory community composed mostly of pacifist Quakers and pro-British Germans. For more complex reasons, however, it was New York that emerged as the greatest Loyalist stronghold in the thirteen colonies. It supplied at various times some 23,500 men to the service of the royal army, a figure equal to that of all the other colonies combined, though New York ranked only sixth in total population.[5]

But even in such apparent refuges of Tory sentiment as New York, the Loyalists were always in the unpopular minority, and it required great fortitude to pursue the course they selected. As a result of their choice, many suffered social ostracism, economic ruin, and even physical torture and death.[6] "The Loyalists were pursued like wolves and bears," remembered a contemporary New Yorker, "from swamp to swamp, from one hill to another, from dale to dale, and from one copse of wood to another."[7] The sad truth of history is that even in the best of causes, as one might believe the Revolution to be, persecution and irrational inhumanity have plagued those who found themselves by choice or otherwise in a despised minority. Ironically, a fear of tyrannical majority rule was a cardinal factor that Loyalists cited in explaining their disagreement with the course of independence. They believed, after all, that they were the true patriots, because their fealty was to a united empire. In remembering the American Revolution, therefore, history must grant to the Loyalists a place alongside those other patriots who believed in secession from that empire.

Before the end of the war in 1783, many Loyalists, especially those who had been active in their resistance to the Revolution, found themselves in intolerable positions. Their property had been destroyed or confiscated and they had lost, in many cases, any hope of social or economic advancement in their communities. Some, like the in-laws of Brigham Young,[8] opted to stay in the United States,

44

Loyalists in New York played a significant role in the British war effort, notably at the Battle of Oriskany in 1777 where they ambushed General Nicholas Herkimer and his Patriot forces (Painting by F. C. Yohn, The Continental Insurance Companies)

but between eighty and one hundred thousand of them returned to England or fled to other parts of the empire, particularly Canada. They flowed into present-day Nova Scotia, New Brunswick, Quebec, and Ontario. In the latter region, then known as Upper Canada, they broke new ground for pioneer settlements and established, together with those who went into the older areas, the basis of a common citizenship that two generations later was to be a fundamental factor in the movement for Canadian autonomy and confederation.[9]

A few of these descendants would return to the United States about the same time as part of a religious movement that announced the establishment of the kingdom of God in the last days.

In June 1832, some Mormon missionaries from Pennsylvania and New York traveled to the village of Ernesttown, a few miles east of Kingston, Ontario. Among them were Joseph and Phineas Young, who had joined the infant restored church of Christ two months earlier with their father, John, and brother Brigham. Phineas, a former Methodist minister, preached in a conference of the

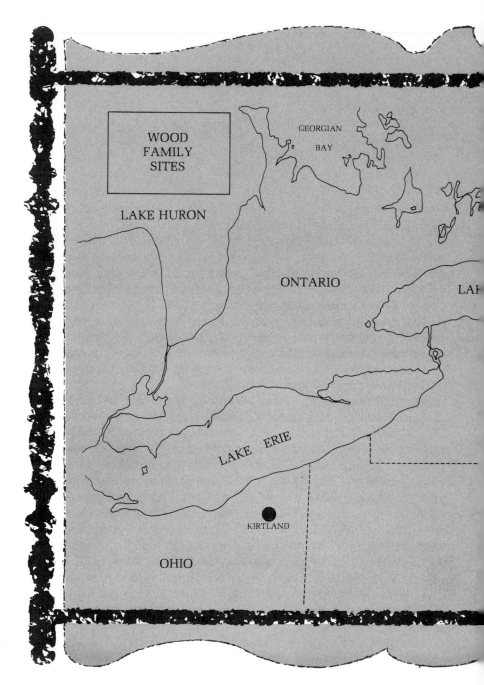

WOOD
FAMILY
SITES

GEORGIAN
BAY

LAKE HURON

ONTARIO

LAK

LAKE   ERIE

KIRTLAND

OHIO

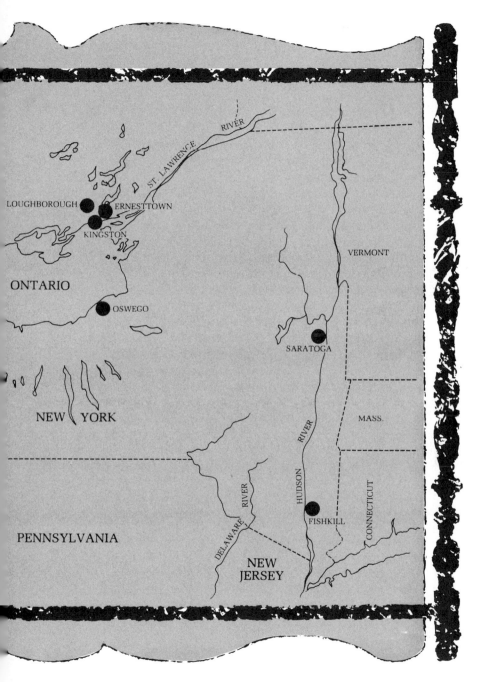

Reformed Methodist Church being held in Ernesttown and thus introduced the restored gospel into Canada. They "labored in Canada about six weeks with great success, raised up the first branch in British America (Ernesttown Branch) and returned home rejoicing. . . ."[10] Among those who heard these pioneer missionaries were a young farmer from nearby Loughborough named Daniel Wood, and his wife, Mary Snider Wood. Opening their home to the elders, the Woods witnessed the remarkable outpouring of the Spirit during meetings held in their house.[11] "Thousands flocked to hear the strange news even so that the houses could not contain the multitude, and we had to repair to the groves," two of the missionaries later recalled. "Hundreds were searching the Scriptures to see if these things were so."[12]

After the departure of the Mormons, the Woods continued to meet with a group of their family and friends to study the scriptures. In the absence of the elders, they became convinced that they required baptism, but lacking an understanding of the authority principle of the gospel, they persuaded a local Methodist minister to perform the ordinance and then continued to meet as believers in Mormonism.[13] In December of that same year, 1832, Joseph Young returned to Upper Canada, this time bringing with him his brother Brigham. The Youngs preached for a period in Kingston and then proceeded to Loughborough, where they further persuaded the Wood group of the restoration. Early in 1833 they baptized Daniel and Mary Wood and some forty others.[14]

The Woods were both descendants of New Yorkers who had left the state after the Revolution. Daniel himself was born near Fishkill in Dutchess County on April 16, 1800. His father, Henry, took the family into Upper Canada in 1803, settling first in Ernesttown, then moving about 1807 to Loughborough and the present location of Sydenham, Ontario, just a few miles north of Kingston.[15] Whether or not the Woods came to Canada as Loyalists is unclear. As late as 1775 Henry's father and grandfather numbered themselves among the patriots, having signed the revolutionary associators list of Ulster County, New York.[16] Nevertheless, the fact that they removed to lands reserved for "United Empire Loyalists" suggests that they had some claim to Tory rewards from the British Crown.[17] Daniel himself claimed Loyalist land in Ontario in 1831 but on the basis of his marriage to Mary Snider, the daughter of John Snider, formerly of Dutchess County, and Elizabeth Amey of

Saratoga, New York.[18] The Sniders and Ameys (Emighs) were "Palatinate Loyalists," descendants of Bavarians whom the British Crown had brought to America as refugees from the ravages of the Thirty Years' War (1618-48) that devastated the Rhineland. Thus, their ultimate fealty to the King during the Revolution was due to traditional gratitude. Both Sniders and Ameys fought under Burgoyne at the battle of Saratoga, for example, and earned beyond question their rights to Tory rewards in Canada as United Empire Loyalists.[19]

Following his baptism, Daniel Wood was ordained an elder in the newly formed West Loughborough Branch and immediately began to preach the gospel near his home.[20] In April 1833, Brigham Young came again into the vicinity, talking about the gathering to Kirtland, Ohio. James Lake of Ernesttown was ready to go at once and persuaded Daniel and his brother Abraham to go along to assist with the move of the large Lake family. Traveling with Elder Young, the Lakes and the Wood brothers arrived in Ohio to meet the Prophet.[21] Daniel quickly determined that he too must unite with the body of the Saints and returned to Canada to sell his possessions. By the summer of 1834, he was ready. With his wife, three children, and a team, he journeyed first to Kingston, where the family boarded the steamer *Great Britain* for the sixty-mile trip across Lake Ontario to Oswego, New York. After enduring a severe storm on the water, they disembarked for Kirtland and a new life in the country their ancestors had been forced to flee. Casting their lot with the Latter-day Saints, they came to know bitterly the sufferings of their fathers, but the die was cast for the family of Daniel and Mary Wood, and there could be no flight from their convictions.[22]

At Kirtland, Daniel and Mary and their three little children stayed for a time with the Lake family, then purchased a small farm four miles south of town where they lived for four years. During this time, Daniel went on a brief mission back to Canada, venturing into the virgin wilderness north of his old home, traveling much of the way on the numerous lakes separating the scattered settlements. After sowing "many good seeds," he passed through Loughborough, preaching to his famiy, and then returned to Kirtland.[23] Coming home was something less than joyous this time, for Elder Wood found the Saints in a precarious situation. No Mormon property was safe in Kirtland, he later wrote. The temple required constant protection, as did the homes of the Church leaders. Mobbers and even government officials would take anything they pleased, saying, "This is Joe Smith's and we take it to pay his debts."[24] Though for different reasons, it seemed that the fate of the Loyalists was falling upon the Saints. They too would have to flee to a new land of inheritance.

The Woods finally managed to leave for Missouri in the spring of 1838. Daniel remembered feeling good about leaving Kirtland for Zion in the West and the promise of peace. They traveled happily along, arriving on June 11 in Daviess County, where Daniel immediately constructed on unclaimed land a log house with a peeled bark roof. The Woods soon discovered, with the rest of the Saints, that they had merely performed the proverbial act of jumping from the frying pan into the fire. The spirit of mobocracy rose so drastically through the summer of 1838 that by the first of August a state of war existed in western Missouri.[25] With both Mormons and their enemies organized into armed camps, highly volatile conditions in the countryside eventually forced the Saints to consolidate at Far West. Then in late October, Apostle David W. Patten and others were killed in a pitched battle with anti-Mormon forces at the Battle of Crooked River. Governor Lilburn Boggs had ordered the Mormons removed or exterminated, and Far West was in a state of siege.[26]

The small town of Far West in late 1838 had become a typical refugee camp. The Woods, for example, had left everything in Daviess County and were forced to live in a log house with some other families. The walls were unchinked, and on one occasion the snow blew in during the night until four inches of it lay on the dirt floor. Being among the men who were standing guard day and night against the arrival of the mob, Daniel had to leave his wife and little children to fend for themselves most of the day and often at night. On October 28, the tension cracked suddenly as a rabble army of more than two thousand men arrived at Far West, under the command of General Samuel Lucas, with orders either to destroy or to vanquish the Mormons. Daniel later recalled the mob-militia setting up camp only a half mile away at Goose Creek, the forming of battle lines on both sides, and the fear. It appeared certain for nearly three days that full-scale war would erupt at any moment. Finally, on the 31st, Joseph Smith agreed to surrender as he realized that hundreds of innocents would otherwise be killed in bloody battle. Thirty years later Daniel Wood remembered that day very well. He re-

Governor Lilburn W. Boggs
(Archives of The Church of Jesus Christ
of Latter-day Saints)

General Alexander W. Doniphan
(Archives of The Church of Jesus Christ
of Latter-day Saints)

called laying down his gun in front of the cursing mob and walking away from the Prophet and the other leaders of the Church who were under guard and soon to be sentenced to be shot.[27] Through the fortunate courage of General Alexander W. Doniphan, who refused to carry out the execution, Joseph Smith escaped death in the Far West public square but spent the next six months in prison while his disciples were hounded from Missouri.[28]

Under control of the mob and bereft of many of their leaders, the Mormons at Far West suffered immensely through the winter of 1838-39. The mobbers, though already well-supplied with items of confiscated Mormon property, allowed only a trickle of food and other provisions to reach the beleaguered Saints. Determined to provide for his family, Daniel Wood sewed to his coat sleeve a red patch such as the Missourians wore to identify themselves. He thereby managed to move about as he pleased and to get supplies for his family and others of the Saints. One day six officers of the militia confronted him and questioned his wearing of the patch. Though he was sure he would be caught, Daniel laughed boisterously and said, "For fun." This convinced the mobbers that he was a "fool" and they let him pass. Through it all, Daniel used a surprising amount of cunning and ingenuity to keep his head above the water of that trying winter, and by February 1839 he had ac-

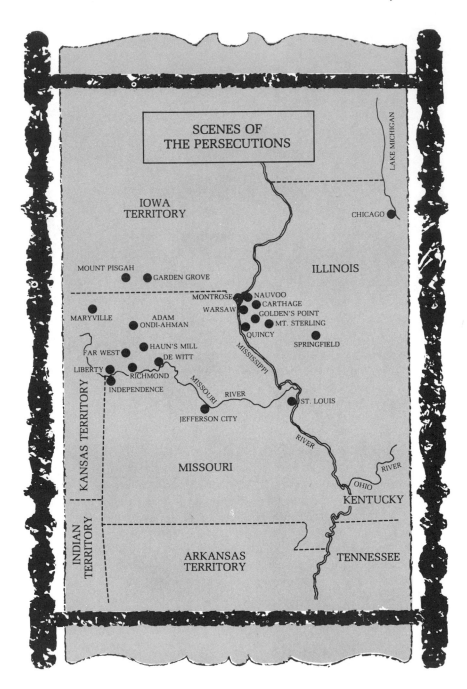

SCENES OF
THE PERSECUTIONS

LAKE MICHIGAN

IOWA
TERRITORY

CHICAGO

ILLINOIS

MOUNT PISGAH

GARDEN GROVE

MONTROSE   NAUVOO
WARSAW   CARTHAGE
MARYVILLE   GOLDEN'S POINT
ADAM   MT. STERLING
ONDI-AHMAN   QUINCY
SPRINGFIELD

FAR WEST   HAUN'S MILL
DE WITT
LIBERTY   RICHMOND   MISSISSIPPI
INDEPENDENCE   MISSOURI   ST. LOUIS
RIVER   RIVER

JEFFERSON CITY

KANSAS TERRITORY

MISSOURI   OHIO   RIVER

KENTUCKY

INDIAN TERRITORY

ARKANSAS
TERRITORY   TENNESSEE

quired a small wagon, a yoke of oxen, and a cow for the removal of his wife and children to Illinois. Fleeing again, the Woods reached the Mississippi River in the midst of the tragic Missouri expulsion and then had to wait three weeks for their turn to be ferried across to a new gathering place in this "land of the free."[29]

In Illinois, they traveled to Brown County near Mt. Sterling, where Abraham Wood had settled. Renting a small farm near his brother's home, Daniel found peace once again. The two brothers united as companions and preached the gospel through the surrounding country. Abraham gradually became dissatisfied, forsook Mormonism, and in 1842 returned to Canada. The loss Daniel felt as this last member of his family left the Church brought him profound sorrow: "I would say to myself, 'My brother is gone and I am left alone.' Then a passage of scripture would occur to my mind when the Lord said that he would take one of a family...."[30]

Daniel soon suffered another loss, however, that such philosophizing could not salve. After moving to Pike County, where he served as branch president, he purchased some acreage in Hancock County near Golden's Point and began to prosper in farming corn and wheat. But persecution and hatred had risen again as it had against the Loyalists during the Revolution and as it had perennially during the brief history of the Latter-day Saints; the Prophet and the Patriarch were murdered, and "standing guard" over property had again become a part of the Mormon way of life. In 1845 teenaged Henry Wood, though sick with "fever and ague," had to stand watch against the mob through a cold night and died shortly after. "His death," lamented Daniel Wood, "was the greatest loss I ever experienced."[31]

Even as they buried the young boy, conditions were worsening rapidly. Mary Wood's last child, Elizabeth, remembered years later how she had watched from a second-story window of their home as the mob burned Mormon houses in the distance.[32]

Realizing that the Church was soon to move again, Daniel decided to make a final visit to his family in Ontario. He journeyed to Loughborough, where he again appealed fervently to his brothers and sisters to accept the restored gospel, but to no avail. Returning dolorously to Illinois, he then moved his family into Nauvoo, having exchanged his property at Golden's Point for teams and wagons. There, in the midst of preparations for the great western exodus, Daniel and Mary received their endowments in the newly com-

Exodus from Nauvoo (Painting by C. C. A. Christensen, Copy by Grant Romney Clawson, Nauvoo L.D.S. Visitors' Center)

pleted Nauvoo Temple and added a plural wife to their household, young Peninah Cotton. Living in a small rented house, the family labored through the winter in anticipation of another journey into the wilderness, knowing from long experience of the hardships to come. For them, as for their Revolutionary War ancestors, considerations of conscience overrode those of comfort.[33]

In February 1846 Daniel and his family crossed the frozen Mississippi into Iowa. As they moved west from the river, the mud was so deep in places that they had to yoke up even their cows in order to keep going. After traveling what Daniel reckoned to be about two hundred miles, the modern "Camp of Israel" arrived at a place they called Mt. Pisgah, where the leaders determined to plant a way-station settlement for use of the migrating Saints following behind. They sent Daniel and some of the other men south into Missouri to obtain provisions. Having very little money with which to purchase supplies, they took furniture, household items, and clothing to barter in the Missouri settlements. As they might have expected, the mission proved perilous, inasmuch as the fires of the Missouri troubles with the Mormons were still smoldering. Indeed, when the Missourians heard of their coming, rumors rapidly

54

extended the small supply expedition into a massive Mormon army coming for bloody revenge.[34]

Nevertheless, by cool and careful action Daniel and his companions managed to accomplish their mission and soon rejoined their families on the trail in Iowa, but not without incident, particularly when it came to the bold Canadian. In Maryville Wood got into a heated conversation with a Missourian

about the killing of Joseph and others in jail and about the usage we received on account of our religion. We had a great deal to say about the Constitution of America and this commenced quite a long discourse. I laid before him how they transgressed the laws of heaven and of America and how they had killed innocent men in jail. And he said they had killed men in England too. I told him I supposed they had. This was incorrect as no Elder or Latter-day Saint has as yet been killed in that country up to this date 1869. I told him that the people there made their own laws and he already acknowledged that the Lord had a hand in bringing about the Constitution of America, and when you transgress His laws it is like touching the ball of His eye.[35]

Though he had apparently accepted Mormon doctrine of the divinity of American institutions, Daniel's background led him naturally into this bit of pungent commentary for which no rational patriot would have blamed him. But it was a different story among the touchy Missourians. Word quickly spread about this brash Mormon visitor, and as Daniel traveled north with the acquired provisions, he learned that a mob was after "the Mormon Wood." Fortunately, one of his companions loaned him a fast horse upon which he made long tracks back into Iowa and to his family camped on the trail west.[36]

Brigham Young and the main body of the camp having already pushed on, the Wood family and some others followed a few days behind and fell even farther back when they heard that Uncle Sam had agreed to enlist five hundred Mormons to form a battalion for service in the Mexican War. It was not cowardice that made them "move very slow," but a mere reluctance to rush forward and volunteer to leave their unfortunate families and friends in the wilderness while they marched to war in behalf of a nation that did not treat them justly. Eventually they arrived at the Missouri River, where "Israel" had camped for the winter. Trading with an Indian a

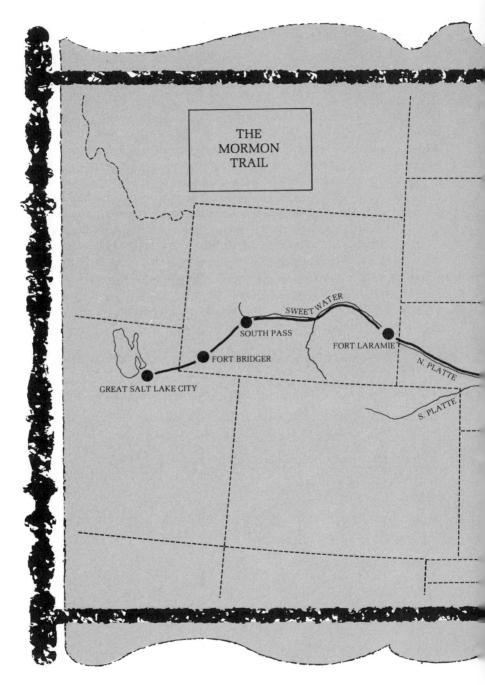

THE
MORMON
TRAIL

SWEET WATER

SOUTH PASS

FORT LARAMIE

FORT BRIDGER

N. PLATTE

GREAT SALT LAKE CITY

S. PLATTE

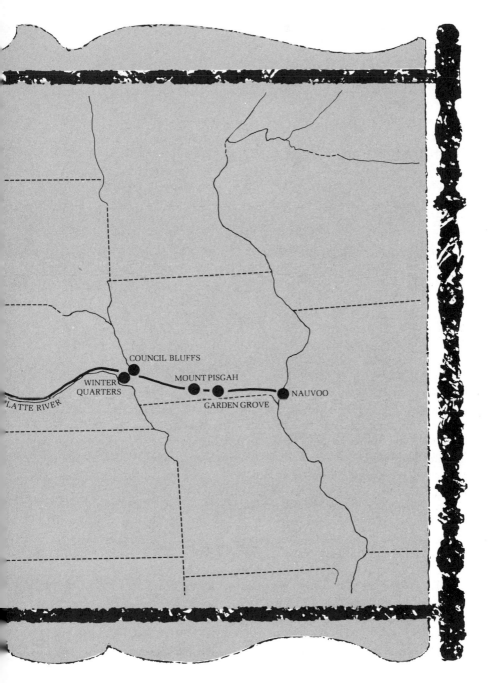

yoke of oxen for a log house on the east bank, Daniel settled his family in for the season at Winter Quarters.[37]

In the spring President Young left with his advance company for the new Mormon homeland in the West. Before doing so, he assigned his old friend and convert from Canada to remain another year in the Pottawattamie country to grow food for the stream of refugees still to come from the East. Laboring thus through 1847, Daniel cultivated some 110 acres near Winter Quarters for the coming Saints, and also prepared judiciously for his own family's trek to the Great Basin. Finally, in the spring of 1848, when the grass on the prairie had grown enough for forage, the Woods headed west in Zera Pulsipher's company with Daniel himself serving as a captain of fifty. His industry while at Winter Quarters and before that in Illinois had left his family well equipped for the trip; he was able to furnish them with four yoke of oxen, three wagons, six cows, a span of horses, and a carriage.[38] They even had a coop full of chickens in the end of one wagon and three pigs in a pen at the back of another, plus an old cat and three geese.[39]

After a few days' journey into present-day Nebraska, the Wood fifty joined a larger company of three hundred wagons headed by Brigham Young, who had returned to lead another body into the promised valley. Also in the party were Daniel H. Wells and Heber C. Kimball, following with another large company. Despite the dust, the heat, and the insects, the Woods traveled along with a surprising degree of exuberance, almost as if generations of expulsion had made such an experience simply a part of life to be expected. The expanse and desolate beauty of the country through which they passed also helped keep spirits high as the pioneers plodded past such landmarks as Chimney Rock and Scott's Bluff. They then transferred from the banks of the Platte River to the Sweetwater and to camp at Independence Rock. There Daniel and several others climbed to the top and sang hymns until past midnight, a strange pack of "Mormon coyotes" silhouetted against the moon. They ultimately pressed on to Devil's Gate, through South Pass on the continental divide, to Big Sandy, the Green River, and finally across the Wasatch range into the Valley of the Great Salt Lake, home at last for the family of Daniel Wood after a forced march spanning two generations and thousands of vexatious miles.[40]

Settling in the wilderness was nothing new for the Woods, but

58

this time they prayed and acted more fervently for permanence. Arriving in Great Salt Lake City in the summer of 1848, Daniel was surprised at its growth and learned that Brigham had already decided that there would not be room enough south of the city for all of the Saints and that some would later have to go north. Understandably weary of shifting around, Daniel turned his family northward around the point of sunburned hills above the infant city into what is now Davis County. There on North Canyon Creek he camped his wagons and took his ax and a team into the mountains to get logs for a house. Just before the snow flew that fall, he completed a squat cabin measuring fourteen by eighteen feet into which he moved Peninah and the children while he and Mary passed the winter in one of the wagons. He still wanted a house in the city, however, and logged all winter so that in the spring he would have the materials to build there. As soon as the weather broke he thus constructed a more substantial building on the southwest corner of South Temple and Second West and sowed wheat on the land now covered by the Salt Palace. There he fought a cricket scourge in 1849 and witnessed the uplifting, if barely sufficient, "miracle of the seagulls."[41] But Daniel's mind often went back to the rich soil surrounding the lower reaches of North Canyon Creek, so he returned that next spring, claiming land one and a half miles west of his first cabin. He thus planted the seeds of a community that later became known as Wood's Crossing, or simply Woods Cross.[42]

By the end of 1850 Daniel had more than a hundred acres surveyed at Woods Cross and had built a fine two-story house, which, with his home in the city, housed admirably his now numerous family. Concentrating on wheat and orchard cultivation, the Woods prospered so much that Daniel was able to add four more wives and to build yet a second dwelling in Davis County.[43] He soon had such a large family that, like Brigham Young, he established a private school for the education of his many children. At last Daniel Wood was realizing a harvest from his persistent faith and effort since the day he joined The Church of Jesus Christ of Latter-day Saints. He lived until 1892 and the age of 92, respected as the patriarch of one of Utah's first families.

Few visitors to his large farm ever forgot the organization and sense of community that existed there. Daniel held a family meeting once a week for which he had constructed a commodious meeting hall complete with bell tower and performers' stage. To it he imported the best teachers, musicians, actors, and sundry cultural events for the edification of his family and workers. The best stock and the finest equipment always came to Woods Cross. Its founder lived out his days grateful for the course he had chosen and happy to have been a part of the building of the kingdom and of the conquest of the great American West.[44]

This story of some Loyalist descendants of the American Revolution and their part in Mormon history could end here, but as with the others considered in this volume, there are numerous additional milestones of heritage among the posterity of Daniel Wood. Mary Snider Wood's youngest daughter, Elizabeth, born in the midst of the Illinois persecutions, married a young English stonecutter named James Moyle and settled with him on the west side of Salt Lake City. During the spring of 1858, as the Utah Expedition (Johnston's Army) approached the valley, Elizabeth, though pregnant, fled the city with most of the Saints in the great "move south" while James remained behind to burn his home if the troops failed to live up to a government promise that they would pass peacefully through and would camp on the western edge of the valley. Within days after returning home in September, Elizabeth gave birth to a son, whom they named James Henry. The youngster early exhibited both a remarkable allegiance to the Church and a keen intelligence. Following a mission to North Carolina, James Henry spent three years at the University of Michigan obtaining a law degree, which thrust him at once into the leading councils of the political life of Utah. Serving several terms in the legislature as a member of the Mormon-dominated Peoples Party, he quickly established himself as a leading statesman in the territory. With statehood in 1896, this grandson of Loyalists numbered himself among the founders of the Democratic Party in Utah, subsequently running twice for governor of the state and for the United States Senate in 1914. Though narrowly unsuccessful in these elective bids, he received an appointment as chief Assistant Secretary of the Treasury in 1917, thus becoming the first Mormon and native Utahn to hold a high executive position in a national administration.[45]

James H. Moyle later served as president of the Eastern States Mission, Democratic national committeeman, Ensign Stake high councilor, state Democratic party chairman, and in countless other high positions in church and government. At the age of seventy-five, he became commissioner of customs in the New Deal administration of Franklin D. Roosevelt. Throughout all of this, he demonstrated an inheritance from the Revolution, though he was the child of Loyalist descendants and a British emigrant. A speech he delivered while serving under Roosevelt revealed at once a full possession both of the Spirit of 1776 and of Mormon concepts thereof:

Every American may well be proud of our heritage, and appreciate living in a land so favored as it is above all other lands, certainly in natural wealth, resources, power, and advanced free government; the greatest democracy the world has ever known, a government, indeed, "of the people, by the people, for the people, and dedicated to liberty," under a Constitution established for the protection of the weak against the strong; to insure the equality of the rights of man; the most favored of all nations in the diversity of its natural resources and products; a land, indeed a great continent, on which kings, emperors, and autocrats have not been permitted to live or their minions endure; a land about which there has seemed to be a Divinity that hedged it about.

Divine Providence has manifestly had a watchful eye over the Nation, which has pioneered, on a large scale, a liberal republic.[46]

James Henry's oldest son by his wife Alice Dinwoodey (a daughter of another British emigrant) was Henry D. Moyle, United States Army officer in World War I, lawyer, University of Utah professor, apostle, and member of the First Presidency of the Church. Speaking in the Tabernacle in 1949, President Moyle displayed his realization of the American heritage, which he consistently portrayed in the light of a Saint's rights and duties as a citizen. "We must rely upon that government for the protection of our principles," he said. "Now these things go to the very root of life itself and of our growth and development in the gospel. We cannot afford to neglect to do our duty as citizens of this great United States and as citizens of the state in which we live." No national chauvinist, however, President Moyle added that those "from the countries outside the United States, so far as the laws of those countries permit, should exercise the same influence [for righteousness] there as we undertake to exercise here under our laws."[47] He often reiterated this theme in his addresses to the Saints, praying for God to "bless us to be wise, to be discreet and discriminating and discerning, and to utilize every force and every asset that we have to

61

James Henry Moyle (Archives of The Church of Jesus Christ of Latter-day Saints)

see to it that our governments are conducted by men who uphold the Constitution unconditionally, who believe in God, who lend obedience to His commandments."[48]

On April 1, 1961, the Wood family association dedicated to Daniel Wood a marble monument in the middle of the old family cemetery in Woods Cross. More than a hundred of Daniel's descendants watched as President Henry D. Moyle, his great-grandson, offered remarks and the dedicatory prayer.[49] It had been a long journey from the Loyalist exodus of Henry Wood and John Snider from Dutchess County, New York, to that spring day at the foot of the Utah Rockies, but the seed that Daniel brought to Zion in 1848 had sprung forth abundantly in the rich soil of the Great Basin until many of the foremost families in Mormondom constructed part of their heritage upon Revolutionary War Loyalism. Their patriot ancestors were those who eschewed rebellion, but who nonetheless staked their all for their country and for their sacred convictions.[50]

Daniel Wood

Henry Dinwoodey Moyle (*Archives of The Church of Jesus Christ of Latter-day Saints*)

Ezra Taft Benson:
A Heritage of Service

By the early fall of 1774 the possibility of armed conflict between Great Britain and her thirteen American colonies had developed into an overwhelming probability. The war clouds that had steadily thickened for a decade, fed by American intransigence to stiffening British controls, were suddenly boiling into a crackling thunderhead over Massachusetts. Citizens of the Bay Colony had competed only with the Virginians in their staunch and outspoken defense of American liberties during the rise of Patriot resistance, matching Samuel Adams for Patrick Henry, John Adams for Thomas Jefferson, and James Otis for George Washington. But it was in Massachusetts, wincing under the threat of "Intolerable Acts" passed against them in Parliament as punishment for the Boston Tea Party, that resistance exploded into open revolt. Angered further by British troops in Boston, the farmers, merchants, and fishermen of Massachusetts in October 1774 organized a revolutionary assembly, the first in the colonies that, just beyond the range of British rule in Boston, collected military supplies, trained militia "minutemen," and prepared in general for battle.

Though several other colonies quickly followed suit, it was against the New Englanders that the King and his Parliament vented their wrath. The royal government did not overlook more universal acts of rebellion, such as the convening in Philadelphia of the First

65

Continental Congress (September 5, 1774) and widespread economic warfare against Britain. But Massachusetts had stuck out its chin, and upon it King George III and Prime Minister Lord North were determined to land a smashing blow.[1]

On April 14, 1775, word reached America that the inevitable had finally occurred in London: Casting aside an appeal for redress from Congress to George III and an unequivocal Patriot "Declaration of Rights," His Majesty's Government had decided to use redcoats and royal marines in the forceful subjugation of Massachusetts and its associated colonies. "The New England governments are in a state of rebellion," the King told Lord North; "blows must decide whether they are subject to this country or independent."[2] So it would be. Greatly encouraging this momentous choice for war was a British confidence that some ten thousand regulars with Loyalist assistance could effectively quash the upstart rebellion in America in a fortnight or so. The British were in for a surprise.[3]

To begin this anticipated conquest of the patriots, General Thomas Gage, royal governor of Massachusetts, received orders from London to round up rebel leaders in the colony. Knowing that elusive fellows such as John Adams, John Hancock, and Samuel Adams would be difficult to corner, Gage planned instead to send troops to Concord where, according to his spies, the Patriots had been stockpiling military supplies for two months. Beyond capturing the stores, the general also believed that any bloodshed incurred during the expedition would serve only to paint the Americans into a scenario of aggression and thus have a demoralizing effect upon the entire rebel effort.[4] Consequently, 700 British soldiers under Lieutenant Colonel Francis Smith left Boston on April 18, crossed the Charles River under cover of darkness, and before sunrise on the nineteenth were marching westward toward Concord, some sixteen miles distant. Despite efforts to conceal their movements, the British were soon graphically aware that the Patriots knew of their presence. Rebel riders, among them the famous Paul Revere, had during the night alerted the villages along the way that the redcoats were coming. When at dawn an advance guard (six companies) of the royal force reached Lexington, a village on the road to Concord, it discovered some seventy Americans with weapons in hand lined up in three ranks on the green. The volatile materials for igniting the fires of war were suddenly at the same point in time and space. Someone inevitably pulled a trigger. The redcoats charged; the Americans fired momentarily and then fled. In minutes it was over. Eight Patriots lay dead and ten more groaned with wounds while a single British private suffered slight injury. It was a small and unspectacular skirmish as wars go, but it furnished the spark that set the blaze.[5]

After a small celebration and the arrival of their main force, the British pressed on to Concord only to find much of their goal, the military stores, already removed by the alerted Patriots. As the redcoats destroyed the remainder, Americans converged on the area and attacked a royal covering party outside the town. After losses on both sides, the British withdrew into Concord, consolidated, and the entire force began to move back to Boston, but not without considerable difficulty. One historian aptly compared their retreat to running the gauntlet.[6] From neighboring communities, hundreds of Patriots, anxious to get into the long-awaited battle for freedom, swarmed upon the British path sniping from every conceivable place of cover until the redcoats had suffered staggering losses. At

At the old North Bridge outside Concord, the Minutemen exchange fire with British soldiers (Painting by A. Lassell Ripley, The Paul Revere Life Insurance Company)

67

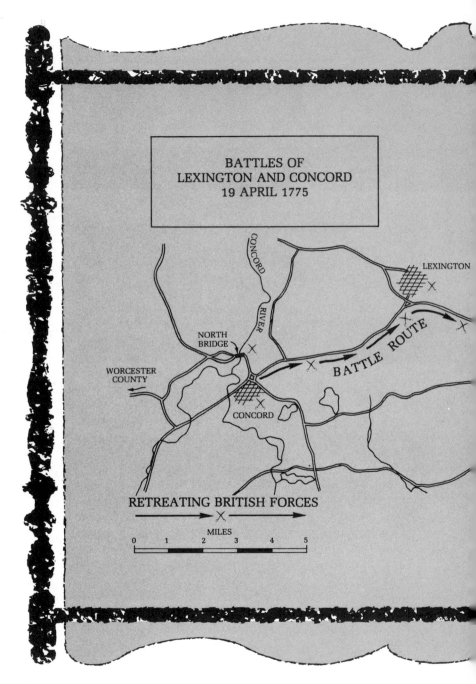

BATTLES OF
LEXINGTON AND CONCORD
19 APRIL 1775

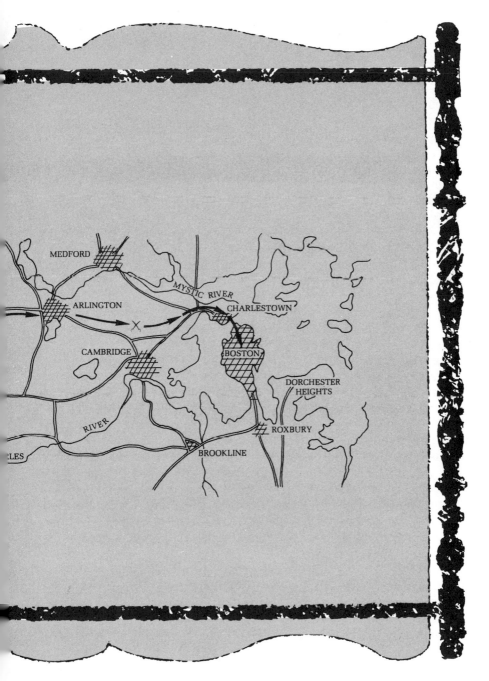

Lexington, Smith's command met a relief column of 1200 men sent from Boston, but more companies of Patriots continued to muster against them. The fighting was often hand-to-hand, and at nightfall the beleaguered British element, minus 273 casualties, arrived at Charlestown peninsula opposite Boston. The Americans had lost 95 men, and had definitely shown their mettle. More importantly, there could now be little doubt on either side that the long-billowing thundercloud had finally burst.[7]

Among the hundreds of "minutemen" who rushed to battle the British on that fateful day was a middle-aged shoemaker named Benoni Benson. He was a lieutenant in the third company of Patriots dispatched to Lexington from Mendon in nearby Worcester County to the west. Among the very first to join the American Revolution, he devoted considerable energy to the success of independence as it traveled its long road to fulfillment. He was, for example, on the committee of correspondence at Mendon. During the revolutionary period these committees were virtual governments in themselves, providing at once for the needs of the local communities and for contributions to the war effort. To serve on such a committee, as did Lieutenant Benson after Lexington and Concord, was a heavy responsibility. Additionally, he worked on a committee in 1780 charged with the duty of hiring "men for the town's quota of soldiers to fill up the Continental battalions." (On that particular panel also sat a neighbor named Jacob Taft; he and Benoni Benson formed an association that would take on added significance two generations later.) Though Benoni seems not to have carried arms regularly subsequent to Lexington and Concord, his son John also mustered to the American cause, serving as an officer in various phases of the struggle for independence. John Benson also held important civilian positions, including two terms as a selectman and prominent membership on various ad hoc committees, among them a commission delegated to the General Court at Boston.[8] In short, the Bensons were dedicated and anxious to serve—traits they passed on to their descendants.

At length the victory was won with the sweat and blood of countless Patriots like the father and grandfather of John Benson, Jr., who subsequently grew up in Mendon, Massachusetts, enjoying with a new generation of Americans the blessings of a free land. His was a tangible heritage from the fires of '76—one he could transmit to his own children.

70

Under heavy fire from the Minutemen, the British retreat through Arlington Heights toward Boston following the battles at Lexington and Concord (Painting by A. Lassell Ripley, The Paul Revere Life Insurance Company)

Another partaker of this inheritance was Chloe Taft, grand-daughter of the Jacob Taft who had served with John's grandfather on the Mendon recruitment committee during the war. She accepted young Benson's proposal of marriage during the first years of the new republic, and before Europe believed that the United States would survive its infancy, the couple had brought forth seven youngsters. The first son and fourth child of the family was born on Washington's birthday, February 22, 1811. They named him Ezra Taft Benson (hereafter referred to as Ezra T.).[9] Little could they have known, as they looked at their red-faced baby boy lying in a rough-hewn cradle in a Worcester County farmhouse, that some four decades later and a half a continent away he would begin his services as an apostle of the Lord Jesus Christ. Nor could they have known that another Ezra Taft Benson, great-grandson of the first, would become president of the Council of the Twelve Apostles and would also serve in the cabinet of a president of the United States. Neither could they have imagined that not far away a five-year-old boy named Joseph Smith was growing to the stature of a prophet. Still, it was a new land with a new promise; startling things were not unexpected.

In 1817 the Bensons moved to nearby Uxbridge. Here Ezra Benson grew up; between stints of New England schooling, he worked with his father on the large family farm where they cultivated apples, hogs, and character. At the age of fifteen, Ezra went to work for his brother-in-law, who operated a hotel in town. Five years later, though only twenty years old, he acquired the business himself, and was operating at the same time his grandfather's farm in Mendon. While thus displaying an early knack for management, he also took time to fall in love, and married Pamelia Andrus (or Andrews). After burying their first two babies in Uxbridge, the young couple decided to move on. They went to Holland, Massachusetts, to try the cotton factory business, but by spring of 1836 the call of the West had reached their ears. Following brief preparatory sojourns in Philadelphia and New Jersey through the next year, they finally set out, traveling by way of St. Louis to a place called Griggsville in Illinois. There, in July 1837, only a few days after their arrival, Pamelia gave birth to a son. But the move was not yet ended. With an associate, Ezra explored a region near the confluence of the Illinois and Little Blue Rivers where he surveyed for a new town to be called Pike. Nevertheless, events were developing close by that would prevent Ezra T. Benson from ever living in his projected town.[10]

Subsequent to working on the Pike project through the summer of 1838, he moved into Quincy, Illinois. As Pamelia was boarding elsewhere as a schoolteacher, he was alone and went to board with some folks named Gordon who called themselves "Latter-day Saints." He also witnessed the daily arrival of refugees belonging to the same group as the Gordons crossing the river from Missouri. The whole countryside, including Ezra Benson, was stirred at their coming. Before many days had passed, the doctrines of this strange religion called Mormonism—modern revelation, a new prophet, restored priesthood—echoed from every corner of western Illinois. Ezra listened intently to his host, Thomas Gordon, to Sylvester B. Stoddard outside of town, and to Erastus Snow preaching in the Quincy courthouse. He was impressed in a bewildered sort of way, though not converted, but he decided to stay near Quincy, leasing some land for a farm about a mile out of town. There, during the winter of 1839-40, he built a house and planted an orchard. Though he was busy, those Mormons, now settling on the river near Commerce, were never out of his thoughts; he admired their zeal and sympathized with their sufferings. Early in the summer of 1840 he went to see some Mormon friends, George D. Grant and Edmond

Bosley, who predicted that Ezra T. Benson would become a Saint. This prophecy disturbed him. He had to know.[11]

In July 1840, another Mormon friend brought word that Sidney Rigdon was going to debate Mormonism with a local doctor of religion and that Joseph Smith himself was going to be there. Ezra determined to be in attendance as well. Though a substitute appeared for Sidney Rigdon, the Prophet was indeed there, and while the two antagonists debated from the stand, Ezra stared at the Mormon leader. When the preacher tried "to make the people believe that Joseph was the false prophet spoken of in the scriptures," Ezra recalled later, "Brother Joseph looked up and smiled very pleasantly— too much so, I thought, to be the character Nelson [the preacher] said he was."[12] More days passed. Pamelia had rejoined her husband and together they went to Quincy to hear Apostles Orson Hyde and John E. Page preach prior to their departure on a mission to Palestine.[13] The Bensons were profoundly impressed. "I never had heard the like before," wrote Ezra.[14] Pamelia, moreover, was thoroughly touched by the Spirit and soon after the meeting sought baptism. After hesitating for a few days, her husband decided to join her, and together they were immersed in the Mississippi River on July 19, 1840.[15]

The Bensons moved into Nauvoo, buying a lot from Hiram Kimball in the spring of 1841, just in time to witness the laying of the cornerstone of the great temple. During that next year as he built his home and worked on the temple, Ezra became well acquainted with some of the apostles who had recently returned from miraculous missions to the eastern part of the United States and to Europe. He quickly caught the missionary fever from such new friends as Heber C. Kimball, and soon requested a call to preach the gospel. In June 1842, preaching his way across the country to his home-state destination, he encountered Elder John E. Page in Philadelphia, but Ezra was disappointed. Something had happened to this apostle. He had evidently lost his desire to serve, having even hired himself to a Protestant congregation as a preacher.[16]

The new missionary pushed on to his former home area around Mendon and Uxbridge only to fall victim to the truism about a prophet being without honor in his own country. "My most intimate acquaintances would not come to hear me," he lamented, "and they acknowledged their disgust at my having become a Mormon, a follower of Joseph Smith. They condemned me without a hearing, without even knowing what I believed."[17] Ezra nevertheless continued to preach in Worcester County until he was mobbed and spat upon at Charlton. He then fled into Connecticut for a time. In the spring of 1843, he became president of the branch at Lowell, Massachusetts, where he presided until fall, and then returned to Nauvoo. On his journey home, he preached at Westfield where, to his delight, Pamelia's sister Adeline came forward to request baptism. The following April in Nauvoo, Adeline Andrus became his second wife as Ezra Benson entered the restored order of plural marriage.[18]

The spring of 1844 was an exciting time in Nauvoo. The temple had risen majestically against the sky, and, equally thrilling, Joseph Smith was running for president of the United States. Ezra Benson and John Pack teamed up as campaigners and drew an assignment to proselyte in New Jersey. There, on a hot July day, they received news that crushed them in a vise of sorrow and shock. The mob had killed Joseph and Hyrum at Carthage, and there was nothing to do but hurry home. In Nauvoo again, Ezra stood in the multitude as Sidney Rigdon and Brigham Young addressed the Saints on the question of succession. The hum of the crowd and the weight of events oppressed his soul until he heard testimony from many around him that they had seen Brigham "transfigured" into the form and voice of the slain Prophet. He immediately pledged his allegiance to Joseph's successor, never questioning the right of the Twelve to lead the Saints.[19]

With the accession of the Council of the Twelve under its president, events among the Mormons progressed rapidly toward their ultimate migration to the Rockies. It was a time when those anxious to serve percolated to the surface more than ever before. Among these new leaders was Ezra Benson, called in late 1844 as Nauvoo high councilor and then on another mission to the East. Assigned to the Boston Conference, he worked through the winter to gather eastern Saints for migration to Nauvoo, where they arrived in the spring of 1845. Then, with his wives, he received his endowments in the temple, after which he was called to assist in giving endowments to others. He labored in the temple every day until early in 1846, when it was time to abandon Nauvoo.[20] "About the ninth of February I started, with my two wives and children, in the dead of winter," he remembered, "leaving my pleasant home and fireside. I left my furniture standing in the house. . . . We crossed the

Mississippi River, leaving our beautiful city and temple."[21] Adding to the travail of the Bensons' exodus was Adeline's pregnancy. At Garden Grove, Iowa, she gave birth in a wagon box to her first son, George Taft Benson.[22]

Further on the trail west, Ezra T. Benson was called as first counselor in the branch presidency at Mt. Pisgah, but it was a short-lived assignment. Early in July 1846 Parley P. Pratt arrived from the main encampment of the Saints at Council Bluffs with a message from Brigham Young: The Lord had selected Ezra T. Benson to fill a vacancy in the Council of the Twelve Apostles. Ironically, it was "the crown of John E. Page," the fallen apostle whom Ezra had encountered in Philadelphia, that Brother Benson was to inherit. "If you accept this office," continued President Young, "I want you to come immediately to Council Bluffs, to prepare to go to the Rocky Mountains."[23] Brigham knew that the journey to come would require a special breed of leader, anxious to serve and willing to strive under grave responsibilities, and he knew that Ezra T. Benson filled the bill. On July 16, 1846, in Orson Pratt's tent on the banks of the Missouri River, the thirty-five-year-old grandson of men of the Revolution was ordained an apostle of the Lord.[24]

Characteristically, Ezra quickly took up his burden—and with zest. In the first party of trekkers, he played a major role in the planning and administration of the historic move west, such that when, late in July 1847, he climbed to the top of Ensign Peak with Brigham Young to survey the new Mormon refuge, he could already feel a sense of satisfaction.[25] In 1850 President Young sent him to Tooele County as head of a colony assigned to mill building timber. While there he served as representative to the territorial assembly (1853-56). Missionary work, however, beckoned again. He left for Europe with Orson Pratt in 1856 to fill a vacancy in the European Mission presidency. There his worth became more evident than ever.[26] "Here is Brother Benson," said a fellow worker. "I have known him for some time, but I never knew the day in my life when I would not lay down my life for him."[27]

The many statements of his character graphically illustrated Elder Benson's perpetual devotion to the cause. "I am all the time digging around the Saints," he told a congregation in Ireland; "I am all the time fanning the flame of Mormonism, and thinking how I can counsel that brother or this sister, and God blesses me."[28] Despite these efforts across the ocean, perhaps his greatest work,

Logan, Utah, at the End of the Nineteenth Century (Painting by C. Eisley, The Church of Jesus Christ of Latter-day Saints)

particularly in view of his posterity, awaited him back home in Cache Valley on the border of northern Utah and southern Idaho.

Elder Benson returned from Europe early in 1858 with Orson Pratt and a group of missionaries. He had built his "Big House" on the corner of Main and South Temple streets in Salt Lake City prior to his mission, but he would have little time to enjoy it, for Brigham Young wanted him to preside over the sixteen Latter-day Saint settlements in Cache Valley. Consequently, the Bensons sold their commodious dwelling to Daniel H. Wells and moved to Logan in March 1860. The verdant valley, originally called Willow Valley, had been occupied by the Mormons since 1855 when Briant Stringham led a party in for the purpose of grazing cattle. It was Ezra's task to expand that activity and to solidify the society and economy of the region. Following his arrival and usual output of management vitality, the valley prospered; its settlements grew in size and number. Interrupted only by brief missions and various journeys on assignment from the Quorum and the Presidency, Elder Benson spent the rest of his short life in Cache Valley. Traveling to Salt Lake City in September 1869, the relatively young apostle collapsed at the home of his friend Lorin Farr in Ogden. In spite of numerous attempts to revive him, he died the night of September 3, a victim of his own immutable energy and eagerness to serve.[29]

Elder Benson's sudden death was a shock to the Church. His family, of course, carried the heaviest burden, and of them perhaps the most affected was George Taft Benson, the oldest son of the apostle and his second wife. Born on the Iowa trail just days before his father became a member of the Twelve, young George had grown up during the greatest years of Ezra Benson's service. He felt a particular closeness to his father, having traveled with him often and having worked almost daily at his side in building a family homestead and church and civic facilities. George was later among those called to expand the Cache settlements northward. In 1884 he moved into what is now Whitney, Idaho, near Preston, leading out in the construction of irrigation projects. For twenty-three years he was bishop of the Whitney Ward, evidence enough (when considered with the responsibility of rearing ten children) that George Taft Benson had inherited his forefathers' capacities for leadership.[30]

George gave his oldest son his own name, but that son in turn decided to honor his apostle-grandfather by naming his first boy Ezra Taft Benson. It was an apt choice, for all the service rendered by the Bensons to their country and to God since the battle of Lexington and Concord was magnified repeatedly in the life of this second Ezra Taft Benson.

The beginnings of his story were unpretentious. Born August 4, 1899, he developed into manhood working on the family's forty acres and learning in the process the fundamentals of sound agriculture from his father, who was also Franklin County commissioner for many years. "I drove a team when I was four years old," wrote Ezra as he reminisced on the rigors of his young life on the farm, "and not many years after this I was riding horses to herd cattle. I learned early to milk cows; we had seventeen Holsteins. This became, and remained, a major responsibility during my growing years—this and digging potatoes and sugarbeets, shocking grain, putting up hay and doing all the other chores that fell to the oldest boy on a farm."[31] He interspersed this practical education with formal schooling at the Oneida Stake Academy and at Utah State Agricultural College in Logan.[32]

By the time of his mission call to Great Britain in 1921, young Ezra was fully aware that he had absorbed in the process of growing up the traditional Benson habits of diligence and perseverance particularly with reference to agriculture. "I grew up believing that the willingness and ability to work is the basic ingredient of successful farming. Hard, intelligent work is the key. Use it, and your chances for success are good. As an adult, this principle deepened into one of the mainsprings of my life."[33]

Such ideas make outstanding men, but Elder Benson, laboring as a missionary in Carlisle, near the English border with Scotland, quickly learned that the price of success also included a surtax of risk. There in 1922 he and his companion were mobbed by a large anti-Mormon crowd and escaped harm only through the intercession of some friendly Britons. Physical strength helped as well: "They surged in on us, but we were both tall enough in most cases so we could almost put our elbows on the shoulders of those around us. They couldn't get us down. . . ."[34] By the time he returned home, he was prepared to become the heir to the tradition of service fostered by the soldier at Lexington and the pioneer apostle who were his ancestors.

Resuming his education, Ezra entered Brigham Young University, graduated with honors, and was awarded a scholarship to Iowa State College in Ames. He also married Flora Amussen, daughter of a Logan jeweler. After obtaining a master's degree at Iowa State in 1927, and following his election to the honor society of agriculture, he returned to southern Idaho to take up his farm and soon became county agricultural agent. So impressive was his work that he was appointed in 1930 as head of the Department of Agricultural Economics and Marketing inaugurated by the University of Idaho Extension Division at Boise. The Bensons had not been in Boise long before the Church also decided to make use of Ezra's talents and willingness to serve. He first filled the position of stake superintendent of the YMMIA, but soon moved into the stake presidency. After a period of graduate work at the University of California, he returned to Boise and soon found himself installed as president of the Boise Stake. In the spring of 1939 he became executive secretary of the National Council of Farmer Cooperatives with headquarters in Washington, D.C., and a year after his arrival there he became president of the newly formed Washington Stake. Once again, his tenure was relatively brief. His abilities and faithfulness dictated another, more weighty calling in the kingdom.[35]

In 1943, when a large regional agricultural cooperative offered Ezra Taft Benson a lucrative position, the Washington Stake president would not accept without a discussion with the leaders of the Church. He consequently journeyed to Salt Lake City, where he learned that President Heber J. Grant himself wanted to speak with him. "President Grant was just recovering from an illness and he received me in his bedroom," he wrote of that surprising day. "He was lying on the bed. As I approached, he took my hand in both of his, looked earnestly into my eyes and said, 'Brother Benson, with all my heart I congratulate you and pray God's blessings to attend you. You have been chosen as the youngest apostle in the Church.'"[36] It was a great opportunity for service, and like Lieutenant Benoni Benson at Lexington in April 1775, Ezra Taft Benson dropped what he was doing to step full-time into the war, this time for men's souls and the advancement of the Church.

His first major battle was not long in coming. At the end of World War II, President George Albert Smith called him on a special mission to Europe, charging him with the spiritual and temporal relief of the Saints in those war-ravaged countries. For ten months Elder Benson worked tirelessly to bless and organize the people and to provide for their physical needs through the workings of the Church welfare plan. In the process he traveled some sixty thousand miles. In Berlin, the apostle went with a German Saint to inspect a shipment of food designated for the aid of the local Mormon population. They took down some of the boxes and opened one of them. "For a moment I was disappointed," Elder Benson wrote later. "It was filled with the commonest of common food, dried beans. As that good man saw it, he couldn't help putting his hands into it, and running it through his fingers, and suddenly he broke down and began to cry like a child."[37] They opened another, this one full of cracked wheat. The German looked at the American through tearful eyes and said, "Brother Benson, it is hard to believe that people who have never seen us could do so much for us."[38] So this farmer-apostle learned what food meant, but this was only a forewarning of the great experience with the massive problems of agricultural production and distribution that awaited him back home in the United States.

In the early 1950s Ezra Taft Benson went to suburban Maryland for the dedication of the Chevy Chase Ward. During a rare moment of free time, he slipped away to the Capitol Building in Washington. "I walked into the huge Statuary Hall where repose so many replicas of outstanding Americans to remind us of the beginnings and growth of our land. For a long time, I looked at the statue of Brigham Young over in one corner; and I meditated on the life of this Mormon pioneer, and on the way our people had flourished in the century since he led them west."[39]

But he had no idea really how far the Mormons had come. On November 24, 1952, President-elect Dwight D. Eisenhower called the startled Mormon leader to his suite at the Hotel Commodore in New York City. Elder Benson knew that Ike wanted him to become Secretary of Agriculture, but the westerner had a whole list of reasons why someone else should fill the lofty position. After listening to his arguments patiently, Eisenhower answered squarely: "We've got a job to do. I didn't want to be president, frankly, when the pressure started. But you can't refuse to serve America. I want you on my team and you can't say no."[40]

Though President Eisenhower did not realize it, that was the most convincing thing he could have said to a Benson, for as they had demonstrated graphically since the Revolution, they were endemically anxious to be of service.

Whether or not observers in Washington agreed with Secretary Benson's philosophies of agriculture and government, they did agree in 1953 that his job was going to be one long row to hoe after another, in the first of which grew politics of the unique American variety. During his initial few days in office the Secretary issued a memorandum on his policies in which he emphasized the principle of hard work, "a full day's work for a day's pay." The press interpreted this innocent call for full effort as a charge that federal employees were not working hard. Concomitantly, Secretary Benson's reorganization plan designed to streamline the department drew heavy slurs from offended bureaucrats and from some reporters who enjoyed quoting his statement out of context. A second row was concerned with the immense problems of agriculture then confronting the United States. For two decades American farmers had grown used to federal intervention that supported prices, absorbed surpluses, and controlled in general agricultural production. Secretary Benson disagreed with this course and determined to change it: "We had too much government . . . in agriculture. It's true that farmers were suffering from price and income troubles. But it was also true that the very governmental policies which were supposed to alleviate those troubles were generally causing greater troubles than the ones they were supposed to cure."[41] Indeed, Ezra Taft Benson believed that freedom "was a God-given, eternal principle vouchsafed to us under the Constitution. It must be continually guarded as something more precious than life itself. It is doubtful that any man can be politically free who depends upon the state for sustenance."[42] It was a simple philosophy; it was a Mormon philosophy.

Thus straddling both these rows, Secretary Benson prepared to devote his full energy to the proposition that "inefficiency should not be subsidized in agriculture or in any other segment of our economy."[43] This philosophy and the vigor with which the Secretary expounded it immediately rankled many comfortable denizens of Washington. Within a month of his inauguration, President Eisenhower was besieged with demands that he fire the outspoken westerner, but most prognosticators who predicted Secretary Benson's exit failed to realize how accustomed to hoeing long rows this tall Mormon had become over the years. They also did not know that the President agreed with his Secretary of Agriculture. Following a straightforward Benson speech at St. Paul, Minnesota, in February 1953, Ike called the Secretary to the White House. "Ezra," he told him, "I believe every word you said at St. Paul. But I'm not sure you should have said it so soon."[44]

Ezra Taft Benson weathered all the storms of eight years in Washington. Controversy is a large part of the American political tradition. His farm policy was one source of constant controversy during his sojourn in the national limelight, as was his outspoken opposition to communism and anything in American society that seemed to lead toward it. He fought hard for his beliefs, and not one of his most ardent opponents could ever truthfully deny that he fought in the open, upon a base of sincere patriotism. Much of his inspiration for action came from the depths of Mormon doctrine concerning the foundations of America. "I love this nation," he said in a speech at Des Moines early in 1953. "It is my firm belief that the God of Heaven raised up the founding fathers and inspired them to establish the Constitution of this land. This is part of my religious faith."[45] A decade later, he wrote,

I believe that the founders of this nation introduced into the world a new concept of government and of the rights of individuals. They bequeathed to us a heritage of freedom and unity that is our most priceless political possession. I believe that we must realize— you and I—the great gift that is ours: this gift of freedom. We must understand that the freedom we possess, though it was bought for us at Valley Forge, and preserved on the high seas by Old Ironsides,

Ezra Taft Benson (Archives of The Church of Jesus Christ of Latter-day Saints)

and maintained at Gettysburg must still be nourished today by you and me with the energy of our daily deeds.[46]

The tenure of Ezra Taft Benson as head of the Department of Agriculture had other aspects apart from the gigantic responsibilities of administration and the formulation of policies for the welfare of the nation—aspects that at the same time revealed his character clearly. He was able, for example, to break down formidable barriers with his down-to-earth demeanor. On one occasion, he drove a four-horse team into a fairgrounds where he was to deliver a speech to a possibly hostile group of cattle raisers. "As we entered the grounds," he remembered, "I loosened the lines and let the horses—and they were a fiery set—run at full speed around the track and back to the platform in front of the grandstand, to the obvious delight of the audience and probable terror of the driver. No matter how poor the speech might be, I had established myself with this group."[47]

Another time he was challenged by some reporters to milk a cow. "So I took my position, grinned at them, and told them to stand back or I'd squirt milk on them. They backed about 10 feet away. I overheard one reporter say, 'He'll never reach us here.' Oh, yeah, I thought. And when I got going pretty well, I suddenly shot a spray of milk and got him good, and some of the cameras, too."[48]

As might be expected, there was a spiritual side to Elder Benson's activities in Washington. Following a tour of drought-stricken Texas in the summer of 1953, for instance, he recommended to the governor of the state a day of fasting and prayer for rain. A few days later he received a note from the governor saying that there had been two inches of moisture. Also enclosed was a newspaper clipping which exclaimed, "Benson Really Has 'Contacts.' "[49] He encouraged the President to institute regular prayers in cabinet meetings, and he prayed continually for wisdom both for himself and for his various associates in the administration. As if to culminate symbolically this element of his service to President Eisenhower, he arranged in October 1958 to have the Tabernacle Choir perform a concert at the White House.

Sitting on the President's right, I was able to share in his delight. Never had I seen him so completely lifted up by music as on this occasion. Again and again, he turned to me to mention his immense pleasure, but especially after two of his favorite numbers, "Battle Hymn of the Republic" and "A Mighty Fortress Is Our God." When the regular concert was concluded, he asked the choir to sing on, and after they had done this for an additional fifteen minutes, he rose and spoke to them and all of us in the warmest tones. The beauty of the performance and the President's reaction brought tears to many eyes.[50]

At this writing, the contributions of Ezra Taft Benson have not come to an end. Several books could well be written detailing the fabric of service to God, man, and country that has been woven from Benoni Benson's role in the American Revolution to the present Ezra Taft Benson's involvement in church and state. The most recent symbol of the Benson family's part in the pageant of history emerged upon the death of President Harold B. Lee in December 1973 when Elder Benson became president of the Council of the Twelve as President Spencer W. Kimball assumed the mantle of the prophet. As President Benson took his position at the head of the apostles, it was yet only another event of many in the long story of service among the Bensons that drifts back in the telling to April 19, 1775, and the road to Lexington, Concord, and freedom.

Daniel H. Wells:
The Price of Liberty

Wars such as the American Revolution tend in later years to wear the apparel of traditional glory. Most Americans remember Lexington and Concord, Saratoga, and Yorktown, and revel in the thought of citizen-soldiers of the Patriot army enjoying the conquest of well-trained and well-equipped British redcoats. It is easy to conjure images of determined colonials, clad in homespun clothing, firing from behind rocks and trees upon the haughty enemy, complete with powdered wigs. It is all a part of Americana and provides interesting symbols of what America has come to mean in the minds of its people—the triumph of the common man over aristocratic tyranny, the ultimate righteousness of an indignant populace, and the final victory of freedom by means of sheer determination and "Yankee Doodle" bravery.

It is not quite so easy to consider scenes of privation and hardship such as Valley Forge, but Americans couch even those in terms denoting glorious sacrifice. The nightmares of frozen feet, acute starvation, and great despair seldom survive the dreams of those who suffered them. Additionally forgotten in the blazes of the war's remembered glory are the many battles lost in the course of winning in the end. Not many Americans realize, for example, that George Washington won few battles, that he was routed from Long Island, crushed before Philadelphia, and narrowly escaped capture and the

85

annihilation of his army at Brandywine. Even more difficult to ponder with any degree of realism is the everyday existence of the private soldier—the boredom, the fears, the loneliness, the disappointments, the sufferings of body and soul in the name of a cause he may not have fully understood. Take, for instance, a young Connecticut lad named David Chapin.

Early in the spring of 1778, word spread about the environs of Hartford, Connecticut, that Congress had commissioned sixteen additional regiments and that some of these were to come from Connecticut. A call went out for volunteers to fill these units on enlistments of three years. Shortly thereafter, in March of that year, David Chapin arrived in Hartford to sign up. Three years was a long time, but he was ready. This thing called liberty was worth the price, whatever it might be. He soon found himself training for combat in Captain Joseph Walker's company of the newly formed Ninth Connecticut Regiment. There was a lot to learn before they met the professional army of King George III. All too soon these green Connecticut boys were marching off with their muskets and rifles slung on their shoulders and the future of America riding on their backs.[1]

David Chapin and his companions headed for Rhode Island, where the British had entrenched themselves at Newport, but the thrill of battle had to wait on the dullness of delay. The Continental strategy eventually scheduled the Battle of Newport for the next season, and the Ninth Connecticut was finally ferried across the Long Island Sound for service on Long Island. Disaster seemed to stalk Chapin's outfit from the beginning. At the Battle of Quaker and Butt's Hills in the summer of 1778, the British overwhelmed the raw Americans and sent them reeling westward toward New York City, also under firm royal control. Barely escaping the British trap, the Americans successfully retreated from Long Island and crossed into New Jersey, where they joined the bulk of the Continental Army under Washington. David and his young comrades had learned painfully the feeling of defeat and headlong retreat. The glory of war they had expected to experience now seemed alien.[2]

In New Jersey conditions only worsened for the Ninth Connecticut and the other Continental regiments. While men like David Chapin dreamed of home and family, there was little to make life bearable in camp. Supplies of food and clothing were minimal at best and only intermittently replenished in dwindling quantities.

Pay came in the form of nearly worthless Continental currency. There was little to do but forage in the countryside, perform mundane camp duties, and wait. Many men deserted. Others gave up more completely and yielded their lives to starvation and disease. Indeed, the encampment at Morristown in the winter of 1779-80 brought greater agonies than had even Valley Forge. That winter was particularly severe, and the troops had only scanty shelters; suffering and death became more fact than fear. The price was heavy for those who persevered, and it had little to do with glory. Yet David Chapin and his Connecticut colleagues bore the vicissitudes well, suffering, as their commander reported, "with the greatest patience and fortitude."[3]

The war went on. With perseverance, perspiration, and the aid of Providence, the Americans eventually prevailed, not by their great battlefield victories, for they were few, but by their incredible determination and desire for freedom. Late in the summer of 1781, the Patriots, with the aid of the French fleet, cornered a large British force under Lord Cornwallis at Yorktown and forced its surrender. The war for independence came at once to an effective end. The King and his Parliament reconciled themselves to the loss of the colonies; they had not been defeated, but the resolve of generals such as George Washington and of privates such as David Chapin brought them to the realization that the Americans would obtain their liberty no matter how long it took, or what price they had to pay. Articles of peace went into effect on January 20, 1783, and all that remained for the end of the Revolution was the evacuation of British troops from the soil of the new nation. On November 21, David Chapin moved with General Washington onto Manhattan Island, a last British bastion, and on the twenty-fifth the Patriots exuberantly paraded southward into New York City from their positions at Harlem Heights as the last of the redcoats left the docks. In symbolic triumph, the Continental Army sensed at last the elusive glory of victory. On December 4, 1783, General Washington took leave of his officers and troops at Fraunces' Tavern and traveled southward to resign before Congress his commission as commander-in-chief. Private Chapin picked up his few belongings and walked home to Connecticut.[4]

The end of the American Revolution was the beginning of what has been called the "Great Experiment." Having cast off their colonial mentors, the incipient Americans perceived a boundless fu-

General Washington's Farewell to His Officers, 1783 (Painting by F. C. Yohn, The Continental Insurance Companies)

ture of opportunity and progress under the enlightened maxims of democratic republicanism. And much of this perception of endless possibilities grew in the soils of the new lands west of the Appalachians, a rough range of mountains that had confined American activities to a relatively narrow strip of coastline. So it was that David Chapin, having fought for the freedom of choice, purchased with some Hartford County friends a large tract of land in the Oneida country of western New York about twelve miles north of Utica. Also involved in the enterprise was Daniel Wells, a descendant of Thomas Wells, who served several terms as governor of Connecticut in the seventeenth century. Daniel was an adventurous pioneer in his own right, having explored "way out west" in Ohio for a new home, but he finally decided to join his Connecticut neighbors in the Oneida project. Western New York held a future both of joy and sorrow for him. There he witnessed the births of five children; then in 1812 he watched his young wife succumb to the rigors of frontier life. In the best of American traditions, folks from the neighboring farms quickly pitched in to help care for the motherless Wells girls. Among these Good Samaritans was David Chapin's daughter Catherine. For her the service was a special pleasure, and in November 1813 she married Daniel Wells. Shortly after, Daniel enlisted in the army. The British, it seemed, were still unconvinced that the United States was a permanent reality. By the time Catherine gave birth to a son on October 27, 1814, the War of 1812 had settled the question.[5]

Daniel Wells died suddenly in 1826, and his twelve-year-old son, Daniel Hanmer Wells, became head of the household. The boy's older half-sisters were marrying and leaving home, so the youngster had to shoulder much of the responsibility for his little sister, his widowed mother, and the family farm. By the age of seventeen, Daniel was a man in every respect, known for his large bones, long limbs, and great shock of red hair. The following year (1832) he decided to follow his father's example and pioneer in the West. Taking his mother and younger sister, he set out for Ohio to buy land, but upon arriving near Cleveland, he found it to be too expensive. The small family remained for a time in the Cleveland area while Daniel taught school and saved money. Finally in the spring of 1835 they pushed on to a bend in the Mississippi River and an Illinois village called Commerce. Here they planted firmly their roots.

In 1837 Daniel married the daughter of a local farmer, and his mother remarried. The families prospered on the rich soil of the river bank, and "Squire Wells" soon became one of the little community's most influential citizens. Among his many friends, for example, was a young Springfield lawyer named Abraham Lincoln. According to the story Daniel always told, the first time he met the future president, Lincoln exclaimed, "Prepare to die! I swore that if I ever met a man who was uglier than I am I would shoot him." To this the unflappable squire replied, "Shoot away. If I am as ugly as you are, then I don't want to live."[6] The pattern seemed to be firmly established for a long future of contentment and stability for Daniel H. Wells and his family in western Illinois. Only occasionally did they hear rumblings about the "Mormon troubles" over in Missouri.[7]

Late in 1838 news reached Commerce that Governor Lilburn Boggs of Missouri had ordered the Mormons out of that state under the threat of death. Soon these persecuted people were flooding across the Mississippi into Illinois seeking refuge from this "exterminating order"; Daniel H. Wells was stunned when he contemplated the injustices and oppression with which the Saints were

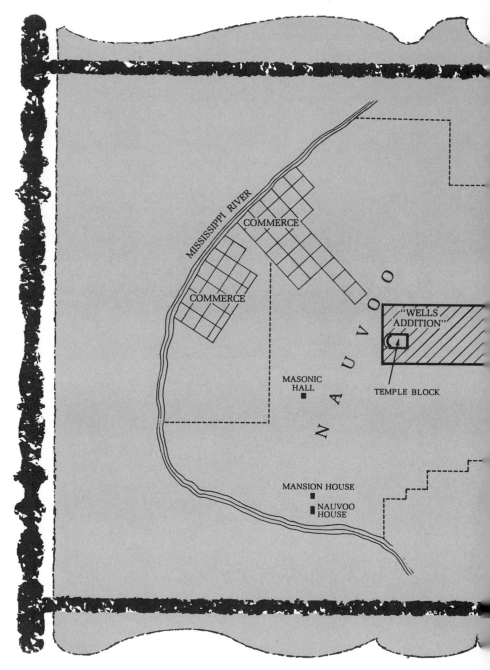

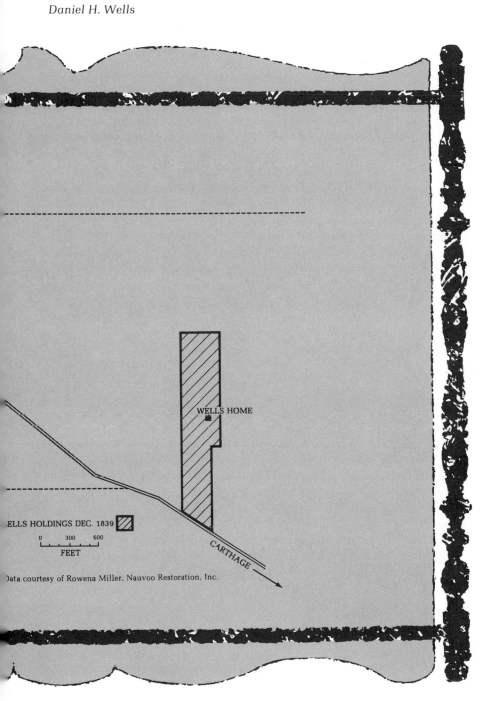

WELLS HOME

WELLS HOLDINGS DEC. 1839

0   300   600
FEET

CARTHAGE

Data courtesy of Rowena Miller, Nauvoo Restoration, Inc.

afflicted. Had not his fathers paid the price of liberty? The squire immediately determined to do all in his power to help the destitute refugees. Working through that winter to find both temporary and permanent homes for the Mormons, he also subdivided eighty acres of his own land near Commerce for a new settlement and sold lots at low prices and on extended terms. The Prophet Joseph Smith, after his release from Liberty Jail, arrived at Commerce, climbed the bluff from the bottom land, and named the place Nauvoo, the Beautiful. And on one of the lots from the Wells subdivision, he projected a new temple of the Lord, to be more impressive and more important even than the one at Kirtland. Soon Daniel's rural village of Commerce had become the bustling city of Nauvoo, the largest community in Illinois, and new institutions and industries were being built under the guidance of Joseph Smith and his disciples. Squire Wells was in the midst of it all, and though not a Mormon, he had gained the trust and confidence of the Saints. Under the remarkable city charter granted in December 1840, he was chosen one of Nauvoo's first aldermen and a member of the city council. He also became a regent of the University of Nauvoo and a brigadier general in the local militia, the Nauvoo Legion. In the short space of two or three years, and though he had not joined the Church, Mormonism had changed significantly the course of the squire's life.[8]

The progress of Nauvoo and the early acceptance of the Saints by the people of Illinois concealed one ominous fact. The Mormons were too united, too powerful politically, and too prosperous to avoid an ultimate clash with the old settlers of the region. As friction increased between the Saints and their neighbors, Squire Wells inevitably reached a crisis of decision whether to join the non-Mormons in the efforts to dislodge Joseph Smith and his followers from their growing position of influence or to cast his lot finally with the Prophet and his cause. Amazed at the disregard of the anti-Mormons for the rights guaranteed all Americans from the age of the Revolution, Daniel did not hesitate in his choice of the latter course. When the mob murdered Joseph and his brother at Carthage in June 1844, he affirmed his allegiance to their beleaguered followers by resisting, though unsuccessfully, the disarmament of the Nauvoo Legion, which left the Saints at the mercy of their oppressors. He then watched as many of his Mormon friends abandoned their homes in the early spring of 1846 and fled westward into the Iowa wilderness. By the middle of the summer, the squire could delay his formal union with the Saints no longer. Professing a hard-won belief in the gospel of Jesus Christ, Daniel was baptized in the Mississippi River on Sunday, August 9, 1846.[9]

The Mormons continued to follow Brigham Young and the Twelve into Iowa, but not fast enough for the mobbers. In September the mob laid siege to Nauvoo. Three Mormons were killed in skirmishes and several others wounded, and eventually Nauvoo's defenders agreed to a cessation of hostilities and a surrender of arms, which were to be returned after the Saints had safely crossed the river. Daniel exerted himself strongly in behalf of peace on that occasion and urged the remaining members of the Church to evacuate Nauvoo rather than die in its futile defense.[10] In so doing he was telling himself to sacrifice the land he had homesteaded a decade before, the city he had helped to build from nothing, and, most of all, his family, for his wife refused to unite with the departing Church. Accordingly, the last of the faithful left the city, but none with a heavier heart than Daniel Wells. He was one of last to leave, and as he crossed the river he was fired upon by an enemy cannon. Retrieving one of the balls, he dispatched it to the governor of Illinois with a message of disgust for the state's disrespect for its own promises of safe conduct and the return of weapons. As had his ancestors, Daniel had come to realize how great can be the price of liberty.[11]

Following his arrival in the Salt Lake Valley in 1848, Daniel H. Wells played an active role in the organization of government in the "State of Deseret." He served on its first legislative council, became state attorney, and took a command in the militia (still called the Nauvoo Legion) with the rank of major general. Later advancing to the rank of lieutenant general, he served with distinction in two "wars." During the Walker Indian uprising in the counties south of Salt Lake, General Wells personally led the legion in its efforts to protect the fragile communities of the region. Later, when President James Buchanan decided in 1857 to replace Brigham Young as governor of the territory and dispatched a large army expedition to accompany the new governor, the Mormons understandably feared a recurrence of mob action under the guise of legality. General Wells took the field and with a handful of men sealed the Echo Canyon entrance to the valley during the ensuing winter.[12]

With the peaceful end of this "Utah War," General Wells resumed his place as a leading actor on the political stage of the territory, serving several terms in the assembly and in most of the conventions that drafted constitutions to accompany Utah's numerous pleas for admission to the Union. "Squire Wells" was known widely for his thorough understanding of the principles of the Constitution and his defense therefrom of the rights of the Latter-day Saints. "We believe and worship as we choose," he once said, "and live under a Government that guarantees unto us that right. Inasmuch as they do not give us those rights, they violate one of the holiest and most sacred provisions of the Constitution of our country, and destruction will be the consequence."[13] He liked to recall that his "fathers of the Revolution fought and bled to secure this holy right" to the freedom of conscience.[14] Yet Squire Wells knew well that "even in this free country some have sought to deprive us of the free enjoyment of the privileges granted unto us in the Consititution of our country, and they will have to pay the penalty for so doing for they trample under foot the Constitution that grants them their own liberties. . . ."[15] Recognizing that the cost of freedom was high, he had long since committed himself to its perpetual maintenance.

Despite Daniel's value as a civil servant to the Saints, there was a more serious calling in store for the former squire of Commerce, Illinois. Sometime following the death of Jedediah M. Grant, who had served as second counselor to Brigham Young for a few months, the President called Elder Wells to his office and asked him to fill the vacancy in the First Presidency of the Church. President Wells was set apart to the position on January 4, 1857, ten years after his baptism in the Mississippi and his decision to follow the Church in its westward search for freedom. Until the death of Brigham Young twenty years later, he worked faithfully for the welfare of the people he had admired from the first time he saw them. But his civic service had not ended with this ecclesiastical appointment. Until 1864, when he departed for a mission to Great Britain, he was superintendent of public works in Great Salt Lake City. In February 1866 he was elected mayor of the city and held that position during successive terms until 1876. With the demise of Brigham Young the following year, Daniel Wells was released from the First Presidency to become a counselor to the Council of the Twelve Apostles. He worked in that capacity and also as president of the Manti Temple until his death on March 24, 1891, in Salt Lake City.[16]

As a final note and perhaps better than any other, the following incident in the life of Daniel H. Wells illustrates his commitment to the ideals of the American Revolution and to the spirit that inspired the signers of the Declaration of Independence to stake their "lives, fortunes, and sacred honor" on the cause of freedom. On May 2, 1879, he was called as a witness in a polygamy case. The federally appointed prosecutor, more interested in embarrassing the Church than in obtaining justice, demanded that President Wells describe the clothing worn during the administration of the temple endowment. He refused and was immediately arrested for contempt. The next day the attorney placed him on the stand again and repeated the demand, to which Daniel replied, "I declined to answer that question yesterday, and do so today, because I am under moral and sacred obligations to not answer; and it is interwoven in my character never to betray a friend, a brother, my country, my God or my religion."[17] He was sentenced to two days in the penitentiary and a fine of $100, but the ultimate victory was his. Upon his release, some 10,000 people met him at the prison gates cheering and waving flags as a tribute to his stand against attempted tyranny of the soul. The entire procession then marched to the Tabernacle, where he received a hero's welcome.[18]

The name of Wells came to have a larger significance in the history of Mormonism's revolutionary heritage even beyond the life of the famous squire. On October 10, 1852, a twenty-four-year-old woman named Emmeline Blanche Woodward entered the household of Daniel H. Wells as a plural wife. Her story is one of the most remarkable among the many to be told of the women of Mormondom. Like those of General Wells, Emmeline's ancestors had shouldered the burden of freedom during the early years of the United States. Her grandfather, Elisha Woodward, was in the Patriot army and in later years took great pleasure in reciting to little Emmeline tales of his experiences during the Revolution. She never forgot the stories nor the circumstances in which the old veteran related them to her.[19] Her father, David, served in the American Army during the War of 1812 as the United States reasserted its independence before the world. Though her father died when she was only four years old, Emmeline sensed as well his participation in the birth and growing pains of the nation.[20] For herself, she quickly displayed an incredible appetite for education. At the age of fifteen she began teaching school and was also baptized a Mormon. The following year, 1843, she married James H.

Harris, the son of a local elder in her home area of Massachusetts. The young couple immediately set out for Nauvoo and a future, particularly for the bride, that no one could have predicted.[21]

Arriving in the city of the Saints on the Mississippi, Emmeline could hardly wait to meet Joseph Smith, Jr. It was a story she would tell her own grandchildren repeatedly:

As we were traveling up to Nauvoo, a lady who knew [the Prophet] very well talked a great deal about him, but I never thought to ask any questions —I sat simply breathless, listening. When we arrived at the city of Nauvoo, a great crowd of people, both men and women, came down to the landing, four or five hundred, I should say, and as we were coming from the boat to the shore, I noticed among them a man taller and larger, it seemed to me, than any other man in the crowd. To me it seemed as if he stood head and shoulders above every man and woman there, and I knew instantly by the feeling I had that it must be the Prophet Joseph. As we came up the landing and stood on the bank of the river among the people, he shook hands with all the newcomers and welcomed them to the city. When he came to me, he also shook hands with me and I think I felt more insignificant at that moment than I ever felt in my life time. I felt as if I could shrink away. I experienced such a wonderful feeling. . . .[22]

If the year 1844 began on the wings of soaring exultation for the young woman, it ended in sinking sorrow. The death of the Prophet came in June; three months later, Emmeline buried her infant son. Her sudden trials were by no means over. Late that fall, James Harris left Nauvoo ostensibly to take care of some business in St. Louis. He never returned.[23]

When Harris abandoned her, Emmeline was barely through her seventeenth year, and compounding her situation were ill health and the increasing persecution of the Saints. Olive Bishop, a cousin of Presiding Bishop Newel K. Whitney, took her into her home and cared for her until the young woman regained her strength. Through this close relationship with Olive Bishop, and anticipating the journey west, Emmeline agreed to join the household of Bishop Whitney as his plural wife. The Whitney family reached Salt Lake City in October 1848 just before Emmeline gave birth to a daughter. Two years later she gave birth to a second child, but the father lived to enjoy his new daughter only a few weeks, for he died in the fall of

Emmeline B. Wells (Archives of The Church of Jesus Christ of Latter-day Saints)

1850. Two years passed again, and the twenty-year-old widow returned to her teaching profession in order to support her small children. But she had come to the attention of Daniel H. Wells, and in October 1852, she became Emmeline B. Wells. She was finally in a situation that could give her intellect the opportunity to blossom.[24]

As soon as Emmeline was in the secure situation of wife to General Wells, her broad literary capabilities and intellectual capacity came rapidly to fruition. She sang in the Tabernacle Choir, wrote prolifically, and became a leader in the advanced movement for women's rights that had emerged in Utah Territory. Indeed, in 1870 Emmeline B. Wells cast one of the first ballots after the franchise had been granted to Utah women. She made much of this symbolic event in the course of her writings, primarily in the *Woman's Exponent*. In 1877 she succeeded to the editorship of that publication, remaining in the position until the final issue came off the press in 1914. She became deeply immersed in the work of the Relief Society and was a moving force in the organization of the Primary and Young Ladies Mutual Improvement associations, but her major interests were never far removed from the political scene. In connection with her participation in the national suffrage movement,

Emmeline devoted herself to the defense of Mormonism and of Latter-day Saint women. She traveled extensively to campaign against the anti-polygamy laws, and at every opportunity she challenged the national prejudice against the Church. In the course of this defense, she corresponded with many influential citizens of the nation and continued to write in every literary forum to which she could gain access. Few informed Americans in the late nineteenth century failed to recognize the name of Emmeline B. Wells.[25]

Perhaps of more lasting significance than all of her work on the national scene, however, were her efforts at home in both the political and religious realms of Utah life. She broke important ground for women as a member of the territorial central and Salt Lake County committees of the Mormon Peoples Party and as a delegate to the constitutional convention of 1882. When the Saints divided along national party lines in preparation for statehood early in the 1890s, Emmeline Wells became an ardent Republican, so much so, in fact, that political historians of the state have called her the founder of the Utah G.O.P. Yet with all of these civic activities to take her attention, Emmeline continued faithfully her service to

South Temple Street, Great Salt Lake City, with the Homes of Brigham Young (left) and Daniel H. Wells (Archives of The Church of Jesus Christ of Latter-day Saints)

the Relief Society. After serving in various positions in the organization, she was called in 1910 as general president, and to this office she devoted the remaining energies of her vibrant life. She was eighty-two when she assumed that demanding position, but she continued to labor in the cause and advancement of women. For Emmeline Wells it was no less a fight for freedom that the Revolution had been. "Aunt Em" died in her sleep on April 25, 1921, at the home of her daughter in Salt Lake City.[26]

Another Wells who prominently played a role in Utah history was born to Martha Harris and Daniel H. Wells in Salt Lake City on August 11, 1859. Heber Manning Wells was graduated from the University of Utah (then Deseret University) at the age of sixteen and immediately followed his illustrious father into public service. He held various public offices until thrust into the forefront of Utah politics during an unsuccessful bid in 1892 for the office of Salt Lake City mayor. From that point the rise of his political fortunes was meteoric. After serving in the constitutional convention that drafted the final document which accompanied Utah's successful application for admission to the Union in 1895, he found himself proposed to head the Republican ticket as its candidate for governor. He accepted the nomination and campaigned vigorously and successfully. On January 6, 1896, this great-grandson of Private David Chapin of the Ninth Connecticut Regiment became the first governor of the state of Utah. He occupied the statehouse for eight years; and though relatively young during this term of service, he gained a large following and managed to govern the infant state with a sagacity that even his opponents had to admire. Following the expiration of his second term, Governor Wells engaged in banking until 1913, when he was elected to the Salt Lake City Commission. He later worked for the Internal Revenue Service in California but soon returned to Utah and a position on the editorial board of the *Salt Lake Herald*. He died in 1938, having demonstrated fully that he was indeed a son of the Revolution.[27]

Heber's youngest full brother, Briant Harris Wells, carried on the Spirit of 1776 among the Wellses in yet a different direction. Briant was born in Salt Lake City December 6, 1872, and was educated in the district schools and at Deseret University. Demonstrating early a clear mind and a certain determination, he received an appointment to the United States Military Academy at West Point in 1889. Only seventeen years old and with a comparatively poor

Briant Harris Wells
(Courtesy Jane Wells Townsend,
White Plains, New York)

Heber Manning Wells
(Courtesy Utah State Historical
Society)

preparation for the entrance examinations, he left for the East early in order to enroll in a two-month crash program at a military preparatory school. After four years of hard work he was graduated from West Point and took a commission in the infantry. His first assignments were in the West, and he was able to visit Salt Lake City often enough to win Mary Jane Jennings as his wife.

The peacetime soldiering came to a sudden end in 1898 when the battleship *Maine* sank in the Spanish harbor at Havana, Cuba. Lieutenant Wells was among the first Americans to arrive in Cuba for the campaign against Spain. In the now famous Battle of San Juan Hill, his "gallantry and efficiency under fire" won for him the Silver Star. A few days later he caught a Spanish bullet and was shipped home for hospital care. Within a month he was up and on his way to the Philippines to aid in quashing the insurrection on the island of Panay. There he demonstrated a certain heritage of Mormonism—hard work. One of his superior officers remembered that Captain Wells appreciated, "as few in our day do, that in military operations there is no difference between day and night when work is to be done."[28] It was obvious that this Mormon great-grandson of the Revolution was going to be a fine soldier.

With the end of the Philippine rebellion, Briant Wells returned to the United States and another period of peacetime preparation for the possibility of war. And it was not long in coming. In 1914 war broke out in Europe, and though the United States government tried to steer a careful course of neutrality, the army anticipated the chance of future American involvement by placing its best officers in training positions. Briant Wells, now a major, became chief of staff in the Sixteenth Division, which had been mobilized on the border with Mexico during the 1916 Pershing Expedition against Pancho Villa. He was serving in that position, training the activated National Guard, when the United States finally declared war on the Central Powers and entered World War I. Major Wells was rushed to Washington for duty on the War Department general staff, but soon received a promotion to lieutenant colonel and the command of a regiment. After training his men at Fort Lee, Virginia, he was surprised to find himself reassigned to the American section of the Supreme War Council in Europe. The reason for this sudden transfer was General Tasker Bliss, who considered him "one of the best qualified officers I have ever served with. . . ." In addition to working under Bliss, Colonel Wells was also assigned as American liaison officer to French Marshal Ferdinand Foch, the Supreme Allied Commander. Eventually, however, Colonel Wells persuaded Bliss to allow him time from staff duty behind the lines to a post on the front. He was consequently tendered the brevet of brigadier general and served as chief of staff under three commanding generals of the Fourth and Sixth Corps. In this capacity he worked through the arduous campaigns in the Woevre Sector, St. Mihiel, and the Argonne. By the end of the war he had earned the Distinguished Service Medal and the total respect of his colleagues, commanders, and subordinates. General Wells had proven, as had his great-grandfather and his father, that when the price of freedom had to paid in the perils of warfare, he had the spirit to do it, and to do it well.[29]

Following the war, Briant Wells returned to the general staff of the War Department and was detailed to the war plans division. Within a year he was its chief and had been rated by "Black Jack" Pershing, then army chief of staff, as number two among the two score brigadier generals he knew. Meriting this kind of confidence, General Wells received in 1923 the most coveted command in the infantry, the Infantry School at Fort Benning, Georgia. During three years at Benning, Wells built the school, both in terms of its advanced training development and in the expanion of its physical facilities, which included the construction of a large athletic field house subsequently named in his honor. He was promoted to major general (two stars) in 1928 after his service at Benning and as assistant chief of staff in the War Department.

In 1930 General Wells took command of the divison at Schofield Barracks, Hawaii, and the following year he became head of the Hawaiian Department of the Army. Here he devoted himself to a revision of the defense plans for the islands, a massive construction program, and a general tightening of operations. But the most significant contribution of General Wells in Hawaii came in the realm of civil relations. He had little patience with racial prejudice, and when he discovered an antagonism between his men and the native and oriental populations of the islands, he bent every effort to see that cordial relations evolved. His success demonstrated itself when, upon his retirement from the army in 1935, a group of native Hawaiians campaigned for his appointment as governor of the territory. He had, however, decided to take a position on the executive council of the Hawaiian Sugar Planters Association. He also became deeply involved in the community life of Hawaii, serving as the first president of the Honolulu Community Theater and as a member of the numerous local civic organizations, including the Hawaiian Historical Society and the Social Science Club of Hawaii. In this way the retired general from Utah spent the remaining days of his impressive life, which ended June 10, 1949.[30]

The outbreak of World War II provided Briant H. Wells with perhaps his greatest opportunity to display a personal inheritance from the revolutionary epoch. After the Japanese bombed Pearl Harbor in December 1941, Japanese-Americans living on the west coast of the American mainland were immediately subject to tremendous persecution. Their loyalty was suspect, not because of their actions but because of their racial background. Americans of Japanese descent were arrested and "reconcentrated" inland in what is surely a shameful episode in the history of the United States. This anti-oriental complex quickly spread to Hawaii, but General Wells, now one of the territory's most respected citizens, spoke vigorously in defense of the Japanese-American group in the islands and expressed his dismay at the actions of those in the States who had given way to hysteria. In large part because of his forceful stand, the persecution never came to Hawaii, and like the Mormons, the Japanese-Americans abundantly proved their loyalty to the United States.[31] It was no wonder that Briant H. Wells, the first Latter-day Saint to hold the rank of major general in the United States Army, had come to the defense of the rights and freedom of worthy Americans. Such action ran in the family.

Edward Bunker:
Heritage of a Name

The most famous name in the lexicon of the Revolutionary War is that of Washington, but not far behind is that of Bunker. In the case of Washington, the cause for fame is a man who served his country as its commander-in-chief during the struggle for independence and who subsequently became the first president of the United States under the newly framed Constitution. The name Bunker, on the other hand, gained its fame at the beginning of the fight for freedom, June 17, 1775, as a place on the Charlestown Peninsula just north of Boston. Then and there, Bunker Hill became an indelible part of the story of the American Revolution.

Following the skirmish at Lexington and the bloody fight between Concord and Boston on April 19, the British retreated from the Massachusetts countryside into the secure confines of Boston to await reinforcements from London and to prepare for what the redcoats believed would be a quick repression of the upstart rebellion. By the first day of June, however, General Thomas Gage, royal governor of the Bay Colony, discovered that all he governed was the city of Boston, and that his domain was surrounded and under siege. On June 12, the governor and his lieutenants decided to wait no longer for more troops en route from England and to move at once against the Americans. Realizing that he was too weak to crush

105

Edward Bunker (Courtesy Winona Wittwer, Centerville, Utah)

the Patriot army surrounding him, General Gage determined to strengthen his position in Boston by garrisoning Dorchester Heights to the south and securing the high ground on Charlestown Peninsula to the north. Fortunately for the Americans, word of the British plan leaked out in plenty of time for Patriot leaders to construct counter-measures, one of which was the immediate occupation and fortification of Bunker Hill, which controlled western approaches to the peninsula. On the night of the sixteenth, a contingent of Patriot militia moved onto the peninsula with this objective in mind, but for some unknown reason, they passed Bunker Hill and set up their defenses on the lower knoll to the east called Breed's Hill. The Americans were unavoidably noisy in their efforts, and by dawn the British command had met in urgent session to consider a new course of action. After various internecine squabbles, the redcoat officers decided upon what J. R. Alden has called a "conventional and uninspired plan" to attack the Americans from the point of the peninsula and thus drive them back to the mainland.[1]

Confident of easy victory, the British landed on the peninsula in the afternoon of the seventeenth under the command of the vain and vigorous Major General William Howe. After wasting considerable time in preparations for a lengthy stay in the area, General Howe finally ordered 1500 redcoats to assault the American right flank, fully expecting the Patriots to take flight. To his great surprise, the outnumbered Yankees instead drove the British back with a series of musket volleys. Indignantly, he reformed his troops and led a frontal assault against the American positions on the hill. This too fell back before the wall of Patriot fire, and the ground was now littered with the bodies of dead and wounded royal troops. Nevertheless, General Howe realized in the midst of his shock that he had the colonials outmanned and that time was on his side. Because of the presence of the Royal Navy in position about the peninsula, the Patriots had no hope for reinforcements, and with just more than 2,000 men, rebel Colonel William Prescott knew he was fighting against odds overwhelmingly in favor of the British. However, he had the advantages of position and fairly good, though minimal, fortifications, and he therefore planned to hold his position and at the same time inflict heavy losses upon the enemy. The British had other ideas. Bolstered by the arrival of more men from Boston, General Howe ordered a third attack on the hill. This time the Patriots lacked the powder to repel a sustained onslaught

Prescott at the Battle of Bunker Hill (Painting by F. C. Yohn, The Continental Insurance Companies)

of redcoat bayonets and were soon retreating toward the mainland. As the day ended, so had the Battle of Bunker Hill, and Governor Gage had captured Charlestown Peninsula. The victory, however, went to the Americans, at least in real terms. They had lost more than four hundred soldiers, but their adversaries, in one of the bloodiest battles of the eighteenth century, had sustained losses totaling over 40 percent of their attacking force. Though they sat on top of their objective, Gage and his officers had little cause for joy. On June 17, 1775, it was even more abundantly apparent than it had been at Lexington and Concord that the Americans meant business, and that it would take more than a few days and a few redcoats to turn the tide of independence.[2]

Even though the main action in the campaign for Charlestown Peninsula occurred on Breed's Hill, control of the larger, more strategically placed mound to the northwest was the objective of the

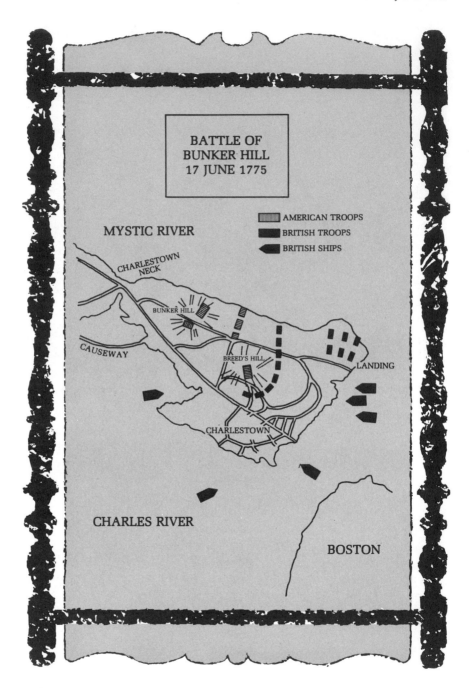

battle. Consequently, the day's combat became known as the Battle of Bunker Hill, and the name of Bunker entered the annals of the revolutionary age as a symbol of early American determination to fight the British for freedom.

The Bunker family was itself one of the oldest in Massachusetts. Within two decades of the settlement of Massachusetts Bay in the early seventeenth century, George Bunker had arrived from England and settled at Charlestown, eventually lending his name to the nearby hill. By the time of the Revolution, the Bunkers were numerous throughout New England, but particularly in Massachusetts, New Hampshire, and the northern section of the Bay Colony, which later became the state of Maine. Massachusetts contributed at least eight Bunkers to the Patriot ranks, including a thirty-three-year-old private from Sedgwick, Maine, named Silas Bunker. He enlisted in 1779 for service in a summer expedition of the local militia and served in the post-revolutionary period as surveyor of highways in Sedgwick. He died in 1829 at Blue Hill, Maine, but not before rearing a large family. His son and namesake followed suit with another large brood, the ninth child and youngest son of which was named Edward. His destiny was enmeshed in the rise of The Church of Jesus Christ of Latter-day Saints as a power in the Rocky Mountains. As a result, the Bunker name came to be as important to the Mormon heritage in the West as it was to the remembrance of the Revolution.[3]

Edward Bunker was born in Penobscot County, Maine, on August 1, 1822. In 1841 he decided to move west, and while passing through Kirtland, Ohio, he met Martin Harris and heard from him the story of Joseph Smith and the foundation of the restored church. Though Edward Bunker was curious, he moved on to Cleveland, where he went to work with the idea of saving money and eventually settling in Wisconsin. But the restoration continued to pursue him. In Cleveland he received from his brother-in-law a copy of the Book of Mormon and a tract called *The Voice of Warning*. He accepted them, sought out a branch of the Church, and was baptized in April 1845. Before long the spirit of gathering drew him toward the main body of the Saints at Nauvoo; he worked his way westward, arriving in July. There he went to work on the temple, which the Mormons were feverishly trying to complete in the face of growing mob violence in the area. Being young and single, he also enlisted for duty in the Nauvoo Legion and assisted in the defense of the city and in the evacuation of the Saints from the surrounding countryside. In the midst of this excitement, he found time to court Emily Abbott, whom he married on February 9, 1846, while the Saints were in the process of deserting the city for a home in the West.[4]

The young Bunker couple was completely without means for the trek west, so Edward went down the Mississippi, where he could earn enough to get them started with the rest of the exodus. He eventually found a way to obtain transportation but ran out of means at Garden Grove, Iowa. There, with some relatives, the Bunkers moved into a one-room log house. Hoping to earn enough in Missouri to outfit themselves with a wagon and team, Edward and a companion traveled southward in search of work. But a more certain solution to the problem of transportation west quickly presented itself. On the way into Missouri, he learned that the United States government had agreed to Brigham Young's request to allow some 500 Mormon men to volunteer for service in the Mexican War, which had erupted that spring. Hurrying home, Edward met some Saints who repeated the news and indicated that President Young had sent a letter to Garden Grove calling for men to assist in the care and movement west of the families of the members of the volunteer battalion. In return, such helpers could use the teams to bring their own families to Council Bluffs. Edward jumped at the chance. He rushed home, confirmed the stories he had heard, and set out for Council Bluffs. Ten miles from the Missouri, messengers met his party with a request for sixteen additional men to complete the Battalion. Reluctantly, and with thoughts undoubtedly centered upon the long separation from his young wife who was expecting their first child, Edward Bunker joined the Mormon Battalion.[5]

After settling into the Battalion camp outside Council Bluffs, Edward heard the story of the unit's origins and its mission. As part of the government's strategy for the defeat of Mexico, Colonel (soon General) Stephen Watts Kearny had been ordered to march into what is now New Mexico, Arizona, and California to secure American control of that region. Commanding the "Army of the West," Kearny had already left Fort Leavenworth, Kansas, for Santa Fe with a large contingent of troops, but in response to a Mormon request he had dispatched Captain James Allen to the camps of the Saints in Iowa to recruit a battalion to follow his expedition. Brigham Young welcomed Captain Allen and his offer to augment finances for the Mormon exodus with army paychecks. President Young and other leaders consequently assisted Allen in the mustering of the Battalion, after which the captain received the brevet of lieutenant colonel, formed up his new command, and moved out for Fort Leavenworth. And so it was that on July 16, 1846, Edward Bunker and five hundred other Mormon men and a number of women and children began what would be one of the longest and most trying infantry marches in American history.[6]

Some two weeks after their departure from Council Bluffs, the Mormons under Colonel Allen arrived at Fort Leavenworth. There the Battalion was outfitted with the tools of war and received a clothing allowance most of which went back to the Church and to families in Iowa. Over a period of three days following receipt of their marching orders, the five companies of the Battalion left Fort Leavenworth for Santa Fe. Within four days members of the Battalion had united on the trail and were marching en masse. Edward Bunker was in Company E, where he put his skills to use as a teamster. While camped at a place called Coal Creek, or Hurricane Point, as the Mormons called it, the Battalion rode out a severe storm, the misery of which was heightened when word arrived that the popular Colonel Allen was seriously ill at Leavenworth and could not join them. On August 22 they named their next camp Allen's Grove in honor of their stricken leader. Learning shortly afterward that he was dead, the members of the Battalion selected Captain Jefferson Hunt to assume command, but within days regular army officers arrived, and under them the Mormons resumed their forced march toward Santa Fe. The new commander, Lieutenant Andrew Jackson Smith, quickly demonstrated his disrespect for the Saints and thus heightened the Battalion's sense of loss over the death of Colonel Allen. They nevertheless fell in daily behind their new leader and pushed on.[7]

On September 10, as they camped on the Arkansas River in the middle of Kansas, the Mormons were visited by the noted traveling historian of the West, Francis Parkman. His journal mentioned the event: "As we ascended the hollow where the water lay, saw the opposite swell covered with wagons and footmen, and the water itself surrounded by white tents, cattle, and wagons drawn up in order. These were other companies of Price's regt., the Mormon Battalion commanded by Col. Smith, and wagons of Mormon emigrants."[8]

111

Parkman's observation is interesting not only for its visual picture of the Battalion in camp, but also because "companies of Price's regt." were part of the Missouri Volunteer Cavalry also heading for Santa Fe. Here in the same place were Mormons and Missourians, a mixture that just a few years before had been as volatile as saltpeter and charcoal. Now they were thrown together in a march to war, this time on the same side. About this time the Battalion learned that General Kearny had taken Santa Fe without resistance; the unit was ordered to proceed directly to the old settlement rather than by way of Bent's Fort as had been planned. It already appeared, as indeed was the case, that the Mormon volunteers were following in the wake of a victorious army whose rapid and easy successes might well prevent its Latter-day Saint reinforcements from firing a single shot in combat.[9]

Whether warfare waited at the end of their journey or not, young Edward Bunker and his comrades had to pay a heavy price in hardship and privation simply to get to the scene of the conflict. By the middle of September, they were in the midst of the Cimarron Desert in what is now southwestern Kansas. One of the soldiers, Henry Standage, remembered walking some twenty miles in intense heat without water and then finally quenching his thirst with muddy water "that the Buffaloes had wallowed in and could not be compared to anything but Buffalo urine, as a great portion of it was of the same, yet we were glad to get this."[10] And the very next day Standage wrote similarly of "toils on this sandy desert," and of finding some welcome "rain water about 2 o'clock, mixed with Buffalo dung and urine; drank some of which seemed to be a blessing."[11]

As might be expected under such circumstances, sickness was a serious problem during the entire march. The army surgeon accompanying the Battalion, Dr. George B. Sanderson, was in addition often more of a hindrance than a help to those who were ill as he tried to force his medicines upon the Mormons, who were more inclined to practice faith and folk remedies. Another of Edward Bunker's compatriots, Daniel Tyler, later recalled his own typical response to a bout with "fever" that made it eventually impossible for him to walk: "The teamsters feared trouble with the Doctor if they allowed him [Tyler] to ride in the wagons unless he was on the sick report, and as he preferred the mercy of the savages to the cruelty and wicked abuse of Dr. Sanderson, with his poisonous drugs, he lay down upon the ground and begged his messmates to leave him, and report him dead and buried."[12] The physician was that terrifying to the members of the Battalion. But Daniel Tyler, Edward Bunker, and the rest learned to take Dr. Sanderson's calomel powders and molasses delivered in a famous "rusty old spoon," and somehow they managed to reach Santa Fe during the second week of October 1846.[13]

As the first of the Mormons arrived in the New Mexico capital on October 9, they encountered a face and figure familiar to many of them in the form of General Alexander W. Doniphan of Missouri, commander of American forces in Santa Fe. General Doniphan had befriended the Saints during their trials in Missouri and had refused, following the surrender of Far West in the fall of 1838, to carry out an order to execute Joseph Smith and other Church leaders. Upon learning of the Mormon approach, the general ordered a 100-gun salute in honor of the Battalion. On October 14, Colonel Philip St. George Cooke assumed command of the unit from Lieutenant Smith, and five days later he marched the Battalion a few miles west of Santa Fe. There he inspected the contingent and decided that almost a hundred men of his new command were unfit for the long march into California. Accordingly, he detached eighty-six men and twenty women and children, and sent them with minimal supplies north to Pueblo (now Colorado). There they would winter with a group of Saints from the southern states who had established winter quarters in anticipation of linking with the main body of the Church on the trail west. Edward Bunker, however, was strong and healthy, and he was detailed as a teamster for the trip to San Diego. Colonel Cooke had outfitted each of the companies with three mule wagons, and the Battalion had in addition several other ox teams and mule wagons, totaling in all about thirty wagons. For a "motley but mobile commissary," the colonel had obtained several head of beef and three hundred head of Spanish sheep. Within a few days, the companies were on their way to the Pacific.[14]

From Fort Leavenworth, the Battalion had followed essentially the old Santa Fe Trail and had little need for experienced guides, but going on to the coast was a different story. The terrain over which they were to travel was extremely rugged and much of it poorly charted. For this reason, Colonel Cooke hired three guides, the chief of which was Pauline Weaver, an old trapper who had worked for the Hudson Bay Company and who knew not only the

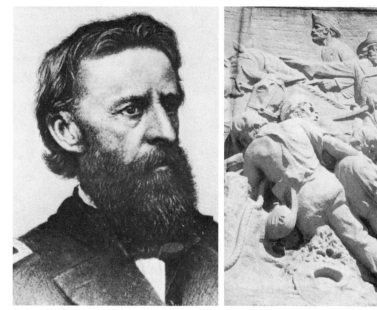

*Colonel Philip St. George Cooke
(Archives of The Church of Jesus Christ
of Latter-day Saints)*

*Detail of Relief on Mormon Battalion
Monument (Sculpture by Gilbert Riswold,
Utah State Capitol Grounds,
Photograph by Dean L. May)*

physiography of the country but also its cantankerous inhabitants, the Apaches. The other two were Antoine Leroux and Baptiste Charbonneau, the latter being the son of the famous Sacajawea who had guided the Lewis and Clark expedition in 1803-1806. Indeed, Charbonneau had been born during the expedition and made most of the trip in a papoose cradle-board on his mother's back. In these capable hands and under the strict leadership of Cooke and his staff, the Battalion moved slowly southward along the west bank of the Rio Grande through Albuquerque and Socorro to the place at which Kearny, a few weeks earlier, had left a sign indicating that the Battalion should leave the river and strike out across the desert to the southwest rather than follow him on down the Rio Grande. On the advice of his guides, Cooke decided to follow the general's tracks for another day or two and then to cut a new wagon road across some of the most desolate country in North America. A wilderness march would be the forge upon which the steel of the Mormon Battalion would be put to the test.[15]

On November 9, the Battalion reached the point where Kearny had left the Rio Grande for the Gila River to the west. At this point, Cooke again inspected his army. Only the toughest outfit would be able to withstand what was ahead, and the colonel cut out of the column the ill and inefficient and sent them to Pueblo to join the earlier detachment. He also pruned his materiel until only the basic essentials remained. The Battalion was now composed of only 340 soldiers, but it was a crack unit, ready for any eventuality. Edward Bunker was one of these men, "hard and lean, deadwood pruned, . . . psychologically geared to a transcontinental trek, . . . uniquely prepared for the dramatic and gruelling desert march that lay ahead."[16] But not even the careful but determined Colonel Cooke and his cautious, even pessimistic, guides could fully anticipate the hardships they would meet. Only the actual experience could paint the picture in real colors.

The march of the next ten days was particularly rigorous. On two occasions the Battalion had to lay over for a day in order to rest men and animals. Cooke, in the meantime, proved himself to be a hard taskmaster and a man of unflinching purpose. The Saints bore his verbal abuse and hard-driving discipline stoically, and even prayed constantly in his behalf. Believing on November 20, for example, that some of the officers had prevailed upon Cooke to turn southward into Mexico in search of "whiskey, tobacco and women," three hundred Battalion members prayed that the colonel would turn west. When Cooke did so the next day, one private exclaimed "God bless the Colonel!"[17] Whether or not inspiration had anything to do with the colonel's choice of routes, the trail that the Battalion blazed across the deserts of present-day New Mexico and Arizona was through some of the most treacherous territory in North America. The men (and three women) crossed the continental divide on November 25 and by the first of December had passed over terrain so rugged that Colonel Cooke called his route a "portage" rather than a trail or road. Indeed, at various times in the arid Guadalupe Mountains the men of the Battalion did practically carry the wagons over the ground. Eventually they reached the San Pedro River, which they then followed westward for several days. Even on the banks of that river they had to cut a path through sand, rocks, and cactus, which made them more road builders than they would ever be soldiers.[18]

On December 11, 1846, the Mormons finally came into combat.

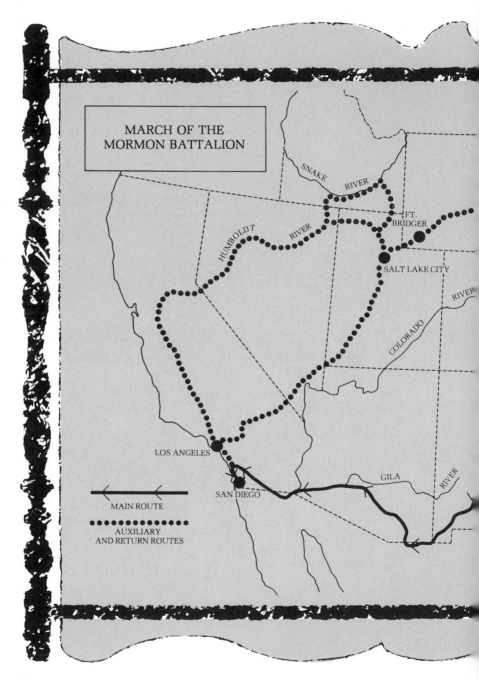

MARCH OF THE
MORMON BATTALION

SNAKE RIVER

HUMBOLDT RIVER

FT.
BRIDGER

SALT LAKE CITY

COLORADO RIVER

LOS ANGELES

SAN DIEGO

GILA RIVER

MAIN ROUTE

AUXILIARY
AND RETURN ROUTES

It was their only engagement of the Mexican War. Known as the Battle of the Bulls, it will never enter the annals of classic warfare, for the enemy was not at all brilliant on the battlefield. While marching along that day, the Battalion was suddenly attacked without warning by a company of wild Mexican bulls. Some men were tossed about, with at least one receiving a nasty gash in the leg. The bulls seemed intent upon devastating the wagons and mules. One animal rode high into the air on the horns of a bull and landed on the other side of its teammate while another of the enemy smashed headlong into a wagon. Despite this determined assault, the Battalion fought bravely and counted, as the dust cleared, only a few minor casualties, mostly among the mules. The enemy, however, lost some sixty to eighty bulls and probably never recovered from its encounter with the Mormon Battalion.[19]

After severe marches and several fortuitous discoveries of water in the desert after they left the San Pedro, Edward Bunker and his fellow soldiers finally arrived at the Gila River, which they followed to its confluence with the Colorado. Along the Gila, on December 21, they picked up the trail of General Kearny once again. As a result, and with the existence of numerous Spanish trails in the area, Colonel Cooke and his men no longer suffered under the necessity of trailblazing. But with this, the colonel hastened the pace. On Christmas day, the Battalion covered eighteen miles.[20] It was a day on which the sufferings of body and soul seemed more acute than ever. Wrote one:

This is rather a strange Christmas to me. My situation with my family in days gone by was called to mind and contrasted with my present situation on the sandy deserts through which pass the Gila and Colorado Rivers. Suffering much at times for the want of water, but still pressing forward with parched lips, scalded shoulders, weary limbs, blistered feet, worn out shoes and ragged clothes; but with me the prospect of the result of my present toils, cheers me on."[21]

Edward Bunker, though he kept no daily record of his Battalion experience, probably had similar thoughts as he imagined his young bride spending Christmas in a half-finished cabin in faraway Iowa. As with soldiers throughout history, his dreams were for the future, when he would see his loved ones again and when the reward for his service would be manifest. Only such thoughts could

118

ease the Christmas pain in the pit of a soldier's stomach.

The Battalion reached the banks of the Colorado River on the morning of January 9, 1847, then proceeded along its south bank as far as it flowed to the west (about ten miles). The next day they started across the river, but so difficult was the crossing that by nightfall they had still not completed the task. On January 11, they pushed into the desert on the Pacific side of the great river, trudging through deep sand that hampered their progress for several days. After a brutal forced march of nearly a hundred miles from the Colorado through what is now known as the Imperial Desert, they reached the Carrizo River, where they demonstrated a resilience that surprised even their commander, who, after giving the men a badly needed day of rest on January 18, could not believe it when he surveyed his "half-starved, worn-out men . . . playing the fiddle and singing merry songs."[22] His determination for speed seemed to wane as the Battalion approached the Pacific. On January 22 he gave the troops another day off at a place called Warner's Ranch near the present location of Palomar Observatory. The goal was in sight.[23]

January 27, 1847, was a day members of the Mormon Battalion never forgot. Like Vasco Nuñez de Balboa, who had discovered the Pacific Ocean in 1513, the battalionists gazed upon that mightiest of seas with reverence and awe for its beauty that "far exceeded our most sanguine expectations."[24] Edward Bunker's reminiscence contained only two paragraphs to cover his experience with the Battalion, since he left to others "the details of the march," but even he mentioned January 27.[25] For the Mormon Battalion, the Pacific's beauty came more from its symbolism than from its intrinsic appearance: it meant their war was over, a war in their case not against men but against the pounding distance of the North American desert, against harsh elements of nature, and against despair and longing.

Following a brief stay at the mission at San Luis Rey near present-day Oceanside, California, the Battalion moved south to San Diego and then northward into Los Angeles, with the exception of Company B, which remained in San Diego for garrison duty. A few men received other assignments, but most of the Mormon veterans of the march were stationed in Los Angeles until July 16, 1847, when the five companies lined up for mustering out. They gave three cheers, collected their pay and belongings, and started for the Great Salt Lake Valley or Iowa, expecting to find their families somewhere on the line of wagon tracks between the two places.[26]

Many have eulogized the service of the Mormon Battalion, but none better than its commander from Santa Fe to the Pacific, Colonel Cooke. Though harsh and demanding, he had gained a respect for his Mormon soldiers, and his letter of congratulations to the Battalion at the end of its march reflected his regard for his troops and their accomplishment:

History may be searched in vain for an equal march of infantry. Nine-tenths of it has been through a wilderness where nothing but savages and wild beasts were found, or deserts where, for want of water, there is no living creature. . . . With crowbar and pick ax in hand we have worked our way over mountains which seem to defy aught save the wild goat, and hewed a passage through a chasm of living rock more narrow than our wagons . . . [while] marching half naked and half fed, and living upon wild animals. . . .[27]

Upon their discharge, some of the Mormons tarried in California. Indeed, some men of the Battalion were working for John Sutter when gold was discovered near his mill in the Sacramento Valley in January 1848. But most, like Edward Bunker, journeyed quickly eastward to join their wives, children, and the body of the Saints. Edward accompanied one of three squads that left Los Angeles, passed through Sutter's Fort, and traced the emigrant trail east over the North Pass of the Sierra Nevada. His group entered the infant City of the Great Salt Lake on October 16, 1847. After a brief pause for rest and resupply, he and some others left the new Zion and hastened eastward. The season being late, they suffered tremendously on their journey back to the Missouri, but·they were accustomed to that. The hunger and hard going were nothing new, and the cold and damp replaced the heat and drought to which they had grown accustomed the previous winter. A week before Christmas, trudging through snow nearly a foot deep, they finally reached Winter Quarters, which they had left a year and a half before. Edward, thinking that Emily was still at Garden Grove, stayed overnight with a friend, itching to move on the next morning. But sunrise brought a pleasant surprise. Emily, her mother, and a fine boy nearly a year old were living only a short distance away. Typically, Edward's autobiography recounted matter of factly what must have been an exultant response to such a discovery: "This was good news, I assure you, and I lost no time in seeking out Emily. . . ."[28]

Once again, and though he had gone on the Battalion journey to insure the opposite, Edward Bunker was without means for the journey west. It had taken all of his army pay just to keep his loved ones during his absence and to get him back to them. He therefore went to Missouri to work for provisions, which he did by splitting rails. Eventually he had enough to obtain a hog and some corn for planting, and the Bunkers moved across the river to Mosquito Creek, where they farmed with some success until the spring of 1850. At last they left for Zion, with the help of back pay from the army, the sale of his military land warrant, and cash from participants in the California gold rush who bought up Edward's corn for six times its value in the States. It had been more than four years since his and Emily's marriage and subsequent flight from Nauvoo. Finally, it appeared, they had reached the top of the hill.[29]

The Bunkers joined the Johnson Company, with Edward serving as a captain of ten, and set out for the Rockies. The trip was uneventful except for an outbreak of cholera that killed eight in the party. They arrived in Salt Lake Valley September 1, 1850, delighted to have reached "our haven of rest." The Bunkers moved northward to settle about a mile from Ogden. There Edward built a three-room log house, fenced his farm, and took a second wife, marrying a neighbor's widow, Sarah R. Browning Lang. He also became one of the first high councilors in the new Ogden Stake in 1851 and was a member of Ogden's first city council. In spite of all he had been through, and despite all his separation from his family, Edward Bunker's pioneer service in building the kingdom was not over. In the fall of 1852 he and seventy others received a mission call to England. When they left they took with them the first publication of the revelation on celestial (plural) marriage. After two years in England Edward became the presiding elder in Scotland, worked there another year, and came home with about five hundred British Saints bound for the Salt Lake Valley. The emigrant party had as its presiding officer Daniel Tyler, one of his companions on the march of the Mormon Battalion. They landed at New York and made their way by land and water to Iowa City, where they were fitted out with handcarts. Edward Bunker was given charge of a company of Welsh emigrants, and once more he knew the hardships of a forced march and consummate physical suffering. Between June 28, 1856, when they left Iowa City, and their arrival in Salt Lake City on October 2,

A Handcart Company (Painting by C. C. A. Christensen, Historical Department of The Church of Jesus Christ of Latter-day Saints)

1856, Edward became well-acquainted with his old traveling companions—heat, dust, insects, exhaustion, hunger, thirst, aching muscles, bleeding feet, and sickness. This time he was responsible for hundreds of persons in addition to himself. Fortunately, the Bunker Company started soon enough and had sufficient provisions to miss the fate of some of the others who started later that summer. But no one can overstate the degree of suffering any handcart company encountered in the cause of the gathering.[30]

Soon after his return from his mission, Edward was called as bishop of the Ogden Second Ward. Again it seemed that life at last was going to enter a "normal" stage. That vision shattered when the Bunker family attended the tenth anniversary in Big Cottonwood Canyon of the entry of the first Mormons into the valley. While there, the Saints learned of the approach of Johnston's Army. "We all returned to our homes," Bishop Bunker remembered of that frightening day, "and prepared for the worst."[31] During the long winter of 1857-58, the Mormons agonized over what might happen

122

in the spring when the snow melted and the troops would be able to fight their way into the valley. President Young and his associates talked continually of combat and preparations for a defense against the onslaught of this new "mob" sent to afflict the Saints.

By early spring Church leaders had faced the inevitability of the United States Army entering the Mormon stronghold that summer. Brigham Young had no desire to see his people destroyed, but he was equally opposed to the idea of turning their homes over to another mob. He developed a plan by which the Saints would evacuate their settlements and move south until the government demonstrated its faithfulness in keeping a promise that the army would pass through the city without molesting the Mormons or their property and then camp some distance to the west. By this action, bloodshed was avoided, but many hundreds left their homes filled with straw for burning and fled southward in a scene familiar to those who had lived through the Ohio, Missouri, and Illinois experiences. The Bunkers traveled from Ogden to Payson, where they remained through the summer until the army, which included, ironically, Colonel Philip St. George Cooke, kept its word. Then, "everything was peaceable and in the fall we returned to our homes."[32]

By the end of the Utah War and the move south, Edward Bunker must have believed that his sacrifices for the kingdom, and those of his wives and children, had been sufficient to warrant some years of ordinary existence (if the life of a Mormon bishop in the nineteenth century fits the term "ordinary"). The Mormon Battalion, the long mission, the numerous treks across the Great Plains, and the move south filled his memory of membership in the Church. But now his family was growing and he had begun to prosper on his farm in Ogden, so much so that in April 1861 he was able to take a third wife, Mary M. McQuarrie, a Scottish immigrant girl. That fall, he was reminded of the predominant aspect of Mormonism under the leadership of Brigham Young—there was little time for rest and relaxation. When the call came to the Bunkers asking them to give up their inheritance in Weber Valley for the sand and rocks of Southern Utah, Edward, Emily, and Mary Bunker were soon on the road to their mission as colonizers. They spent the first year in Toquerville, Utah, after which Sarah joined them and Edward was called to preside as bishop at Santa Clara in Washington County, Utah's Dixie.[33]

At first, the hardships at Santa Clara began to take on familiar characteristics. There was hunger and physical privation as a result of crop losses, but Bishop Bunker and his people persevered. Within a few years his community had established its viability. During the twelve years that he served as bishop in Santa Clara, he pushed out into new areas, settling Clover Valley, Nevada, and buying land in Panguitch, Utah. By distributing his family through these communities, he soon built a comfortable estate. Then came President Brigham Young to introduce the United Order, and Edward contributed all he owned, including a bountiful crop of grain. A year later "the Order broke up," and the bishop found himself without even enough grain to sustain his family through the next winter. "The Lord knows we obeyed that principle with pure motive," he told himself, "and He will not let us suffer."[34] Carrying this attitude and an ax, he and his sons went to the mountains, where they cut and hauled to St. George enough wood to pay for provisions to get the family through to the next harvest. "So you see," recalled the bishop, "the Lord abundantly blessed us for our integrity."[35]

Edward Bunker's willingness to sacrifice and to undergo severe hardship was typical of his attitude, but unfortunately the toll of hard life eventually demanded payment. In 1874 he was released from the bishopric at Santa Clara because of deteriorating health that prevented him from "having sufficient resources to keep [his] family together."[36] By now, he had grown used to moving, and besides, he wanted to make a new settlement further south on the Virgin River so that he could try the United Order experiment again. With President Young's permission, he organized a company with some of his sons and friends and settled in 1877 near a place called Mesquite in present-day Clark County, Nevada. They named their settlement, appropriately, Bunkerville, and Edward Bunker again found himself serving as bishop. But his health continued to fail, so in the spring of 1882 he left for a rehabilitating trip through Arizona and Mexico. His son, Edward, Jr., who had been born in Iowa while his father marched with the Mormon Battalion, succeeded him as bishop at Bunkerville. After an absence of two years, the elder Edward Bunker returned to southern Nevada at last ready to settle into a peaceful existence. "I am resting from my labors," he wrote in 1894, "and am associated with a goodly portion of my family. . . ."[37] That was really as much as this man desired.

Elder Francis M. Lyman ordained Edward Bunker a patriarch

on September 10, 1900, but pushing on was in the blood of this Battalion veteran, former handcart company captain, and Dixie colonizer. The next spring he organized another pioneering company and moved to Colonia Morelos, Mexico. There, on November 17, 1901, Edward Bunker died.[38] But his illustrious surname, from Bunker Hill, Massachusetts, to Bunkerville, Nevada, remained as part of the heritage of history connecting the Latter-day Saints to the age of the American Revolution.

John Brown:
Out of the Ordinary

On March 17, 1776, the British evacuated Boston. They had endured a taxing siege of nearly a year, and the royal commander, General William Howe, realized that holding Boston while the Patriots controlled the interior of New England was a military feat of little importance. He also knew that the American ranks were burgeoning each day, and that his situation, in military parlance, was untenable. But Howe had no intention of quitting, nor did his departure by ship for Halifax with his regulars and several hundred Loyalists signal a real victory for the Patriot cause. Lexington and Concord, Bunker Hill, and such overt acts of rebellion as the convening of the Second Continental Congress in the spring of 1775 had given the British an assurance that the colonists meant business. The events of 1775 had also stiffened royal resolve. Howe, for one, would not easily erase from his mind an image of British troops dying on the slopes of Breed's Hill. His thoughts, as he watched Boston fade into the distance, were upon a return to the rebellious colonies and smashing defeat for George Washington and his army of rabble.[1]

The climactic events of 1775 also had a stirring residual effect upon the Americans themselves. Prior to the fights in Massachusetts, even the most radical of the Patriot leaders were loathe to mention independence. Once Americans had died in combat with their

127

British cousins, however, the conviction grew rapidly that there was no possible reconciliation, and that two separate nations were at war against each other. Added to this came news that the British had employed foreign mercenaries to help put down the rebellion and that King George had announced a state of war. As a consequence, a complete separation from the mother country became at once the final objective of the war already in progress. "Nothing is now left," wrote a North Carolina Patriot, "but to fight it out."[2] From the dawning of such a realization upon the bulk of the Patriot leaders, events moved rapidly through the spring and early summer of 1776 to July 4, when Congress announced the signing of the Declaration of Independence. The revolutionary struggle was henceforth in a state of warfare.[3]

Commissioned as commander-in-chief, George Washington assumed a great portion of the Patriot burden. His task was to draw from the ranks of ordinary men soldiers who could withstand the concerted attack of the most powerful army and navy in the world. He would have to train them in the field and on the anvil of actual battle. There would be few rewards, poor pay, and even little praise, for war seldom brings the glory it promises; only the attendant misery and horror are guaranteed. Washington knew what he was asking of his Continentals, and he fully expected that much. As a result, few men stayed by his side through the entire course of the war. Desertions were common, especially during periods of privation and defeat, periods that covered most of the seven-year war. In addition, most of the enlistments were for short terms, and when they expired, the men often went home, whether there was a battle the next day or not. But the Virginian believed at the outset that there were some very uncommon men among the Americans, men who would stick it out for as long as it took to convince the King and Parliament that the United States would be free. By July 4, 1776, George Washington had staked his life on that belief. On that same day, General Howe and thousands of British regulars landed on Staten Island south of New York City. Washington's conviction was about to meet its first crucial test.[4]

New York, with its harbor and strategic location, held tremendous advantages for its occupants in war. Howe and his brother, Admiral Richard Howe (commanding the accompanying battle fleet), amassed on Staten Island every bit of manpower and logistics they could acquire through the rest of the summer until they could

128

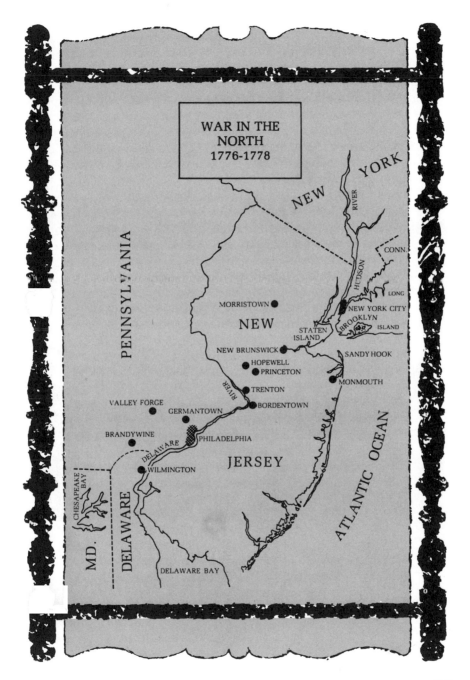

WAR IN THE
NORTH
1776-1778

NEW YORK

PENNSYLVANIA

HUDSON RIVER

CONN.

LONG

MORRISTOWN

NEW YORK CITY

NEW

BROOKLYN

STATEN
ISLAND

LONG ISLAND

NEW BRUNSWICK

SANDY HOOK

HOPEWELL
PRINCETON

MONMOUTH

TRENTON

VALLEY FORGE

GERMANTOWN

BORDENTOWN

BRANDYWINE

DELAWARE RIVER

PHILADELPHIA

JERSEY

WILMINGTON

CHESAPEAKE BAY

MD.

DELAWARE

ATLANTIC OCEAN

DELAWARE BAY

count nearly 35,000 well-equipped troops at their disposal for the capture of New York. In the meantime, Washington had moved the bulk of his army from Boston to New York and was doing all he could to fortify the city's defenses. When the Howe brothers arrived on Staten Island, the American situation was hopeless, but the British delayed their attack, hoping that the Patriots would respond to a conciliatory offer from London that amounted to nothing more than a colonial surrender. When the redcoats finally launched their attack on August 22, the Continental Army was not much better prepared for holding New York, but it was infinitely better prepared for something more important—survival.[5]

After landing on Long Island with 20,000 men, Howe sent his British and German regulars against the American positions on Brooklyn Heights on the night of August 26. By morning, the Patriot line had crumbled and General Israel Putnam, commanding the American forces on the island, realized that he was facing annihilation. Outnumbered and in poor position for even an adequate holding action, Putnam was in full retreat before noon, leaving behind some 2,000 casualties and a thousand others doomed to surrender. Washington assumed direct command of the forces now retrenching

General Francis Marion, the Swamp Fox (Painting by F. C. Yohn, The Continental Insurance Companies)

130

along the East River for a hard defense of Manhattan. Fortunately for the Americans, Howe refused to listen to his officers, who were urging him to overrun the Patriot position. Failing to recognize the opportunity at hand to crush the mass of the rebel force in one blow, the British general decided instead to lay siege to the city. Reassessing his own position, Washington saw that there could be no victory without an army, so getting his troops out of contact with the overwhelming British force became the greater part of valor. With the cooperation of a stiff northerly wind and a low tide to keep Admiral Howe from cutting off his escape, Washington managed to ferry his men across the river onto Manhattan during the night of the twenty-seventh. On September 12, the Americans withdrew to northern Manhattan with the British in pursuit. The battle of Long Island was over; the British had captured New York City, but Washington and his army had survived. Escaping into New Jersey, the Americans overcame the British at Trenton and Princeton, then went into winter quarters at Morristown nursing some very serious wounds. They were nevertheless convinced that the war could be won in spite of what appeared to be great odds against success.[6]

Only a few men who suffered with General Washington through those first trying days of defeat would remain with him until the war was over six years later. They were not ordinary men, for defeats were to be the rule rather than the exception. That was what it took to win in the end, and Washington knew it. One of those uncommon men who persevered through it all was a young officer from Pennsylvania named James Chapman. During the disastrous fight on Long Island, Chapman was nearly killed when a British rifle ball missed him only by hitting the hilt of his sword.[7] Another uncommon man was Benjamin Brown, an infantry officer from North Carolina. He had three brothers in arms by the end of the war; one of them lost his life. At home was another brother, John, who was but twelve years old when the war ended in 1783.[8] Chapman and Brown were among a handful of men who witnessed the war through its entire course, from the nearly fatal defeat at Long Island to the exultation of final victory at Yorktown. Through the rest of their lives, the revolutionary heritage they would impart to all they knew was a rare one. Benjamin's young brother John and James's little girl Martha partook eagerly of the inheritance.

Following the war, James Chapman moved to Virginia, and in 1797 across the mountains into Tennessee, settling at King's Station near the present city of Gallatin in Sumner County. In 1800 he purchased a large tract of land and, with his wife and nine children, embarked upon a life of freedom and security; but before the year ended, he had succumbed to pneumonia. That same year his daughter Martha married young John Brown, who had moved into Tennessee in 1795. Martha subsequently bore John fourteen children over a period of twenty-three years. The twelfth, born on October 23, 1820, they named John.[9] To the Browns, little John's birth was the most important event of that year. They had no idea that a few months before, a teenage boy in New York had told his family he had talked with the Lord, and that a restoration of the fulness of the gospel of Jesus Christ was about to take place in the milieu of freedom their fathers and brothers had fought to secure.

When John Brown was still a toddler, the family pulled up stakes after living in Sumner County for nearly three decades. The movement of the Browns was typical of two important themes in early nineteenth century America—rapid settlement and new land in the West. "The country soon became thickly settled," John recalled years later, "and my father's family became so large that the small tract of land, which consisted of one hundred acres, was too small for them to dwell on; consequently, he concluded to move to a new country."[10] In 1829, when John was nine, his father purchased a section (640 acres) in southern Illinois, where the family established a prosperous farming operation. Tragedy, however, stalked the Browns in Perry County. Within seven years of their arrival there, the father, three brothers, and two sisters were dead, and by the spring of 1837, the rest of the children had left home, leaving young John and his mother to run the farm. In spite of her need for him at home, Martha wanted her last son to have every opportunity, and so at the age of seventeen he was sent back to Tennessee for an education. There, while living with an uncle and attending the Rural Academy at Gallatin, John joined the Baptist Church after becoming persuaded through a study of the Bible that immersion was required for effective baptism. Returning home, he soon converted his mother and most of his family to his new faith, but he also noticed "some very strange men in the country preaching a new doctrine, causing great confusion among the people."[11] Young Brown thought these persons—who were called Mormons—were troublemakers, and their presence only deepened his concern over religion and heightened his lingering desire to become a Baptist minister. But he knew something was missing. He was ripe for the harvest.[12]

John Brown was teaching school in the spring of 1841 in Perry County when a Mormon elder arrived at the door of his schoolhouse and requested its use for a meeting. Reluctantly, he agreed. He listened to the missionary for three days, arguing fiercely the entire time, but suddenly realized that this man, George Dykes, spoke what had to be the truth. Late in July 1841, John Brown was baptized a member of The Church of Jesus Christ of Latter-day Saints. His friends and family expressed great shock, and shortly thereafter, his little schoolhouse mysteriously caught fire and burned to the ground. He bid farewell to Perry County and traveled northward to Nauvoo, where his fellow Saints were gathering, arriving in October 1841. There he became acquainted with Joseph and Hyrum Smith and other Mormon leaders. With his faith thus entrenched, he accepted a mission call to the southern states in 1843 and journeyed through Kentucky, Tennessee, Alabama, and Mississippi. In the latter area and within only a few months, he and his companion baptized more than one hundred persons. While on this mission, in May 1844, he married Elizabeth Crosby, sister of William Crosby, a well-to-do Mississippi farmer and one of his converts.[13]

Learning a month later of the martyrdom of the Smiths, John returned to Nauvoo, where he went to work on building the temple and after dark patroled the city as part of the "Whittling and Whistling Club" that guarded the streets at night to keep order in place of the police force that had been abolished along with the Nauvoo Charter. The Browns had just finished building a house when, amid driving persecution, they were forced to flee the City of Joseph in the exodus of 1846. Having property in Mississippi, they returned there with a message from the Council of the Twelve for the 150 Mormons in Monroe County, Mississippi. The main body of the Church would leave Nauvoo and temporary camps in Iowa in the spring of 1846 for the Great Basin. John Brown, though only twenty-six years old, was instructed to lead some of the Mississippi Mormons to Wyoming, where they would meet the advance company of Latter-day Saints. He directed the gathering of supplies and wagons, and on April 8, 1846, a band of forty-three persons with nineteen wagons rolled out of Mississippi as the advance company of the migration from the South. William Crosby, president of the Running Water (Mississippi) Branch of the Church, was elected captain and, with his brother-in-law, John Brown, led the company into Independence, Missouri, on May 26, after traveling 640 miles from their place of departure. There they were joined by a group of six wagons and fourteen Tennessee Saints under Robert Crow. Crow's wife was Elizabeth (Betsy) Brown, the daughter of John's uncle Benjamin, one of the extraordinary men who persevered with General Washington through the long course of the Revolutionary War. The Crows had joined the Mormon Church in 1838.[14]

As these southern Saints traveled along the Platte River across Nebraska, they expected to find the advance company of Mormons who would, they thought, have left the Missouri River ahead of them. But they did not find them, nor did they receive any word of them. Indeed, some months passed before they learned that the main group of the Saints had camped at Winter Quarters and had decided to wait until 1847 before moving west. Elders Brown, Crosby, and Crow, perplexed by this lack of evidence, decided that the lumbering Nauvoo wagons had moved faster than they expected and were on the trail ahead of them, so they hurried on. Fearful of the Indians but excited by the scenery, the southerners killed buffalo and antelope to sustain themselves. Shortly before they reached Chimney Rock on July 6, 1846, they encountered some travelers headed back from California who informed them that there were no Mormons on the trail ahead of them. Disappointed, they determined to winter at the first suitable place they could find. Being the first Mormon company into the West was a distinction they failed to appreciate at the time, for the idea of winter alone in the wilderness overshadowed all other considerations.[15]

A few miles from Fort Laramie they met a leathery-skinned French trapper, John Reshaw. Dressed in Indian leggings and fringe, hair down to his shoulders, Reshaw indicated that he was going to Fort Pueblo on the headwaters of the Arkansas River in present-day Colorado, and that they were welcome to accompany him there. He recommended it as a good place to winter because a few mountain men and their wives lived there and would probably have a supply of corn, beans, and squash that they might trade for some of the Mormons' surplus. Having few other options, John Brown and his people followed Reshaw to Pueblo, entering the fort on August 7, 1846. The Puebloans, who had been in contact with Santa Fe, told them of the Mormon Battalion and that the main body of the Saints would remain in Iowa and at Winter Quarters until 1847. Recognizing the realities of their situation for the first time, the little com-

Every Mormon elder on the Plains was a "Pioneer Clergyman" (Painting by Austin Briggs, The John Hancock Mutual Life Insurance Company)

pany of Mormons from the South began to make preparations for the winter. As John remembered,

we counseled the brethren to prepare for winter to build them some cabins in the form of a fort. The mountaineers said they would let them have their supplies, corn for their labors, etc. Those of us who had left our families stopped here until the 1st of September. We organized the company into a branch and gave them such instructions and counsel as the spirit dictated, telling them to tarry here until they got word from headquarters where to go. They were much disappointed as they expected to get with the main body of the church. We comforted them all we could and left our blessing with them.[16]

Francis Parkman, who had previously visited the camp of the Mormon Battalion, observed the activity at Pueblo that fall and wrote:

135

We saw the white wagons of the Mormons drawn up among the trees. Axes were sounding, trees falling, and log-huts rising along the edge of the woods and upon the adjoining meadow. As we came up the Mormons left their work, seated themselves on the timber around us, and began earnestly to discuss points of theology....[17]

George Ruxton, whose book *Life in the Far West* became a basic source on the West in the 1840s, said that the Mississippi Mormons "erected a street of log shanties, in which to pass the inclement winter. These were built of rough logs of cotton-wood, laid one above the other, the interstices filled with mud, and rendered impervious to wind or wet."[18] Ruxton made a point of remarking that the Mississippians "were a far better class than the generality of Mormons, and comprised many wealthy and respectable farmers. . . ."[19] Most of them, he said, "were accustomed to the life of woodmen, and were good hunters. Thus they were enabled to support their families upon the produce of their rifles, frequently sallying out to the nearest point of the mountains with a wagon, which they would bring back loaded with buffalo, deer, and elk meat. . . ."[20]

After these initial preparations were underway, and as soon as they were assured that the families were secure for the winter, John Brown and four others left on September 1 for the South to get the

Pioneer Fort on the Trail West (Painting by Barna Meeker, Archives of The Church of Jesus Christ of Latter-day Saints)

136

rest of their people who wished to migrate. During this journey, they met the Mormon Battalion and then traveled for a while with some government teamsters headed back from Santa Fe. They reached Mississippi late in October and began efforts to get their families ready for a spring trek to the Rockies. (John Brown, William Crosby, John D. Holladay, George Bankhead, and Daniel Thomas had left their wives and children behind the previous spring.) Happy as they were to see their loved ones, their thoughts were never far from the small band of Saints they had left on the Arkansas River in Colorado.[21]

The Mormons at Pueblo had in the meantime added to their log cabin village a churchhouse for meetings, religious services, and socials. According to Ruxton, the local mountain men sometimes joined these festivities because of the "really beautiful Mississippi girls who sported their tall graceful figures at the frequent fandangoes."[22] Indeed, observed Ruxton, "dancing and preaching go hand in hand in Mormon doctrine, and the temple," as he called the meetinghouse, "was generally cleared for a hop two or three times a week, a couple of fiddles doing the duty of orchestra."[23]

In October the Pueblo Saints were happy to greet a detachment of the Mormon Battalion comprising some 154 persons. Unable to cross the desert with Colonel Cooke and the rest of the Battalion, these Mormons had heard of the southern Saints and their encampment on the Arkansas while drawing supplies at Bent's Fort, fifty miles below Pueblo. Their subsequent arrival at Pueblo was particularly joyous because many of the Battalion members had friends and relatives among the Mississippians. The leader of the Battalion detachment was Captain James Brown from North Carolina, who had also been in Mississippi as a missionary. Captain Brown put his men to work, and soon they had constructed a row of eighteen additional log cabins to house the soldiers and the few wives accompanying them. With that, the Mormon colony contained 275 people and was well-prepared for a winter sojourn of relative comfort and pleasantry.[24]

Back in Mississippi, John Brown and his partners received a message from Brigham Young requesting that they leave their families in the South another year and come immediately to Council Bluffs to aid the apostles in the pioneer trek to the Rockies. On January 10, 1847, John once again bid adieu to his wife, and with seven other men, four blacks and three whites, he set out for the

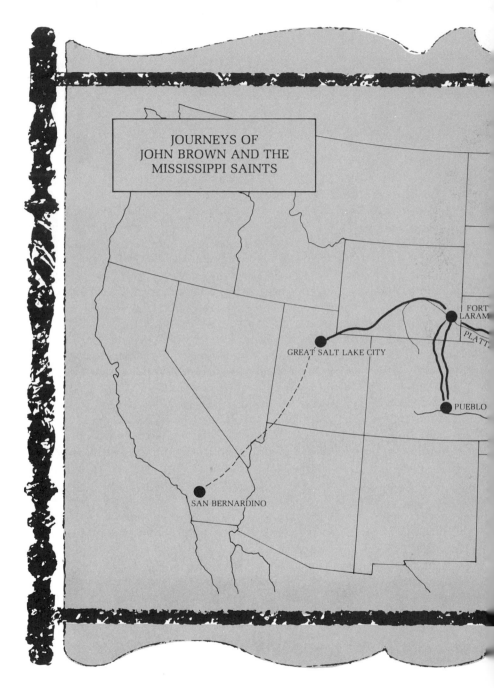

JOURNEYS OF
JOHN BROWN AND THE
MISSISSIPPI SAINTS

FORT
LARAM

PLATT.

GREAT SALT LAKE CITY

PUEBLO

SAN BERNARDINO

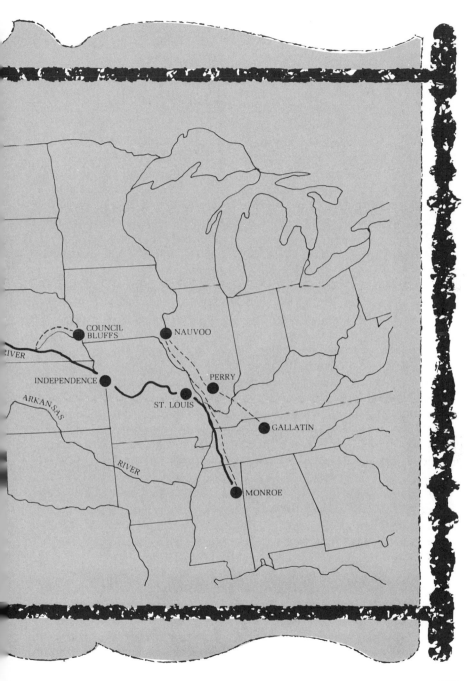

Bluffs, a distance of a thousand miles. At Winter Quarters, he was appointed head of the hunting party that was to furnish meat for the advance company. Accordingly, he fitted out with two wagons, three mules, four oxen, and two cows, all of which he had brought with him from Mississippi. Accompanying him were two blacks from Mississippi, Oscar Crosby and Hark Lay. A third black, Green Flake, also joined the advance company, driving a wagon and livestock belonging to another southerner, James M. Flake. (Indeed, it was in Flake's white-topped carriage that Brigham Young was riding when at the mouth of Emigration Canyon he made his famous "This is the place" pronouncement.) On April 16, 1847, the company, consisting of 143 men, three women, two children, and 73 wagons, was on its way to the Rocky Mountains. Having led the Mississippi Saints over much of the same projected route the previous summer, John Brown was an extraordinarily valuable member of this party of "original" Mormon pioneers.[25]

Traveling every day but Sunday, and without too much difficulty, Brigham Young and his trekkers arrived at Fort Laramie on June 3. John Brown was thrilled to find waiting at the fort seventeen Pueblo Saints, Battalion members, and southerners under Captain James Brown and Robert Crow. Eleven men and six women had been sent to Laramie to intercept the first company and were concomitantly pleased to have President Young order them in with the advance party for the journey into the Salt Lake Valley. Concerned for the Saints still waiting at Pueblo, the President also directed Amasa M. Lyman and three others to go to the Arkansas and lead the group up the trail to the Salt Lake Valley. He did so and reached the valley on July 27, three days after Brigham Young.[26]

The first men in the advance company to see the Salt Lake Valley were John Brown and Orson Pratt, who, while scouting ahead of the main party on July 19, 1847, ascended Big Mountain from where they could see the valley and a corner of the Great Salt Lake. For details of the few days that so concern Latter-day Saints in their pioneer celebrations, John Brown left the following:

> On the 21st we passed over the little mountain onto the last creek. Here the main camp came up with us, and Orson Pratt and Erastus Snow went a little way into the valley. Some of us climbed onto the mountain where we had a full view of the lake. On the 22nd some eight or ten of us went into the valley to explore. We

found it covered with rich vegetation in the vicinity of the streams, and the low-lands were green and beautiful. On the benches the grass was dry and a great variety of soil, all watered by streams from the mountains. From the base of the mountain several hot springs issued whose waters are highly impregnated with salt, sulphur, soda, etc. There were hosts of black crickets all over the valley and apparently harmless.

In the afternoon the camp came into the valley. On the 23rd we moved north about three miles and camped on the south side of City Creek, a little south of what is now called Immigration Street. A meeting was called and arrangements made to put in some seeds. Several committees were appointed to attend the various departments of business. All went to work with zeal characteristic of Saints, and by night there were several acres of ground ploughed and other preparations in proportion.

Next day, being the 24th, the President came into camp about noon. We were all together once more and on the spot we had so long been toiling for. President Young's health [he had mountain fever] was much improved. He said we were on the spot where the city was to be built. He knew it as the place he had seen in vision. Said we might explore the mountains over and over again and each time return to this place as the best. This day we got in some seeds, the first put in.[27]

So John Brown had had the uncommon experience of leading the first band of Mormons into the West in 1846 and then of being among the first Saints to arrive in the Valley of the Great Salt Lake in 1847. But his travels were by no means at an end. Back in Mississippi still waited his wife, Elizabeth. Consequently, on August 26, he started back east with Brigham Young, traveling in the same wagon with George A. Smith. From Winter Quarters he journeyed southward, arriving in Mississippi in December. He wintered with his wife in Monroe County and prepared once again to cross the plains. Under his leadership the remainder of the Mississippi Mormons left on March 10, 1848, headed for St. Louis and Council Bluffs, where they joined Amasa M. Lyman's company for the trek to the new Zion. When John Brown's group of thirteen Mississippi families arrived in the valley in October 1848, there were then about 250 southerners, both whites and blacks, in the area.[28] Elder Lyman surveyed an area ten miles southeast of the city, and most of the southerners settled there. They called their community Mississippi Ward, or Holladay Settlement, after John D. Holladay, its first bishop.[29]

John Brown remained in Utah, but most of the Mississippians, including Bishop Holladay, migrated as a group to southern California in March 1851, with Amasa Lyman and Charles C. Rich. There, in a colony of some 450 Saints that founded the Mormon settlement at San Bernardino, they lived in wagon homes, planted gardens, and built a stockade fence around a plot of irrigable land that they planted to grain. They also built a road to the San Bernardino Mountains to bring timber with which they constructed sawmills, gristmills, and a tabernacle. The area proved to be remarkably fruitful. John Holladay, for example, planted a bushel of hard red wheat he had obtained in Taos, New Mexico, and reaped an incredible 110 bushels. The Mormons remained in San Bernardino until 1858, when a majority of them obeyed Brigham Young's call, during the invasion of Johnston's Army, for them to return to Utah. Most of the returning Saints relocated in Southern Utah, where they raised cotton, grapes, and other semitropical products. Later, many of them, southerners still, pushed into Arizona establishing settlements along the Little Colorado and Gila rivers. Many of their names are prominent in Arizona to this day.[30]

John Brown also participated in this general expansion of the "Great Basin Kingdom." Late in 1849, Parley P. Pratt selected him to assist an exploring expedition into Southern Utah. John headed a party of fifty men in this group, which scouted natural resources and located places for settlement. Returning to Salt Lake City in February 1850, he became a director of the Perpetual Emigrating Fund Company established to assist financially in the gathering, and in the fall of 1850 went to the Nebraska frontier as its agent. He carried with him on that trip $5,000 in gold for the purchase of oxen and supplies for the immigration. The next summer he conducted a large train of Saints to Utah. This was his eighth crossing of the Great Plains over a period of five years.[31]

In November 1851 he was elected to fill a vacancy in the first territorial legislature, but the next spring Brigham Young called him to go to New Orleans, where he was to meet 2,500 immigrants from Liverpool, conduct them up the Mississippi River in steamboats to Keokuk, Iowa, and then lead them across the plains to the Salt Lake Valley. With that he had made the pioneer journey ten times. But like his revolutionary forebears, John Brown was a man out of the ordinary, and his people could afford him little rest. In 1855 he moved to Lehi, from which settlement he was elected to the legislature again. In the spring of 1857 he accompanied President Young to Fort Lemhi, on the Salmon River in Idaho, and in the fall of that same year served in the militia as it attempted to forestall the arrival of Johnston's Army in the valley during the Utah War. After this adventure, he filled a mission to England with Elders Lyman and Rich (1861-62). Upon his return, in February 1863, he became bishop of Pleasant Grove and finally settled into a quieter life, serving in that role for twenty-nine years (1863-91) with two years out for a mission presidency in his native southern states (1867-69).[32]

John Brown lived an active secular as well as ecclesiastical life. In addition to serving several terms in the Utah legislature, where he advocated women's rights and better education, he was a colonel in the militia, mayor of Pleasant Grove, and county commissioner for two years. Elizabeth Brown kept pace with her energetic husband, bearing ten children and finding time for the taxing job of Relief Society president in Pleasant Grove for many years.[33]

John Brown died at Pleasant Grove, November 4, 1896, the year Utah gained statehood.[34]

His heritage was one of uncommon loyalty, purpose, and diligence. "If Uncle John ever had a lazy hair on him," remembered a nephew, "he shed them all before I knew him. He never knew when he was tired or when I was tired either."[35] He also left many children who were demonstrably partakers of his dynamic lifestyle. Among his sons was the noted Utah physician and surgeon, John Zimmerman Brown; another, James Lehi Brown, became a professor of education at Brigham Young University. A grandson is Russel B. Swensen, history professor at BYU and Ph.D. in history from the University of Chicago; a granddaughter married Alexander Schreiner, organist for the Mormon Tabernacle Choir. Numerous others of his descendants have made and continue to make important contributions to the institutions of Mormondom and of America.

Perhaps the most notable example of John Brown's unusual heritage from the revolutionary age, through his roots in the South, to the building of the West and the kingdom of God, was in the life of his daughter Amy. Born in Pleasant Grove on February 7, 1872, Amy grew up in the refined atmosphere of John Brown's pioneer

Orson Pratt (Engraving by Frederick
Piercy, Archives of The Church of
Jesus Christ of Latter-day Saints)

Amy Brown Lyman
(Archives of The Church of Jesus Christ
of Latter-day Saints)

home, imbibing her father's propensity for learning and rarefaction.
(During the last years of his life, John read Bacon's *Essays*, Plu-
tarch's *Lives*, works of Emerson, and other classics of English literature.) The daughter of John Brown's third wife, Margaret, Amy was
also the granddaughter of George Zimmerman, an erudite German
immigrant whose prowess as a linguist was well-known throughout
Utah. It was no surprise, then, when she began to exhibit while yet a
toddler a thirst for education that was finally quenched to some
degree in her early teens when she encountered the mind of Karl G.
Maeser at the Brigham Young Academy in Provo. In addition to
studying under the venerable professor at the academy, she also
boarded at his home in Provo, continuing her education at his feet
outside the classroom. Following her graduation from BYA in
1890 at the age of eighteen, she was hired as an instructor in the
training school at the academy and was eventually appointed to the

faculty to teach physical education and domestic science. In 1894, at the age of twenty-two, she became matron of the academy and handled remarkably well the awesome task of supervising the coeds there. It was abundantly apparent by the time John Brown's daughter left the academy later that year to teach in the Salt Lake City schools that she had inherited her ancestors' extraordinary qualities of mind and leadership.[36]

Just before her father's death in 1896, Amy Brown married Richard R. Lyman, son of Elder Francis M. Lyman of the Council of the Twelve. Immediately after their marriage, Richard joined the engineering faculty at the University of Utah, where he became the first teacher in the new State School of Mines and Engineering. He later took sabbatical leave from Utah in order to pursue advanced degrees at Cornell University in New York, from which he received his Ph.D. in 1905. This period in the East gave Amy her first opportunity for the extensive travel she had sought to round out her education. While Richard studied, she took advantage of her presence in the East to visit cultural centers and to enjoy a period of leisure to its fullest extent. And it was a good thing, because shortly after the Lymans returned to Utah, she was called to the general board of the Relief Society, and the course of the rest of her life was set in the path of Church service. A few years later (1913), she became the Relief Society's general secretary; she served later as counselor to President Louise Y. Robison (1928-39), and then succeeded her as general president of the society in January 1940.[37]

In the meantime, Richard R. Lyman was called to the Council of the Twelve, and Amy had added to her responsibilities the duties of companion to an apostle. Her public life in the secular realm was also very active. From her Relief Society work she acquired an intense interest in social welfare, particularly the extension of casework into the efforts of the Church. This involvement ultimately led her into association with professional welfare workers and organizations. She was a charter member of the Utah Conference of Social Workers (of which she served a term as president) and belonged to such national groups as the National Conference of Social Work, the American Association of Social Workers, and (as an honorary member) the American Mental Hygiene Association. She also served a term in the Utah House of Representatives in 1923 and was on the board of directors of numerous community operations, such as the Public Health Committee and the Utah Tuberculosis Society.

Concomitant with this local activity, she was active in the national women's movement, attending sessions of the National Council of Women. Her effective involvement in civic and religious activity was unquestionably, and in characteristic Brown fashion, out of the ordinary.[38]

A close associate characterized Amy Brown Lyman as "a modern woman ... which implies that she believes in developing all of her powers and placing them where they can best serve her in the modern world."[39] The idea of developing powers for coping with the world is the crux of practical Mormonism. John Brown had had a remarkable understanding of that idea, and he taught Amy and his other children that at the gospel's center is the ability to learn, to absorb greater light as it is available and as the mind is prepared for it. Before Amy Lyman died on December 5, 1959, she had echoed in her life and thought the core of her father's philosophy as he had expounded it a century before in the *Millennial Star*:

The introduction of the gospel in these last days has been upon the same principle that it was introduced to the world anciently. A small lesson was first given: when that was received another was given, and then another; and being different degrees to truth, they were varied and apparently contradictory. Consequently, there was and is a continual change or increase of knowledge, just as there is with the school-boy in learning the exact science of arithmetic, which, although perfectly true, yet in its practical workings is apparently contradictory. The teacher first sets the pupil to learn simple addition, and tells him to add the figures together. He works at this until he understands it. He knows nothing of other rules; but, of course, he thinks it is all addition. The teacher next gives him a sum of subtraction, and tells him to subtract, or take one line of figures from another. Now the pupil is puzzled: he cannot understand what this means. It is directly the reverse of what he was told before. He is perplexed in his mind, consults his mates, goes again and again to the teacher, who is patiently waiting for the tender mind to grasp the principle; and after much exertion, and perhaps several days of hard study, he begins to understand the rule. This experience adds to his knowledge; and thus he goes on from rule to rule, having a new principle to meet and learn in each succeeding rule, until at length he completely masters the science.[40]

146

Like all of the other extraordinary men and women who have participated in the building of The Church of Jesus Christ of Latter-day Saints, John Brown played a unique role, one that amassed in its course an impressive inheritance, not only for his own family, but for the Saints as a whole. Just as Benjamin Brown and James Chapman contributed to the heritage of which John Brown partook by their participation in the birth of the Republic, John Brown also passed an exemplary legacy to his posterity, and to us all.

Christeen Golden Kimball:
Bearing a Legend

Late in the fall of 1776, George Washington and the main body of the Continental Army were in hasty retreat across New Jersey after surrendering New York City to the British. The premium had become simple survival for the Patriots and their cause. Reaching the Delaware River, the American general and about three thousand men quickly crossed over into Pennsylvania and then collected all the boats they could find on the river in order to deny their use to the advancing redcoats under General Charles, Lord Cornwallis. When the British subsequently reached the Delaware, they decided to go into winter quarters after establishing outposts on the east bank with strong points at Trenton and Bordentown. Washington, still smarting from his recent defeats, determined to take the offensive by which he hoped to regain control of western New Jersey, and by which his own legend of dogged genius would be born.[1]

With the retreat from Long Island, many of the Virginian's "summer soldiers and sunshine patriots" had disappeared. "These are times," wrote Tom Paine, "that try men's souls. . . . He that stands it *now*, deserves the love and thanks of man and woman."[2] In preparation for his assault upon the royal positions on the east bank of the Delaware, Washington sent an urgent appeal for reinforcements to the northern army at Albany and to General Charles Lee

149

operating on the other side of the Hudson. By December 20, Washington had more than six thousand men ready to fight. Among them were not only regulars from north and east but also militiamen from Pennsylvania and New Jersey who were responding magnificently to the commander-in-chief's call for aid.[3] At Hopewell, in nearby Mercer County, New Jersey, for example, a farmer named John Goldy had watched as five of his sons hurried off to join Washington before Trenton.[4] This kind of response was more than the general could have expected, but because of it he was ready for a planned series of surprise attacks across the river.

On Christmas night, 1776, Washington set his plan into motion. Leading 2,400 men himself, he crossed the Delaware at a ferry just above Trenton while other American units carried out coordinated maneuvers around the city. The royal troops, most of them German or Hessian mercenaries, were totally unprepared for the Patriot action even though they had been warned of an impending attack. In the course of the resulting rout, the Hessian commander and the bulk of his troops were forced to surrender after brief resistance. Fearing a British counterattack, Washington then withdrew back into Pennsylvania, but by New Year's Eve had reoccupied Trenton. In the meantime Cornwallis, who had gone to New York to celebrate Christmas, was dashing angrily toward the Delaware, gathering troops as he went. On January 2, he entered Trenton, leading a column of six thousand redcoats. Again the Patriots retreated in order to remain a viable fighting force. They left their campfires burning to deceive the British and marched quietly around the redcoats in the darkness, arriving at Princeton as the winter sun rose on January 3. There they encountered three royal regiments, which, after a hard fight, they finally defeated. From Princeton, Washington led his men to Morristown for a winter encampment. There he could easily defend himself and prepare for the campaign of 1777.[5]

The significance of the victories at Trenton and Princeton could not be overstated. Though they accomplished little in terms of substantive military achievement, they had a profound effect upon the morale of the Patriots. "A few days ago," wrote a young British observer, "they had given up the cause for lost. Their late successes have turned the scale and now they are all liberty mad again. . . ."[6] The self-concept of the Patriot troops had changed. They were no longer losers and underdogs, but tough, Yankee Doodle troopers

Washington at Valley Forge (Painting by F. C. Yohn, The Continental Insurance Companies)

who just might lick the most powerful army in the world. While optimistic, the Americans had also grown accustomed to the necessity of sacrifices for freedom. John Goldy, for his part, saw only two of his five sons return to the farm at Hopewell after the battles at Trenton and Princeton.[7] With such personal losses, Goldy and others like him could not think of turning back and thereby rendering their precious oblations meaningless.

Nearly half a century after the battles at Trenton and Princeton, members of John Goldy's family were still living on the family farm in Mercer County, New Jersey. The sacrifices of the revolutionary age had been transmuted into legend. The children who grew up on the family farm at Hopewell loved to hear about the five heroic sons of Grandfather Goldy—how they had left barefooted one day to join Washington at the Delaware; how they had only one gun among them ("the longest barrel shotgun in America"); how one of them "killed several British officers"; and how "three of them disappeared and were never heard of again."[8] No one noticed or cared that the battles for western New Jersey occurred in the *winter* of 1776-77, making the idea of fighting barefoot rather unlikely, or that killing several enemy officers with one muzzle-loaded weapon, even if it was the longest one in America, was close to impossible. What mattered was the story, the legend, and the identifying element of the present it had become.[9] The youngsters at Hopewell, like Americans of the succeeding two hundred post-revolutionary years, listened intently to such legends, and believed them for all they said about their country and themselves.[10]

Among the believers in the legend of John Goldy's sons was Christeen Golden, born on her grandfather Goldy's farm at Hopewell on September 12, 1824.[11] After finishing twenty years of tutelage under the schoolmasters of farm life and heady family tradition, Christeen was visiting in Philadelphia when she happened to hear a story of another sort than the one with which she had grown up—a story that was to her even more believable and more far-reaching in its potential for affecting her life. Preaching a sermon was Jedediah M. Grant, a "Mormonite" missionary from the West. Renowned among the Latter-day Saints for his potent oratory, Elder Grant was in fine form that day in Philadelphia, for young Miss Golden was immediately converted. Following her baptism, she took some Church works back to Mercer County, excited in the prospect of sharing her new faith with her family. Completely rejected there, she returned to Philadelphia and from there traveled to Nauvoo with Elder Grant and his wife.[12]

Arriving on the banks of the Mississippi, Christeen became acquainted with the dynamic apostle Heber Chase Kimball. Elder Kimball, second to Brigham Young in the Council of the Twelve, was a fascinating person; the more the young woman from New Jersey learned about him, the more impressed she became. Others shared her impression. "The unwavering integrity, the benevolence, and urbanity of President Kimball," said one commentator, "endeared him to the hearts of the Latter-day Saints universally. . . ."[13] Thomas L. Kane found Elder Kimball to be "a man of singular generosity and purity of character."[14] But some aspects of his personality gave him a reputation for being coarse and impetuous. He loved to participate in the vigorous oratory of early Mormonism and was not afraid to express his opinion in words most familiar to himself and his frontier listeners. Heber's dedication to the cause of the Latter-day Saints often brought forth the aggressive and bumptious language that made a Kimball sermon something his audiences never forgot. "Am I afraid?" he once asked. "No; but I am afraid to do wrong. I feel joy in my heart to be valiant and tell you the truth; and I pray that God my Father and his Son Jesus Christ may bring the evil upon [our enemies] that they desire for this people."[15] By the time Christeen Golden met him, Brother Heber's lack of patience with opponents of his church and people had become legendary among the Saints.

As Christeen Golden learned of Heber C. Kimball's personality, she also learned of the background that had brought him to the ranks of the Saints and then into the councils of Mormon leadership. He was born in Vermont on June 14, 1801. His parents, Anna Spaulding and Solomon Farnham Kimball, had grown up, like her own parents, during the age of the American Revolution. "At the close of the Revolutionary War," Heber reported, "my father was thirteen years old, and I can remember his rehearsing to me some of the scenes of the war."[16] After the Revolutionary War, the Kimballs had pushed westward into New York, seeking new lands and new opportunities, but the economic difficulties that accompanied the War of 1812 struck a severe blow to the Kimball family. By 1820, when Heber was nineteen, the family had lost its property, and the boy was on his own. He eventually joined his brother, who was a potter for a period of apprenticeship that took him to the village of Mendon in Monroe County, New York. There he purchased his brother's business, married Vilate Murray from neighboring Victor, became a Free Mason, and joined the Baptist Church.

In 1827 Heber and Vilate befriended the family of John Young, which had just moved into Mendon. The Kimballs were particularly attached to young Brigham. The two men became close friends, and their many conversations often revolved about religious issues. When five Mormon elders appeared in the vicinity of Mendon late in 1831, Brigham and Heber and their families listened to the story of a new scripture, a modern prophet, and a restoration of the priesthood. Experiencing numerous gifts of the Spirit, the Kimballs and Youngs were quickly converted to the new religion. On April 15, 1832, Heber was baptized into the restored church of Christ. He was ordained an elder, and with Joseph and Brigham Young (who had joined earlier), he presided over the small branch in Mendon. The life of a potter was suddenly a secondary calling; or, more accurately, Heber would become a potter of men.[17]

In the fall of 1832, Heber and the two Youngs journeyed to Kirtland, Ohio, to meet Joseph Smith, the Prophet. Elder Kimball summarized their visit with Joseph in a few words that clearly indicated the Prophet's impact: "We had a precious season and returned with a blessing in our souls."[18] Having thus felt Joseph's spirit, few Latter-day Saints wanted to be far from him, and Heber C. Kimball worked from that point toward getting his family ready for a move to Kirtland. A year later, the Kimballs and their two children, along with widower Brigham Young and his two daughters, traveled by wagon to Ohio, arriving around the first of November, 1833. They found the Church in the midst of building the temple and warding off increasing persecution. Brigham and Heber became instantly involved in both enterprises, serving the Prophet faithfully and learning all they could about the scope and meaning of his mission.[19]

In May 1834, Joseph Smith gathered two hundred men for the purpose of "redeeming Zion" in Jackson County, Missouri. The personality and predilections of Heber C. Kimball dictated that he should be among them, and on May 5, he left his wife and children in Kirtland and followed the Prophet. During the course of this march of "Zion's Camp," many of its members became impatient with the Prophet's leadership and with the failure of the camp to accomplish what they supposed to be its mission—the forceful capture of Jackson County. In addition, many of them fell victim to the ravages of a cholera epidemic. The ultimate result of the experience was the trial of the faith of its surviving members,[20] and among those who stood unwaveringly by Joseph Smith through it all were Heber Kimball and Brigham Young.

On February 14, 1835, Joseph assembled the remaining members of Zion's Camp and declared that the Lord had directed that he organize a modern Quorum of Twelve Apostles from the faithful members of the camp. Following prayer, the Prophet and the three witnesses to the plates of the Book of Mormon chose twelve men as special witnesses of Christ in the last days. The two friends from Mendon, Brigham and Heber, thus were named as apostles of the Lord. They were subsequently ordained by the three witnesses to the Book of Mormon, Oliver Cowdery, David Whitmer, and Martin Harris. When the quorum was organized with seniority according to age, Elder Young ranked third and Elder Kimball fourth.[21] Not three years after their baptisms, the two elders thus found themselves in the forefront of a major movement in American religious history. They would quickly prove themselves equal to the task.

In the decade following his call to the apostleship, and before Christeen Golden met him in Nauvoo, Heber C. Kimball became a leading figure in the community of the Saints. His missionary labors were particularly remarkable: during an 1837-38 mission in England, for example, Elder Kimball and his companions baptized some two thousand people in the space of eight months. He passed through the Missouri persecutions of 1838-39, and in September 1839 left his small family in a shack on the banks of the Mississippi River in Illinois for another mission to Europe with his friend Brigham.[22] The scene of that departure has since become a part of the Mormon legend of missionary sacrifice. In the words of B.H. Roberts,

Elder Kimball left his wife in bed shaking with ague [a malarial fever], and all his children sick. It was only by the assistance of some of the brethren that Heber himself could climb into the wagon. "It seemed to me," he remarked afterwards in relating the circumstance, "as though my very inmost parts would melt within me at the thought of leaving my family in such a condition, as it were, almost in the arms of death. I felt as though I could scarcely endure it." "Hold up!" said he to the teamster, who had just started, "Brother Brigham, this is pretty tough, but let us rise and give them a cheer." Brigham, with much difficulty, rose to his feet, and joined Elder Kimball in swinging his hat and shouting, "Hurrah, hurrah, hurrah, for Israel!" The two sisters, hearing the cheer came to the door—Sister Kimball with great difficulty—and waved a farewell; and the two apostles continued their journey, without purse, without scrip, for England.[23]

Returning to Nauvoo in July 1841, Elder Kimball quickly immersed himself in the work of the Church. He also built a beautiful home and accepted the principle of plural marriage as taught by the Prophet Joseph Smith. When Christeen Golden came to Nauvoo in 1844, Heber had nine wives. Having studied his character and knowing his capacity as a servant of the Lord, she consented to become his tenth. So evenly did Elder Kimball run his polygamous household, however, that Christeen "knew not her number" among the wives.[24] He eventually had additional wives, but according to one of his numerous grandchildren, "no family in Israel, in its domestic relations, better exemplified the true nature and purpose of the polygamic principle, than the family of Heber C. Kimball."[25]

After the assassination of the Prophet and the Patriarch, Heber assisted Brigham Young in the governing of the Church until the exodus of 1846-47, when he accompanied the advance party to the Salt Lake Valley. He returned that fall to the Missouri River, where the Twelve met at Council Bluffs on December 27, 1847, to reorganize the First Presidency after having led the Church for three years as a quorum. President Brigham Young was sustained as successor to Joseph Smith; he then chose as his first counselor Heber C. Kimball, the good friend and companion with whom he had joined the Church nearly fifteen years before in New York. The next spring Heber led a company of Saints across the Great Plains to the new Zion in the West. In that company was Christeen Golden Kimball, anxious as ever to be of value to her husband and to the building of the kingdom.[26]

In the harsh environment of Utah in 1851, Christeen bore Heber C. Kimball a daughter whom they named Cornelia, and two years later, on June 9, 1853, she had a son. At the time, Christeen was living at the "Kimball Mansion" on Main Street just north of Temple Square, an appropriate place for the birth of a legend. The Kimballs named the boy Jonathan Golden after his maternal grandfather, but the "Jonathan" gave way to the more colorful second name, and J. Golden Kimball was abroad among the Saints.[27] His father, in the meantime, had further enhanced his own position as a leader of larger-than-life proportions. In addition to his ecclesiastical responsibilities, Heber served as chief justice of the Provisional State of Deseret and as lieutenant governor to Brigham Young. With

Heber Chase Kimball (Archives of The Church of Jesus Christ of Latter-day Saints)

156

the organization of Utah Territory, he became a member of the first territorial assembly. But it was in the realm of oratory that Elder Kimball gave his best service to President Young and the Saints. He made numerous predictions about the future of the Church and its Great Basin Kingdom, leading Brigham to dub him "my prophet."[28] Not even President Young claimed rhetorical abilities above those of Heber Kimball. "When I arise to speak," explained Elder Kimball, "I have never a premeditated subject; I let God, by the Holy Ghost, dictate me and control me, just as the musician would his violin."[29] He was able in one breath to bless his people with profound reverence, and in the next to condemn their enemies with vitriol. "I never use rough words," he once said, "only when I come in contact with rough things; and I use smooth words when I talk upon smooth subjects. . . ."[30]

J. Golden Kimball grew up in the shadow of such a father, partaking of his freewheeling inheritance of loyalty and reverence on one hand, and intense, biting coarseness on the other—an open willingness to say what was on his mind. "For fifteen years of my life I was disciplined and instructed by my father," Golden wrote years later, "which has been an anchor to my soul. The things I was taught in my childhood (Father died when I was fifteen years old) have been the anchor of my soul; and the Holy Ghost has brought them to my remembrance."[31]

Christeen also had a great influence on the growing boy and his brother, Elias, and sister, May Margaret. (Cornelia died at the age of four.) "Mother was simple, plain, and cheery in her living and manners and most generous, hospitable, and kind in her nature," remembered Golden. "I don't believe there was ever a mother who was more anxious than she was that her sons should live good lives, go on missions, and be honest, honorable, and upright."[32] But Christeen Kimball had little idea that after she became a widow, on June 22, 1868, her son Jonathan Golden would inherit her husband's place in the pantheon of Mormon folk heroes. Indeed, for the first few years after Heber's death from the effects of a buggy accident, it was doubtful whether Christeen and her three children could ever rise from the poverty and struggle into which they sank as Heber's estate disappeared among the many Kimball heirs. Golden was attending Deseret University in Salt Lake City when his father died, and over the protests of his mother, he quit in order to support her family. "Mother sewed for Z.C.M.I. [Zion's Cooperative Mercantile

Institution] at those early starvation prices," Golden recalled, "kept boarders with poor surroundings and accommodations, as by this time we had been boosted out of Father's mansion and lived in a two-room house."[33] Young Kimball hired himself as apprentice to a freighter, becoming in the process one of the best mule skinners (or drivers) in the Salt Lake Valley. Within a few years, he had built his own hauling and contracting business, but, in his own words, "we starved out. Just couldn't make it."[34]

In 1876 Christeen and her boys decided to leave Salt Lake City for a new start in the Bear Lake country to the north where several of Heber's other sons had colonized under the direction of Brigham Young and Charles C. Rich, the apostle. There, in a squat dugout at Meadowville some four miles from Bear Lake, they "commenced a fight for life."[35] As little May Margaret grew, so did their ranch, and by 1890 Christeen Kimball and her three children were owners of a prosperous cattle and horse operation that belied the long periods of suffering that had built it. In that vigorous atmosphere, J. Golden became a tough pioneer, a cowpoke, the image of the West. It was during this period of his life that he acquired the language patterns that became inexorably a part of the Kimball legend. On one occasion during these wild years, the Kimball brothers were on a lumbering expedition for the construction of the Logan Temple. While working on that project they were prohibited from swearing, and Golden was trying hard to overcome his mule-skinner speech habits. But a team of oxen he was driving refused to respond to his whip and shrill voice. He lost his temper and said what came to his mind. If his father was famous for that trait, Golden would be more so, and those oxen got a preview of the legend of J. Golden Kimball. "And, boy, how I did cuss! did I wax eloquent? I'm afraid I did. But did those oxen sit up and take notice? They sure did; every one of them got down to business. You see, they were Church oxen, and when you talked that language to them, they understood it."[36] For the next fifty years, not only oxen but people sat up and took notice whenever this rangy son of Heber opened his mouth.

In the midst of their rough-and-tumble existence as cowboys of the old West, Golden and Elias never escaped the influence of their mother, who had visions of her boys being educated and holding responsible positions in life. Her hopes were fulfilled beginning in 1881 when Dr. Karl G. Maeser visited the Bear Lake settlements recruiting for Brigham Young Academy in Provo. The boys were immediately impressed after the years of listening to Christeen pray for their upward progress in life. They sold some of their ranch belongings and saved money until they had enough to move the family temporarily to Provo. For two years Golden listened intently to Professor Maeser, absorbing in the process all the wisdom the great educator could impart to a rough boy from the country. Truly his father's son, Golden excelled in oratory, and by the spring of 1883 he had won numerous speech contests at the academy. Word of his abilities reached Salt Lake City, and on April 6, 1883, at the age of thirty, J. Golden Kimball received a call to go to the Southern States Mission. A month later he was traveling in Virginia, preaching the gospel.[37] The road from a cussing western cowboy to a humble missionary in the South was as short as Christeen Kimball and Karl Maeser could make it, but J. Golden liked to believe that he never walked that road all the way, and that there was always a little bit of both characters living genially in his soul.

During his mission, Golden contracted malaria, and John Morgan, the mission president whom he served as secretary, tried to release him several times. "Brother Kimball," said Morgan, "you'd better go home. The mission is very hard-run for money. It will cost twenty-four dollars to send you home alive, but it will cost three hundred to send you home dead."[38] Golden refused to leave early, and successfully completed a full term of service. Though still in poor condition upon his release, he determined to keep a promise to his mother that he would go to New Jersey to preach to her folks in Mercer County. He visited there for five weeks, both talking and listening. While preaching Mormonism and collecting names for temple work, he also partook of the same traditions upon which his mother had been raised, hearing with pride the enhanced legend of John Goldy and his heroic sons of the Revolutionary War. He then returned to the ranch in Bear Lake valley more than ever both Golden and Kimball.[39]

Shortly after his return from the South, Golden married Jeanette (Jennie) Knowlton, and they moved to Logan in the late 1880s. Subsequently, Christeen and her children began the gradual exchange of their holdings in Rich County for land in Cache Valley. They also speculated in Canadian land, but were unsuccessful. In 1891, J. Golden received another call to the Southern States, this time as mission president, and a year later, President B. H. Roberts of the First Council of Seventy called him to come to Salt Lake City, where he was ordained one of the Seven Presidents. His being a General Authority gave the blossoming legend of Golden Kimball a fruitful place to expand, but he had yet to finish his second mission. He was finally released in 1894 and was succeeded in his presidency at Chattanooga, Tennessee, by his brother Elias. "The two of us spent ten years in the South, and when we came back, we didn't have a thing but our families and our lives," wrote Elder Kimball. But, he added, "I have got all that I deserved and a good deal more."[40]

Within a few months of Golden's release from the mission presidency, Christeen Kimball, then in her seventies, grew progressively weaker, and on January 30, 1896, she died, content in the realization that her two boys had grown into men and Saints, one a General Authority and the other a mission president. "Her life was one of continual devotion and sacrifice," Golden wrote in 1912. "I love her memory more than I do anything else at this date."[41]

J. Golden Kimball died on September 2, 1938, when the automobile in which he was riding crashed outside of Lovelock, Nevada. But the legend of J. Golden Kimball, like the legends of John Goldy and Heber C. Kimball, lived on. "In a Mormon circle," wrote folk historian Austin Fife, "if you come out with the dictum about believing more in a swearing saint than in a praying rogue, you are sure to evoke the image of J. Golden Kimball."[42] Wallace Stegner, writing about "Mormon Country," added that some called Golden "the Will Rogers of the Church." Stegner disagreed. "He should never have been compared with anyone, because J. Golden was an original."[43]

In every group of Mormons, there are J. Golden Kimball yarns, full of earthy humor and plain language, bridging the gap between the lofty ideals of the true church and the ultimate humanity of its members. Thomas Cheney, the noted Utah folklorist, made a life's work of collecting elements of what he called "the Golden Legacy." He believed that J. Golden Kimball was easily the best-known Mormon in the world at the time of his death, next to the president of the Church.[44] In short, during his half century as a General Authority, Golden Kimball said enough unique things and exhibited enough gutsy strength of mind that the people could not forget him. Pious men and women grimaced when he cussed, but laughed at his jokes and plain humanity. No one missed his messages, for they came across in few and plain words. He preached a no-nonsense brand of devotion to the cause of Christ, and pretention and ostentation were often the target at which he threw his most pointed barbs.

As with all legends, the story of Golden Kimball often had little to do with "fact." But no Mormon sage telling a tale beginning with "One time J. Golden Kimball was at a conference in St. George," cared whether it really happened or not. With Golden, it could have happened, and that made the yarn worth telling. "Now he lives in the minds and memories of men," wrote Cheney, "in their oral and written words, as a kindred spirit, who saw incongruities in human behavior, dichotomy in apparent truths, blotches of ugliness in patches of beauty. And though he was an animal, he felt his eternality and aspired to be a god."[45] What ultimately made J. Golden Kimball into legend was his pungent kinship to every Saint, struggling between the earth and the sky for eternity.

No treatment of the heritage of Christeen Golden Kimball would be complete without the telling of a couple of J. Golden yarns, but even artists like Stegner and Cheney could not paint the deep colors of a Kimball story as told by the Mormon folk. Stegner tried to do so with the following:

In St. George, when he was stumping with an apostle to raise money, the two high dignitaries showed up in town on the monthly fast day. There hadn't been an apostle in town for a long time. His coming put a burden on the good farmers of Dixie. They were gaunt and sad-eyed as they came to the meeting. . . . The Word of Wisdom and the midsummer heat rode heavily on them. They sat glumly while the apostle inched his way like a measuring worm through a tedious sermon. By the time J. Golden arose they were restless and a little resentful. It was a hundred and ten in the hall; they steamed slowly, waiting for the inevitable and dreaded time when [contributions would be mentioned], wondering how small a donation they could get away with.

"Brethren and Sisters," J. Golden said, "you have heard good counsel. I don't aim to add much to it, even if I thought I could." He paused, his skinny six-feet-three leaning forward over the pulpit. "I know times are hard," he said. "I know it's a fast day. I know it's hot as hell. But I want to prophesy, Brothers and Sisters . . . ," and his hand went up in a gesture of benediction, "I want to prophesy that if you shell out, and shell out handsome, Apostle Lyman and I will get out of town in half an hour." They paved the platform with silver dollars.[46]

Jonathan Golden Kimball
(Archives of The Church of Jesus Christ
of Latter-day Saints)

Helen Mar Kimball Whitney
(Archives of The Church of Jesus Christ
of Latter-day Saints)

According to Cheney, the following J. Golden story was first told about Heber C. Kimball, but could be true of either father or son. It seems that Golden urged a young man who had just purchased a team and wagon to sell it and go on a mission. The fellow hesitated, hating to give up his most prized possession.

"Don't worry," answered Elder Kimball, "if you will accept this call, the Lord will provide you a better team and wagon when you return."

This satisfied the young man and he went on the mission. Two years later he returned, worked a while and waited, but financial pinch made getting the team quite impossible. In desperation he went to Elder Kimball and said, "You prophesied that if I went on a mission the Lord would provide me a team and wagon when I returned. I've been home a year now, and I can't earn enough to get them."

J. Golden led him out to his corral and sent him away with his own team and wagon.

Later, back in his house, his wife reprimanded J. Golden for his being so generous. "Hush up," Golden answered. "If the Lord won't keep his promises, then, by hell, I will."[47]

162

Jonathan Golden Kimball, Ben E. Rich, and Elias S. Kimball (Archives of The Church of Jesus Christ of Latter-day Saints)

Other Kimballs have helped to form the broad foundation of Mormon leadership. Golden's full brother Elias Smith Kimball, after serving a second term in the Southern States Mission, 1894-98, was appointed by President William McKinley as chaplain of the Second Regiment of Volunteer Engineers in the Spanish-American War, which was commanded by Colonel Willard Young of Utah. Elias was thus the first Latter-day Saint to serve in the United States military as a chaplain.[48] Following the war he lived for a period in Logan, but shortly after the turn of the century he moved to Blackfoot, Idaho, where he was called as stake president on January 1, 1903. Only seventeen years old when he accompanied his mother, sister, and brother Golden on the pioneering expedition to Bear Lake valley, Elias consequently attained to manhood in J. Golden's long but thin shadow, and the relationship between the two was always intense and full. Indeed, Elias understood the workings of his legendary brother perhaps better than anyone else. "He is nervous and high-tempered and has made a mighty effort all his days to

Orson F. Whitney (Painting by John Hafen, Archives of The Church of Jesus Christ of Latter-day Saints)

David Patten Kimball (Archives of The Church of Jesus Christ of Latter-day Saints)

164

master himself," said Elias of his brother. "No man in the world knows him as well as I do. I love him with all my heart."[50] It was a love that J. Golden fully reciprocated. Elias S. Kimball died June 13, 1934, at the age of seventy-seven, in Salt Lake City.

There were, in all, sixty-five sons and daughters of Heber Kimball, and all of them lent materials to the building of the Kimball tradition among the Latter-day Saints. Two of Vilate Murray Kimball's ten children, for example, played particularly interesting roles in the early history of the Church in the Rocky Mountains. Her third child and second daughter, Helen Mar, was born in Mendon, August 22, 1828. She was five years old when the family moved to Kirtland with Brigham Young, and was in her teens when Heber took a second wife. Her father explained the doctrine of plural marriage to her in June 1843. "Had I not known he loved me too tenderly to introduce anything that was not strictly pure and exalting in its tendencies," she later wrote, "I could not have believed such a doctrine. I could have sooner believed that he would slay me, than teach me an impure principle."[51]

Helen subsequently heard the Prophet Joseph Smith expound the principle. Thoroughly converted to the righteousness of the new order of marriage under auspices of the priesthood, she determined to defend it and her people with all of her might. Opportunities to do so quickly appeared. After her marriage to Horace K. Whitney in the Nauvoo Temple in February 1846, the exodus into the wilderness, and the deaths of her first three children, Helen watched as her own husband entered the order of plural marriage; she stood staunch as the United States government and American society attempted, because of polygamy, to dismantle the Church and deny the Saints their rights as citizens through the last half of the nineteenth century. Whenever criticism of the Mormon people and the practice of polygamy arose, Helen Mar Whitney was in the forefront of the defense. Her favorite theme in this effort revolved about the ideals of the revolutionary age, that "her ancestors died fighting for the liberty which is denied to some of their children, by men who have usurped authority and become oppressors."[52] In addition, Helen was characteristically incensed over current ideas about the inferiority of women, and she often editorialized in various publications for women's rights.

Another of her important contributions to the Mormon heritage came with the birth of a son on July 1, 1855, Orson Ferguson

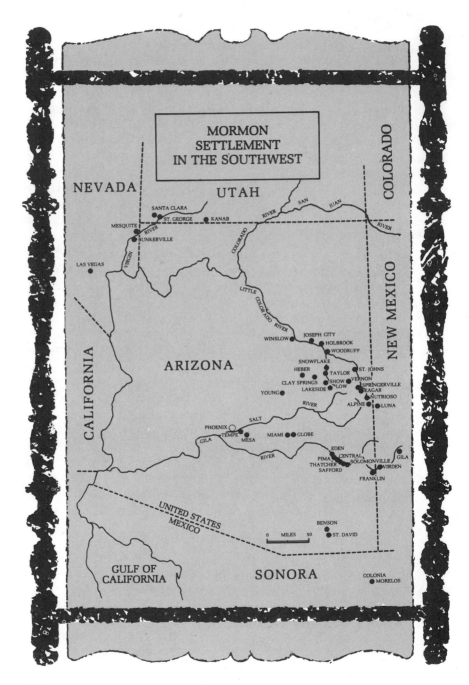

MORMON
SETTLEMENT
IN THE SOUTHWEST

Whitney. He became an outstanding educator and literary figure in Utah, writing prolifically and eventually joining the Council of the Twelve in the footsteps of his famous grandfather. Elder Whitney's articulate writings, many of them still serving as standard works on Utah history and biography, bore eloquent testimony to his mother's heritage as a Kimball.[53] She died on November 15, 1896.

Helen Mar was not the only child of Vilate and Heber Kimball to make significant contributions to the Church. On the night of August 23, 1839, in a log shack at Commerce, Illinois, Vilate gave birth to a son whom she named David Patten Kimball in honor of one of her husband's colleagues in the Council of the Twelve, David W. Patten, who was killed during the Missouri persecutions at the Battle of Crooked River, October 25, 1838. In 1848, at the age of nine, David came to Utah and, within a few years, though still a youngster, had developed into a trustworthy teamster. As J. Golden inherited his father's legendary strength of mind, David P. Kimball became known for his powerful body and physical courage, two more of the storied traits of Heber C. Kimball. He first gained notice when at the age of eighteen he accompanied a group of young men sent from Salt Lake City to rescue the ill-fated Martin handcart company, which was stranded on the Sweetwater River in Wyoming in the face of deepening winter weather. The astonishing story of how David Kimball and his friends George Grant and Allen Huntington carried virtually every member of the stricken company one by one across the icy river quickly spread through Mormondom. President Young, when he heard it, wept and then sealed the three heroes to "an everlasting salvation in the Celestial Kingdom" for their almost selfless courage. David was married shortly after the Sweetwater incident and went to Tooele County to run Heber's ranch near Grantsville; then in 1863 he went on a mission to England. Upon his return he engaged in the freighting business until 1864, when Brigham Young called him to bolster the settlements in Bear River valley, where he settled at what is now Paris, Idaho. He worked there until the mid-1870s, when he took a colonizing mission to Arizona, helping to build the extensive Mormon colony in the Salt River valley. On November 22, 1883, just after his call as first counselor in the new St. Joseph Stake presidency, David P. Kimball died while visiting in Salt Lake City.[54]

Thirty of Heber's grandsons wrote patriotic chapters in the Kimball story by serving in the United States military during World

War I. J. Golden, in his preaching, liked to add that all thirty returned home safely.[55] A thirty-first grandson was in college in 1917 when the United States entered the war in Europe. He left school and went home to await induction at Thatcher, Arizona, where his father, Andrew Kimball, a son of Heber and Ann Alice Gheen, was president of the St. Joseph Stake. While expecting momentarily a call to join his cousins under arms, Spencer Woolley Kimball worked in a bank and courted Camilla Eyring from nearby Pima. His draft notice never came, for the war ended in 1918, and Spencer and Camilla decided to get married. He subsequently helped develop a thriving insurance and real estate business, but he was soon more involved in the work of the Lord. After first serving as stake clerk, he became a counselor in the stake presidency, and in 1938, when the stake divided, he became president of the new Mt. Graham Stake. Five years later, he followed his grandfather into the Council of the Twelve, being ordained an apostle at the age of forty-eight by President Heber J. Grant.[56]

As an apostle, Elder Kimball devoted extensive time to the budget and missionary committees, but he had gained from his father, a long-time missionary among the Indians, a fervent desire for the strengthening of the Church's Indian programs. He consequently served as head of the Church Indian Committee for twenty-five years.

However, Elder Kimball had another much less welcome burden to bear, suffering enough illnesses, at his son's counting, "to make one wince simply at the listing—typhoid fever, smallpox, Bell's palsy, years of boils and carbuncles, a major heart attack, cancer of the throat resulting in the removal of most of his vocal cords, recurrence of cancer requiring radiation treatment, heart disease requiring open-heart surgery to replace a valve and transplant an artery, and most recently Bell's palsy again."[57] Yet, the son added, his father "had hidden wells of strength upon which he calls so often and so substantially that one begins to think, erroneously, that they are inexhaustible."[58] That typical Kimball strength manifested itself continually during Spencer Kimball's three decades in the Council of the Twelve, but never so much as it did after December 30, 1973, when he succeeded Harold B. Lee as president of The Church of Jesus Christ of Latter-day Saints. President Kimball once characterized a true prophet as one "who gives example—clean, full of faith, godlike in his attributes with an

168

Spencer W. Kimball (Painting by Lee Greene Richards, Archives of The Church of Jesus Christ of Latter-day Saints)

untarnished name, a beloved husband, a true father."[59] He was unconsciously describing, more closely than anyone else, Spencer Woolley Kimball.

A human legend may be defined as "one around whom [marvelous] stories and traditions have grown up," or "one having a special status as a result of possessing or being held to possess extraordinary qualities. . . ."[60] George Washington, the sons of John Goldy, Heber C. Kimball and his children and grandchildren, and a prophet of God—all fit the description. They are all part of a Mormon legacy brought to mind by the name of a girl from New Jersey who became Christeen Golden Kimball when she married an apostle of the Lord in 1844, in the United States of America.

Hartman Rector, Jr.:
Let It Be True

Following the   British defeat at Saratoga, New York, in October 1777, the Revolutionary War in the North settled into stalemate. In the South, however, the British generals heightened their activity, hoping to capitalize on what they believed to be overwhelming Loyalist sentiment below the Potomac River. France had recently entered the conflict on the side of the Patriots, and King George's men wanted to subdue the southern portion of the rebellious colonies before the French presence could have much effect.

Although the expected support from the southern populace failed to materialize, the redcoats were in firm control of Georgia and South Carolina by the summer of 1780, having easily rolled back American resistance from Savannah to Charleston and northward into North Carolina. That summer, while Patriots in the two southernmost colonies turned to guerrilla warfare under such leaders as Francis Marion, "the Swamp Fox," the British army under Sir Henry Clinton and Lord Cornwallis was threatening to push the Continental Army from North Carolina and even Virginia. But the Americans were stiffening their resistance to the royalist incursion into the southern colonies. On June 23, 1780, the Continental Congress unanimously pledged "to support the liberty and independence of every one of its members,"[1] and by the end of July a

171

large army of Patriots, both Continentals and militiamen, mostly from Delaware, Maryland, and Virginia, was moving southward to meet the British threat. The stage was set for the most decisive battles of the war, and for Great Britain, "the world turned upside down."[2]

Under command of General Horatio Gates, the Patriots marched into South Carolina to a point thirteen miles north of their first objective in the southern campaign, a British post at Camden. There they camped for a few days, preparing for the surprise assault on Camden, which they launched on the night of August 15. On that same night, a slightly smaller force of royal troops under Lord Cornwallis left Camden for a surprise attack upon the Americans. The two groups' only surprise came the next morning when they suddenly met each other at Saunder's Creek. Gates, believing correctly that his troops outnumbered those of Cornwallis, ordered his left wing to attack. The British commander realized that his assailants were militiamen whom he could overwhelm with a counterattack, so he turned his regulars against the advancing Patriots. It was quickly apparent that Cornwallis had gambled well, for the Americans were soon fleeing in disarray back into North Carolina.

When Gates finally reassembled his army in Hillsborough some sixty miles north of the battle scene, he could count only a fourth of his original force. The result was disastrous. Cornwallis quickly capitalized on his victory thrusting easily into North Carolina. On September 7 he entered Charlotte without resistance. From there he planned to sweep through the rest of the colony and link with British forces in Virginia, thus completing in one crushing blow the conquest of the South. While in Charlotte, however, the adventurous Briton learned that an auxiliary force of more than a thousand Loyalists had been destroyed at King's Mountain in western Carolina on October 7. Disappointed, Cornwallis retreated to Camden, where he remained for almost three months, planning a new offensive into North Carolina.[3]

With the British retreat, Patriots reoccupied Charlotte and received a new commander from Congress, General Nathanael Greene. The new leader found only fifteen hundred soldiers in Charlotte, half of whom were veterans of the rout at Camden. Knowing that such a force could not stand against Cornwallis and his growing army, Greene nevertheless decided to take the offensive. He split his army, sending one element under General Daniel

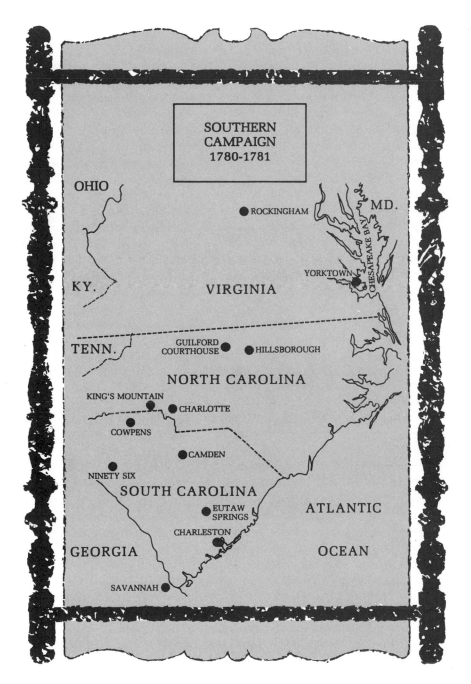

SOUTHERN
CAMPAIGN
1780-1781

OHIO

KY.

TENN.

● ROCKINGHAM

MD.

YORKTOWN ●

CHESAPEAKE BAY

VIRGINIA

GUILFORD
COURTHOUSE ●   ● HILLSBOROUGH

NORTH CAROLINA

KING'S MOUNTAIN ●   ● CHARLOTTE

COWPENS

● CAMDEN

NINETY SIX ●

SOUTH CAROLINA

● EUTAW
SPRINGS

CHARLESTON ●

ATLANTIC

GEORGIA

OCEAN

SAVANNAH ●

Morgan to the southwest to harass Cornwallis on his flank. On January 16, 1781, Morgan met a thousand redcoats at a place called the Cowpens and, by virtue of superior battle position, managed to smash the British force while suffering comparatively light casualties. Infuriated, Cornwallis rushed forward in an attempt to cut off Morgan's escape, but the Americans moved quickly, reuniting with Greene and the main body of the Patriot army at Guilford Courthouse, North Carolina. They then crossed the Dan River into Virginia, where they were reinforced by four hundred Continentals and numerous militiamen. In the meantime, Cornwallis had not received the aid from the North he had expected, nor was he able to rally the North Carolina Loyalists to his side in sufficient numbers to offset the burgeoning American army. Still believing his forces superior to those of Greene, he therefore accepted a challenge to meet the Americans in battle at Guilford Courthouse on March 15. The ambitious lord again gambled wisely. While he lost some 500 men killed or wounded, he managed to rout the Patriot militia and forced the Continentals to retreat. Cornwallis jubilantly marched to the coast and then northward into Virginia. He did not know that although he had won the battle, he was about to lose the war.[4]

General Greene realized that Cornwallis had considerably weakened the British position in the South by his successful, though costly, operations in the Carolinas, and that royalist forces in the Deep South could not withstand a concerted Patriot campaign to dislodge them with Cornwallis and the main British army maneuvering in North Carolina and Virginia. After Guilford, Greene thus linked his forces with those of Marion and Light-Horse Harry Lee; by the middle of May the Patriots had surrounded the British outposts guarding Charleston and Savannah and had laid them under siege. Greene himself waited for the British to surrender their post at Ninety-Six, but fell back after the Loyalist garrison there was reinforced on June 20. But the remainder of the British outposts had surrendered by that time, and royal holdings in the Deep South amounted only to Charleston, Savannah, and a few nearby towns. On July 3 the British also evacuated Ninety-Six in order to concentrate in Charleston. The victories of Cornwallis during the previous spring were suddenly empty and meaningless, but Greene was not yet satisfied. Anxious to capture Charleston, he amassed his forces and moved upon the South Carolina capital. On September 8 he met an equal force of about 2,300 British troops at Eutaw Springs.

After a see-saw battle, Greene was defeated once more, but again he profited more than the victors, for the British were sufficiently weakened to prevent them from mounting any type of offensive. As a result they retreated to Charleston, Savannah, and St. Augustine, where they waited hopefully for news of a Cornwallis victory in Virginia. It never came.[5]

Greene's troops also waited for news from the North. A few hardened veterans of the bloody campaign that began over a year before at Camden were still with Greene and had suffered the losses along with him at Guilford, Ninety-Six, and Eutaw Springs. Yet somehow they had a smell of victory. They had fought too hard and too desperately for all to come to naught. Too many good men had died, and as they hovered about Charleston keeping the royalists bottled inside,[6] they prayed for success elsewhere, for the war to reach an end that might vindicate their sacrifice. They prayed for freedom, for justice, and for what they were convinced was ultimate truth—the set of principles embodied in the Declaration of Independence. Only a final victory would confirm those truths, and they prayed most fervently for that.

Among these Continentals was a thirty-year-old trooper from Rockingham County, Virginia, named Isaac Garven. As he performed his duties outside Charleston, his thoughts were back home in Virginia. He wondered about Cornwallis and his men. Could the Patriots in the Old Dominion stop the Tories and their string of victories? Garven had faced their fire and steel many times, but he knew they could be defeated, and that it had to be done. The United States would be free, and if the war had started in Massachusetts, it might as well end in Virginia.[7]

While Greene had by attrition reconquered almost all of the Deep South, Cornwallis had decided in recompense to secure control of Virginia. By May 23, 1781, he was in Petersburg at the head of an army of seven thousand men. His superior, General Clinton, looked on from New York with great trepidation, knowing that Cornwallis had abandoned the Deep South and that the French fleet might appear in Chesapeake Bay, rendering extremely precarious his subordinate's position in Virginia. He urged Cornwallis to move into Pennsylvania, but the brash lord refused and began operations against rapidly responding Patriot forces under Governor Thomas Jefferson, Marquis de Lafayette, and "Mad Anthony" Wayne. At first Cornwallis manhandled Lafayette's army, but soon he found it

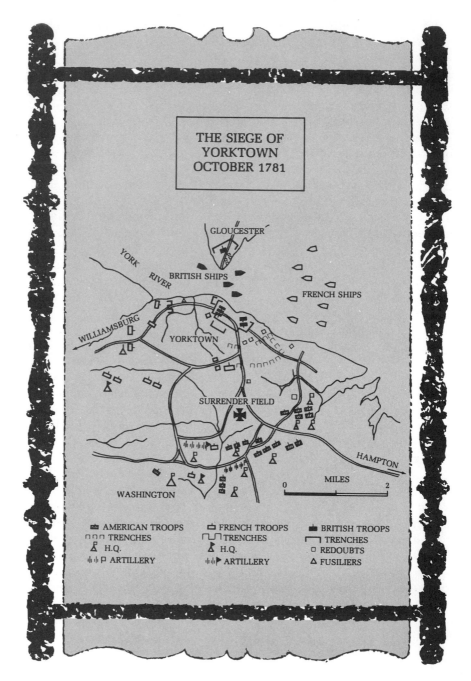

THE SIEGE OF
YORKTOWN
OCTOBER 1781

GLOUCESTER

YORK

RIVER

BRITISH SHIPS

FRENCH SHIPS

WILLIAMSBURG

YORKTOWN

SURRENDER FIELD

HAMPTON

MILES

0   2

WASHINGTON

⊡ AMERICAN TROOPS   ▱ FRENCH TROOPS   ◗ BRITISH TROOPS
⊓⊓⊓ TRENCHES   ⊓⊔ TRENCHES   ⊓ TRENCHES
⚑ H.Q.   ⚑ H.Q.   ▫ REDOUBTS
⫼⫼⊓ ARTILLERY   ⫼⫼▶ ARTILLERY   △ FUSILIERS

difficult to maneuver in the field without a firm base of operations. He chose Yorktown, a port city on the Chesapeake, where he began to erect fortifications late in July 1781. By the first of September, he was well entrenched at the mouth of the York River.

Meanwhile, Washington had been planning a joint Franco-American assault upon New York, but when he learned of a French naval plan to occupy the Chesapeake, he boldly transferred the bulk of his army into Virginia, hoping to trap Cornwallis at Yorktown. The allies executed superbly their land-sea operation, and by the middle of September, Cornwallis was backed against the sea by sixteen thousand American and French troops, many of them hardened veterans of half a dozen years of war. The British general quickly realized that without reinforcements he could escape only by sea, but the French fleet had indeed sealed the bay. Stripped of his brash confidence, Cornwallis begged Clinton to relieve him.

After lengthy preparations and planning, Clinton sailed from New York on October 17 to rescue his repentant subordinate, but on that same day—four years to a day after the surrender of Burgoyne at Saratoga—Lord Cornwallis asked Washington for terms, and two days later he capitulated with his entire force of seven thousand men. On the field of surrender, the British band played somberly an

The First Shot at Yorktown (Painting by Clyde O. Deland, The Continental Insurance Companies)

Robert Morris, the superintendent of finance in the Revolutionary government whose financial reforms in the early summer of 1781 contributed substantially to the American victory at Yorktown (Painting by Ben Stahl, The John Hancock Mutual Life Insurance Company)

English tune called "The World Turned Upside Down." For the British Empire, the earth had reversed itself, and the American people had by their determination and courage severed colonial ties with their powerful and still admired mother country. After Yorktown, the war was virtually over. Isaac Garven and his companions waiting in South Carolina could go home to a free Virginia and a free America. After a continuous series of intervening nightmares, the initial dream had come true.[8]

Subsequent to the surrender of Cornwallis at Yorktown, British strategists realized that although they might win most of the battles in America, they could not win the war. While warfare outside of small skirmishes ground slowly to a halt into 1872, peace negotiations, which had been underway in Europe for several years, quickened in pace. Within a few months of Yorktown, the basic details of the Treaty of Paris (1783) had been worked out. One of its most important articles dealt with boundaries that could have crushed the United States into a narrow strip of land between the

Appalachians and the Atlantic. But the British were willing to draw the boundary along the Mississippi River in the West. This incredible concession gave the Americans a much vaster territory than they had ever controlled and opened to them an almost inconceivable amount of new land for settlement and expansion. Other than the actual winning of independence, this addition of so much territory to the new nation was perhaps the most profound result of the Revolutionary War.[9]

Isaac Garven, shortly after his discharge from Greene's command in December 1781, heard, like so many of his fellows, the call of the fresh land in the West. In December 1834, fifty years after his service in the Patriot army of the South, Isaac was living in Lincoln County, Kentucky, about fifty miles south of Lexington. There, at the age of seventy-one, he applied for a pension from the federal government for his service in the war. He remembered clearly the events at Camden, Guilford Courthouse, Ninety-Six, and Eutaw Springs.[10] He had told the story of the crucial southern campaign of 1780-81 many times. His children knew it well. But three months after his pension application, Isaac Garven died, leaving to his sons and daughters the task of perpetuating the story of his role in the Revolutionary War and its significance.[11]

In the 1830s, even farther west, a drama with another meaning was taking place in the new state of Missouri. The disciples of Joseph Smith were moving into the western counties of the state for the purposes of "establishing Zion," and there were few non-Mormons in Missouri who had not heard of this peculiar religion and its dedicated adherents. One of Isaac's sons, Steven Huston Garven, had settled in Randolph County in the north-central section of the state, and had plenty to do, while running his modest farming operation, without worrying about the build-up of "Mormon troubles" to the west. Most Missourians regarded the Latter-day Saints as merely another group of hard-working immigrants and did not participate in the dreadful persecutions that drove them finally into Illinois at the end of the decade. Indeed, as the Mormons were crossing the Mississippi during the winter of 1838-39 to escape the mobocracy of a few vitrolic Missourians, Steven Garven was thinking more about his wife, Janette Brooks, who was about to give birth. On February 11, 1839, as the Mormons were settling near Commerce, Illinois, Janette Garven bore Steven a son whom they named William Brooks. The tragic scenes of the Mormon expulsion from Missouri were far beyond the thoughts of the Garvens of Randolph County.[12] Thus, as young W. B. Garven grew up on the family farm, the Mormon experience in Missouri was a matter of interesting history, but not much else.

In 1848, when W. B. was nine years old, the United States acquired from Mexico a vast chunk of territory in the Southwest, which added (with Texas) some 1,200,000 square miles to the national domain. Two years earlier, the Americans had also gained clear title to Oregon south of the forty-ninth parallel. This rapid expansion of the United States to the Pacific had been exciting, but it also brought to the horizon fearsome clouds that threatened to destroy the nation on the eve of its greatest territorial extension. The divisive issue of slavery, which politicians had for three decades refused to discuss, suddenly became an all-consuming difficulty as both North and South clashed in what they believed was a life-and-death struggle to determine whether slavery would be allowed into the new territories.

As the decade of the 1850s progressed, it became tragically clear that the deep gulf between the North and the South on this and other issues would ultimately lead to physical violence. By 1858, when William Brooks Garven turned nineteen, the dispute over slavery had become, in the words of Senator William H. Seward of New York, "an irrepressible conflict between opposing and enduring forces, and it means that the United States must and will, sooner or later, become either entirely a slaveholding nation or entirely a free-labor nation."[13] That meant a war between the states and between brothers—a civil war. Nothing in the history of the world is more bitter and as spiritually devastating as internecine warfare.

In Missouri, as in all of the border states (or slave states that did not secede), the Civil War struck particularly hard, as friends and neighbors and even members of the same family often found themselves on opposing sides. The Missouri Garvens were typical. Ten of them joined the Confederate Army, while fourteen others fought for the Union.[14] In Randolph County, several companies were raised for each side in the conflict, but William Brooks Garven stayed on the farm, perhaps choosing a neutral course, as his associates, some in blue and some in gray, marched off to war.[15]

It was a heart-wrenching time for the United States. Before it was over, a million Americans were dead and countless other

180

carried home wounds of body and soul that never healed. When the Union was finally secured in 1865, Americans had killed more Americans than all the enemies of the United States would kill during the rest of its history to the present. So terrible were those four years of war that one of every three men who donned a uniform during its course became a casualty. The last and greatest casualty, President Abraham Lincoln, had dedicated the war to a "new birth of freedom," and when it ended, the United States had a fresh start. This "Second American Revolution," as Charles Beard called it, charted a new course for the United States, one that led it into the world as a powerful and dynamic nation that could aspire to and achieve greatness.[16]

W. B. Garven in the meantime married and established himself in a prosperous Missouri farming operation. By the turn of the century, he had raised a fine family but had also buried his first wife. At the age of fifty-nine he married Lucy Ellen Mason and began a second family. Prospering financially, he did business with the Farmers Bank of Renick, where he associated closely with the vice-president of the institution, a neighboring farmer, Joel Legrand Rector. Rector also traced his origins to Virginia and Kentucky, and the two families grew close. On August 18, 1918, Joel's twenty-two-year-old son, Hartman, tied the Garvens and Rectors together officially when he married the first child of William's second family, Vivian Fay. Vivian, nineteen, had taught school during the year before her marriage. It was a doubly joyous time for the young couple inasmuch as the war in Europe had ended and Hartman had come home safely from his service in the U. S. Army. Only the death of William B. Garven on April 2, 1919, at the age of eighty, dulled the luster of their new life together. But the great-granddaughter of Isaac Garven had had plenty of time to ingest the true meaning of her heritage as a child of the Revolution and of America.[17]

Like their parents before them, the Rectors planted their roots in the loamy soil of northern Missouri. Their first son, Hartman Rector, Jr., born August 20, 1924, grew up as a farmer's son in Randolph County, and he loved it. It never occurred to him that he would be anything but a farmer the rest of his life. During the winters he attended school first in the small grade school and then at the high school in Moberly, and during the summers he sweat alongside his father while he coaxed a modest living from the family farm.

The biggest time of the summer around Moberly was the Fourth of July. Young Hartman loved that, too. "When I was growing up," he later recalled, "there were no limits on the size of firecrackers. We took great delight in laying a stick of dynamite on top of a log, lighting it, and then going back quite a distance. We rattled all the dishes on the shelves of every home in the little valley in which I lived."[18] On the serious side, he realized as well that the Fourth of July meant freedom— "real freedom, the freedom to act, the freedom to pray, the freedom to love and *know* what we're doing."[19]

Because of his heritage, because of who he was, Hartman Rector, Jr., gave the concept of freedom a lot of thought. He liked to visit his Grandmother Garven in nearby Renick and listen to her tales of the past. Lucy Garven was a descendant of the Revolutionary War herself, coming from the Marshall, Mason, and Rhodes families of Virginia, but she also liked to tell the youngster about religion. She had a big Bible that she loved to read to him while he sat on her lap. Before he was very old, Hartman had an appetite for more of the truth, but "he knew not where to find it."[20]

As he grew into young adulthood, the pattern of Hartman's life seemed to be well-fixed until it was interrupted by the outbreak of World War II. He joined the navy with the goal of becoming a pilot, and from that point his life's pattern altered drastically. During pre-flight training he began to attend church services and to read and think a great deal about religion, but a full understanding seemed always to elude his grasp. "The desire to know the truth was intensified as I studied and prayed and as I attended first one church and then another, but there was something missing in all of them for me."[21] As he progressed in his training as a navy pilot, he was able to outline in his mind several "questions and irritations" concerning religion and became convinced that when he saw the "plain truth" he would recognize it.[22]

In 1947, after four years in the navy, Hartman went home to Moberly, married Constance Kirk Daniel, "the beautiful little dark-haired girl" whom he had loved for years, and moved onto the Rector family farm. During their courtship, they had discussed religion often and agreed to a joint search for spiritual truth with a pledge "never to cease to grow."[23] With their marriage, the search continued and intensified. They read the Bible together and considered its questions and answers through the births of their first two children. Then came the Korean War and a new call to service in the navy. The Rectors moved to San Diego, where Hartman's squadron was based, but shortly thereafter he was assigned to Hawaii for training.

Soon after his departure, two Mormon missionaries knocked on Connie Rector's door. "In one of her letters to me," Hartman wrote later, "she mentioned that two young men had called on her and asked a lot of questions about religion, to which they also then seemed to have all the answers."[24] On his first evening home from Hawaii, he heard from Connie the early history of Joseph Smith. As he listened to this tale of a young religious leader who just over a century before had passed within miles of his grandfather's home, he could not believe in modern visions and revelations and laughed at Connie's seemingly fanciful tale. But when he saw how impressed she was, he agreed to read the Book of Mormon. He knew almost at once that his quest was about to end. "While reading First Nephi, I remember saying to myself, 'Dear God, let this be true, please let this be truth—for if it is, it answers all the questions I have been trying to answer all my life.' I hadn't finished Second Nephi when I knew it was true."[25]

The Rectors studied the gospel in San Diego during Hartman's few days of leave. When he sailed for Asia in January 1952, he was loaded with Mormon books and pamphlets. On February 25, 1952, he presented himself for baptism at the Japan Mission home in Tokyo. There in the garden he was baptized "in 30-degree weather, seven thousand miles from my home in Missouri. . . . My search had come to an end."[26] Connie entered the waters of baptism four days later in San Diego.[27] Though an ocean apart, they wished to go together into the kingdom of God.

With the end of the Korean War, Hartman Rector, Jr., decided to remain on active duty partly because of his love of flying and partly because of the free time service in the military afforded him to work in the Church. While serving in the navy, he attended Murray State College in Kentucky and universities in California, Georgia, and Minnesota. During his period of military duty, the Rectors also took time to prepare to receive their temple blessings, and they were sealed together in the Mesa Temple in May 1953.[28]

In 1958 Elder Rector completed a tour of shore duty at the Pentagon and then left the navy to accept a position in the United States Department of Agriculture under Secretary Ezra Taft Benson.

At this time the growing family was living in the Virginia suburbs of Washington, D.C., where both Hartman and Connie settled into busy lives of work, rearing children, and serving in the Church. Hartman soon became a Washington Stake missionary, having been ordained a seventy in May 1956 by Elder George Q. Morris. During four years of labor he baptized nearly fifty persons. After subsequent service as stake mission president and in various other positions, Hartman Rector, Jr., became senior president of the 542nd quorum of seventy in the Potomac Stake.[29]

He was serving in that position when in early 1968 President David O. McKay summoned the Rectors to Salt Lake City for an interview. As they sat in the outer office wondering why the Prophet of the Lord wanted to talk with a pair of converts from Missouri, they noticed a distinguished-looking young man and his wife also waiting to visit with President McKay. Through their nervousness, the Rectors noticed that their fellow sufferer was six and a half feet tall, and they learned that he was Loren C. Dunn, first counselor in the New England Mission presidency, director of communication for the New England Council for Economic Development, and the husband of Sharon Longden, a daughter of Elder John Longden, Assistant to the Twelve. While visiting with the Dunns, Connie turned to Hartman and said with a smile, "If you two are interviewing for the same job, we'll be on the first plane home."[30] But when Hartman was ushered into the presence of the Prophet, he discovered that it was not for an interview but for a calling, the same one issued to Elder Dunn—a call to the First Council of the Seventy, to become one of the General Authorities of the Church. At the end of the meeting, President McKay took Elder Rector's hand and said, "I want you to know that the Lord loves you and so do we."[31] It had been only sixteen years since Elder Rector had discovered the restored church, and now it would be his responsibility to assist in disseminating its message to the world.

In the summer of 1971, Elder Rector was called to preside over the newly formed Alabama-Florida Mission with headquarters in Tallahassee, Florida, but he was called back to Salt Lake City a year later as the missions of the world were placed under the direct supervision of the First Council of the Seventy. In this changed arrangement of responsibility, President Rector and his six colleagues on the council traveled more extensively abroad than before. This experience had a profound effect upon this descendant of Private

Isaac Garven of the Virginia Line of the Continental Army. He became increasingly impressed with the role of the United States in the building of the kingdom as he journeyed about the missions of the world; the blood of men like Garven and the greatness of the America that sprang from it took on a new meaning.

"We're beginning to see [that this] is no longer an American church," he said at the close of one of those trips abroad. "It is an international, universal kingdom of God that bids fair now to be on the way to blanket the earth with truth as the waters cover the mighty deep, as the prophets have said." But, he asked further, "why do you suppose the Lord organized the kingdom in the United States? So he could finance it. The kingdom has to be financed."[32]

However, Elder Rector knew there were many other reasons. It was apparent, for example, that the United States was furnishing the great bulk of the missionary force to the world. In light of these factors, he could see clearly his heritage both as Latter-day Saint and as American. "To me, it's obvious why the Lord established this country, this land. With his own hand he has done it." He continued: "The work must be done. And we're free to do it because we have this kind of nation as our heritage. We know more about freedom, I presume, than anyone knows—except, I guess, maybe one doesn't really know about freedom unless he's lost it. But we know about freedom because we *have* experienced it."[33]

So Hartman Rector, Jr., a twentieth-century convert, contributed to the heritage of the Latter-day Saints in the Spirit of 1776. He was, after all, a partaker of the inheritance of Isaac Garven, one of the Patriots who suffered through the southern campaign of 1780-81, in which campaign Cornwallis was forced to entrench at Yorktown. By forcing his surrender, the army of the United States verified the truth of the revolutionary cause and secured a nation from which could go forth the word of God in the last days. It was therefore possible for a man like Hartman Rector to serve as a General Authority of the church of Jesus Christ and at the same time express deep regard for the United States. "Another reason why I love the USA is that she has produced some great men," he once said, "great men that you can hold up as an example, that you can look to for leadership. George Washington, whom many call the father of this country, was such a man."[34] But great persons need not be famous in the sense that Washington was famous. Asael Smith, Solomon Mack, John Young, Daniel Wood, Benoni Benson,

David Chapin, Silas Bunker, Benjamin Brown, John Goldy, and Isaac Garven were also great men, at least to their descendants and to such latter-day patriots as Hartman Rector, Jr. As Mormons believe, the restored gospel must go forth to all the world; the United States of America, its revolutionary heroes, and their descendants among the Saints have provided the impetus for this "call to repentance."[35]

Hartman Rector, Jr., also perceives a place in the Revolutionary War heritage for children of more recent immigrants, whose American lines do not run through the years of the Revolution:

> The [American] people have come from all nations. The mixing of the blood of all the children of God has taken place here. Isn't it apropos? That's how you get strength. Anybody who knows anything about raising cattle knows that you have to bring in outside blood lines every now and then to build strength in the stock. Of course, it's the same way in the kingdom of God. That's the reason we need to keep bringing in the converts, mixing them with the blood in the Church so the blood of Israel will be kept strong and viable.[36]

Speaking at the Provo Freedom Festival on June 30, 1974, President Rector passed a challenge to American Saints that summarizes well the point of this book:

> We need to give. That's the message of the Fourth of July, as far as I'm concerned. It is, once again, a looking back to that time when our forefathers were willing to pledge their lives, their fortunes, and their sacred honor to bring this nation to pass. Many gave their lives to do it, but it was worth it. When you die in this kind of cause, I think you've got a ticket to the highest degree. "Greater love hath no man than this, that a man lay down his life for his friends."
>
> We're called of the Lord to give, worldwide. . . . We can do it because this is the land choice above all other lands. We can reach out to other peoples, and they can feel the touch of the Master's hand through us because that's what we're called to do.
>
> We are blessed above all other people. But we're not blessed to sit down with our blessing and hold it and hug it to our breasts; we are blessed to give it away. . . . That's the gospel of Jesus Christ and that's the philosophy of this country.[37]

186

George Washington (Painting by Harold Von Schmidt, The John Hancock
Mutual Life Insurance Company)

If two centuries of American history and a century and a half
of Mormon history mean anything at all, they provide a heritage of
giving, of love unfeigned, and of selfless dedication to the ultimate
exaltation of humanity. Within that concept is the Revolutionary
War heritage of the Latter-day Saints.

Notes

COMMENT ON SOURCES

Trying to weave the Mormon story, which began in the 1820s and 1830s, into the history of the American Revolution of the late eighteenth century required such a long sortie into a wide variety of documents and historical writings that it precluded any intensive study of materials relating to the entire scope of this volume. Because of the nature of this book, I have felt free to rely upon the works of others, where possible, for a presentation of the history of some Latter-day Saints and their Revolutionary War ancestors. In cases of questionable accuracy of secondary sources, or for purpose of verification, I consulted primary sources, such as diaries, contemporary documents, and the like. Some of the essays required much more primary research than others, and the new material presented consequently varies proportionately. Each chapter in the book raised different research requirements, and this, as well, is reflected in the footnotes, which were designed to give the interested reader guidelines for tracing the course I took in discerning as closely as possible what probably happened in the part of the past I was considering. I hope that in repeating and documenting the beliefs of other historians concerning that past I have avoided attaching credit or blame to someone else for my own ideas, however accurate or inaccurate.

In discussing the various facets and events of the Revolution at the beginning of each essay, I have relied heavily upon John Richard Alden's contribution to the New American Nation Series, *The American Revolution, 1775-1783* (New York: Harper & Row, 1954), which is probably the best single synthesis in existence of scholarly thinking on the Revolution. There are many other important works on the revolutionary period without which an understanding of America's birth would be much more difficult. Not as detailed as Alden, but an excellent survey, is Edmund S. Morgan, *The Birth of the Republic, 1763-89* (Chicago: University of Chicago Press, 1956). More involved studies that have contributed to my work on this volume include Richard B. Morris, *The American Revolution Reconsidered* (New York: Harper & Row, 1967); Eric Robson, *The American Revolution in Its Political and Military Aspects, 1763-1783* (London: Batchworth Press, 1955); and Allan Nevins, *The American States During and After the Revolution, 1775-1789* (New York: Macmillan, 1924). Because my study of the war dealt almost exclusively with its military history, also invaluable to my efforts was John C. Miller, *Triumph of Freedom, 1775-1783* (Boston: Little, Brown, 1948), which contains an excellent set of maps. Additionally influential in this regard were Charles K. Bolton, *The Private Soldier Under Washington* (Port Washington, N.Y.: Kennikat Press, 1964); Francis V. Greene, *The Revolutionary War and the Military Policy of the United States* (Port Washington, N.Y.: Kennikat Press, 1911); Piers Mackesy, *The War for America, 1775-1783* (Cambridge, Mass.: Harvard University Press, 1964); and Willard M. Wallace, *Appeal to Arms: A Military History of the American Revolution* (New York: Harper, 1951).

For the details of specific themes or incidents, I consulted for each chapter some narrower studies and have in each instance cited them carefully in the essay's notes.

The history of The Church of Jesus Christ of Latter-day Saints is incredibly well documented. From its inception, the Church kept detailed records, believing such activity to be a commandment of God. In addition, a great number of Latter-day Saints have kept careful records of their lives in the form of diaries and reminiscences. For this reason, a historian mining the resources of the Mormon Church Archives in Salt Lake City often finds himself overwhelmed by the unbelievable wealth of resources available for study. A small book such as this one has revealed perhaps one drop of the veritable ocean of material on deposit in the Church Archives for the study of Latter-day Saint history. Again, the notes for each chapter reveal the degree to which I have probed various records applying to the subject at hand.

The storehouse of material in the Church's Genealogical Society Library in Salt Lake City was also a great help in the preparation of *Latter-day Patriots*. The fine collection of microfilm publications was particularly valuable when it came to such things as pension records and service indexes. Family group sheets on deposit there were often helpful in determining relationships and time/place factors. Finally, the society's excellent collection of local histories provided me with easy access to obscure information that often played a significant role in the stories I was writing.

With regard to Mormon history already published, I seemed continually to be consulting such standard publications as Joseph Smith's *History of The Church of Jesus Christ of Latter-day Saints*, ed. by B. H. Roberts, 7 vols, 2nd ed. rev. (Salt Lake City: Deseret Book Company, 1964); B. H. Roberts, *A Comprehensive History of The Church of Jesus Christ of Latter-day Saints, Century I*, 6 vols. (Salt Lake City: Deseret News, 1930); and Andrew Jenson, *Latter-day Saints Biographical Encyclopedia*, 4 vols. (1901; reprint ed., Salt Lake City: Western Epics, 1971). I was also grateful for the numerous biographies of Mormon figures that have been prepared over the years as well as for the growing body of periodical literature on Mormon history in such journals as *Brigham Young University Studies, Dialogue: A Journal of Mormon Thought, Journal of Mormon History*, and *Utah Historical Quarterly*.

Among the most useful sources of material for this book were the minds of my colleagues in the Historical Department of the Church. On numerous occasions their work and understanding provided immeasurable input without which the process of gathering information for *Latter-day Patriots* would have been a seemingly interminable task.

CHAPTER 1

[1]D&C 101:79-80.

[2]D&C 101:76-78; 98:4-10; 134.

[3]1 Nephi 2:20; 13; 2 Nephi 1:5-11; 10:19; Alma 43:48; Ether 2:7-12, 15; 13:2.

[4]Joseph Smith, Jr., *History of The Church of Jesus Christ of Latter-day Saints*, ed. by B. H. Roberts, 7 vols., 2nd ed. rev. (Salt Lake City: Deseret Book Co., 1964), 5:526. This work has often been cited in the past as "Documentary History of the Church." Based largely on a lengthy manuscript compiled between 1839 and 1856 by various clerks, it was finished to appear as the work of Joseph Smith himself while being adapted in reality from the great bulk of documents created by others as well as the Prophet during his lifetime.

[5]Whitney R. Cross, *The Burned-Over District: The Social and Intellectual History of Enthusiastic Religion in Western New York, 1800-1850* (Ithaca, N. Y.: Cornell University Press, 1950), pp. 139-41. Cross adds on page 150, however, an assertion that the Church, its personnel, and its doctrines were not really frontier products, but, like Joseph himself, "belonged rather to that Yankee, rural, emotionalized, and rapidly maturing culture which characterized western New York so markedly in the second quarter of the nineteenth century." See also Sidney E. Ahlstrom, *A Religious History of the American People* (New Haven, Conn.: Yale University Press, 1972), pp. 501-509, who admits (p. 508) that Mormonism's "numerical growth, economic adaptation, internal divisions, external hostility, and heroic exploits [render] almost useless the usual categories of explanation. One cannot even be sure if the object of our

consideration is a sect, a mystery cult, a new religion, a church, a people, a nation, or an American subculture; indeed, at different times and places it is all of these."

⁶Smith, *History of the Church*, 5:498.

⁷Archibald F. Bennett, "The Ancestry of Joseph Smith the Prophet," *Utah Genealogical and Historical Magazine* 20 (January-April 1929): 72, 74; John Henry Evans, *Joseph Smith: An American Prophet* (New York: Macmillan, 1933), pp. 20-21; John A. Widtsoe, *Joseph Smith, Seeker after Truth, Prophet of God* (Salt Lake City: Deseret News, 1951), pp. 99-100.

⁸Joseph Fielding Smith, *Asahel Smith of Topsfield, Massachusetts, with Some Account of the Smith Family* (Topsfield: Topsfield Historical Society, 1902), p. 88.

⁹Bennett, "Ancestry of Joseph Smith," p. 14, quoting *Massachusetts Soldiers and Sailors in the Revolutionary War*, 14:537.

¹⁰*Salem (Massachusetts) Gazette,* November 22, 1785, quoted in Evans, *Joseph Smith,* p. 22; Mary Audentia Smith Anderson, *Ancestry and Posterity of Joseph Smith and Emma Hale* (Independence, Mo.: Herald Publishing House, 1929), pp. 55-58; Bennett, "Ancestry of Joseph Smith," p. 15. See Richard L. Anderson, *Joseph Smith's New England Heritage: Influences of Grandfathers Solomon Mack and Asael Smith* (Salt Lake City: Deseret Book Co., 1971), pp. 89, 188.

¹¹Evans, *Joseph Smith*, pp. 22-23.

¹²Elmer Cecil McGavin, *The Family of Joseph Smith* (Salt Lake City: Bookcraft, 1963), pp. 18-20.

¹³Mary Duty Smith's brothers, Moses, Mark, and William Duty, also served in the army out of Windham. Bennett, "Ancestry of Joseph Smith," p. 28.

¹⁴Charles Henry Jones, *History of the Campaign for the Conquest of Canada in 1776* (Philadelphia, 1882), p. 198, cited in Richard Anderson, *Joseph Smith's New England Heritage,* pp. 92, 193; ibid., p. 92

¹⁵Richard Anderson, *Joseph Smith's New England Heritage,* pp. 92, 192-93; Audentia Anderson, *Ancestry and Posterity of Joseph Smith and Emma Hale,* p. 59.

¹⁶Bennett, "Ancestry of Joseph Smith," p. 11. See also Smith, *Asahel Smith,* p. 89.

¹⁷Asael Smith to Jacob Towne, January 14, 1796, Essex Institute, Salem, Massachusetts, quoted in Richard Anderson, *Joseph Smith's New England Heritage,* pp. 118-23; Smith, *Asahel Smith,* p. 91; McGavin, *Family of Joseph Smith,* pp. 11-12. See also Daniel 2.

¹⁸Asael Smith's Address to His Family, April 10, 1799, Topsfield Historical Society, Topsfield, Massachusetts, quoted in McGavin, *Family of Joseph Smith,* p. 17; Smith, *Asahel Smith,* p. 95; Richard Anderson, *Joseph Smith's New England Heritage,* pp. 124-40.

¹⁹McGavin, *Family of Joseph Smith,* pp. 9-20; Joseph Fielding Smith, *Essentials in Church History,* 22nd ed. rev. (Salt Lake City: Deseret Book Co., 1971), p. 25.

²⁰Ibid.

²¹Solomon Mack, *A Narrative of the Life of Solomon Mack, Containing an Account of the Many Severe Accidents He Met with During a Long Series of Years, Together with the Extraordinary Manner in Which He Was Converted to the Christian Faith* (Windsor, Vt., c.1810), pp. 5-9, reprinted in Richard Anderson, *Joseph Smith's New England Heritage,* pp. 34ff. See also Evans, *Joseph Smith,* p. 25; Bennett, "Ancestry of Joseph Smith," p. 50.

²²Mack, *Narrative,* p. 9.

²³Evans, *Joseph Smith,* pp. 25-27.

²⁴Mack, *Narrative,* pp. 10-14. See also Richard Anderson, *Joseph Smith's New England Heritage,* pp. 12-18. The *New England Chronicle* reported that thirteen of Solomon's uncles on his mother's side served in the Revolution—all six-footers and "very brave men." Evans, *Joseph Smith,* p. 25. It is also interesting to note that

Solomon's son, Stephen, became a brigadier general in the revolutionary army. Bennett, "Ancestry of Joseph Smith," p. 51.

[25]Evans, *Joseph Smith*, pp. 25-27. See also Lucy Mack Smith, *Biographical Sketches of Joseph Smith, the Prophet, and His Progenitors for Many Generations* (Liverpool: Orson Pratt, 1853), pp. 15-44.

[26]Writers have devoted considerable effort to the study of the ancestry of Joseph Smith, some to prove a disreputable background and others to demonstrate the opposite. Among the latter were Mormon apostles George Q. Cannon and John A. Widtsoe. Elder Cannon, in his *Life of Joseph Smith the Prophet* (Salt Lake City: Juvenile Instructor, 1888), pp. 31-32, asserted that the men in Joseph's ancestry "were devout and generous, measurably prosperous in a worldly sense, and several of them were brave and steadfast soldiers through the Colonial campaigns and the Revolutionary struggle." Elder Widtsoe, in *Joseph Smith*, p. 100, added, "During the Revolutionary period and before, many of Joseph Smith's ancestors, on both paternal and maternal sides, took courageous and unflinching part in the movements, including army service, that led to the formation of the United States of America." More recently, and by means of exhaustive research, Richard L. Anderson permanently dispelled the myths about the unworthiness of the Prophet's ancestry. He concluded that Asael and Solomon were honorable men, responsible in large degree for the character of their "prophet-grandson," and, quoting from Duberman's *Charles Francis Adams*, asserted that the Smiths and Macks were "true New Englanders" after the model of the Adams family, "earnest, certain men, capable for better or worse, of instilling in a child firm beliefs and positive standards." (*Joseph Smith's New England Heritage*, pp. 155-58.)

[27]See Fawn M. Brodie, *No Man Knows My History: The Life of Joseph Smith, the Mormon Prophet* (New York: Alfred A. Knopf, 1945), pp. 5-6.

[28]In addition to those works cited previously, see, for a further sampling, E. W. Tullidge, *Life of Joseph the Prophet* (New York, 1878); Harry M. Beardsley, *Joseph Smith and His Mormon Empire* (Boston: Houghton Mifflin Co., 1931); Ivan J. Barrett, *Joseph Smith, the Extraordinary* (Provo, Utah: Brigham Young University Extension Division, 1954); Leon R. Hartshorn, *Joseph Smith: Prophet of the Restoration* (Salt Lake City: Deseret Book Co., 1970); B. H. Roberts, *Joseph Smith the Prophet-Teacher* (Salt Lake City: Deseret News, 1908); I. Woodbridge Riley, *The Founder of Mormonism: A Psychological Study of Joseph Smith, Jr.* (New York: Dodd, Mead & Co., 1902); Daryl Chase, *Joseph the Prophet as He Lives in the Hearts of His People* (Salt Lake City: Deseret Book Co., 1944); Hyrum L. Andrus, *Joseph Smith, the Man and the Seer* (Salt Lake City: Deseret Book Co., 1960). Those interested in Mormon history await anxiously works underway on the life of the Prophet by such scholars as Dean C. Jessee, Jan Shipps, and Marvin Hill.

[29]Martin B. Hickman, "The Political Legacy of Joseph Smith," *Dialogue: A Journal of Mormon Thought* 3 (Autumn 1968): 22-27. See also the work of Hyrum L. Andrus and G. Homer Durham.

[30]Smith, *History of the Church*, 2:6-7.

[31]Ibid., 2:12-13.

[32]Ibid., 2:13.

[33]Ibid., 6:56.

[34]Ibid., 6:56-57. This unabridged excerpt is from a sermon that Joseph preached from a stand east of the unfinished Nauvoo Temple on October 15, 1843, as reported by Willard Richards. The Prophet was here dealing with what was perhaps the most biting political issue of the day—that is, whether the Constitution, under the "strict interpretation," delegated *all* powers not specifically enumerated within it to the states, or whether, under a "broad interpretation" that Joseph espoused, the federal government ought to be involved in such matters as the protection of civil liberty, the

abolition of slavery, etc. It is a conflict in many respects still unresolved.

[35]B.H. Roberts, *A Comprehensive History of The Church of Jesus Christ of Latter-day Saints, Century I*, 6 vols. (Salt Lake City: Deseret News, 1930), 1:468-88.

[36]Ibid., 1:488-97.

[37]Smith, *History of the Church*, 3:304. This letter contributed Sections 121, 122, and 123 to the Doctrine and Covenants.

[38]Smith, *History of the Church*, 6:293. Elder Taylor said this in the course of his April 1844 conference address.

[39]*Times and Seasons*, October 1, 1843. See also Smith, *History of the Church*, 6:40.

[40]Smith, *History of the Church*, 6:99. See also ibid., 6:115-16.

[41]See ibid., 3:320-22.

[42]Ibid., 3:320-21.

[43]See Roberts, *Comprehensive History of the Church*, 2:1-28.

[44]Smith, *History of the Church*, 4:23-24.

[45]Ibid., 4:24.

[46]Ibid., 4:39-42, quotation on p. 42.

[47]Ibid., 4:78-80.

[48]Ibid., 4:80.

[49]Ibid., 6:197-209. See Richard D. Poll, "Joseph Smith and the Presidency, 1844," *Dialogue: A Journal of Mormon Thought* 3 (Autumn 1968): 17-21. See also pp. 28-36 of the same issue of *Dialogue*.

[50]Smith, *History of the Church*, 4:198-99.

[51]Ibid., 6:200.

[52]Ibid., 6:205.

[53]Ibid., 6:208.

[54]Roberts, *Comprehensive History of the Church*, 2:227-37.

[55]Smith, *History of the Church*, 6:498-99.

[56]Journal of Joseph Smith, as kept by Willard Richards, June 18, 1844, Ms., Church Archives, Historical Department of The Church of Jesus Christ of Latter-day Saints, Salt Lake City, Utah, hereinafter cited as Church Archives.

[57]Smith, *History of the Church*, 6:499.

[58]Ibid., 6:500.

[59]*Conference Report*, October 1912, p. 8. The speaker was Joseph F. Smith.

[60]George Albert Smith, "Perpetuating Liberty," *Improvement Era* 53 (February 1950): 93.

CHAPTER 2

[1]Susa Young Gates and Mabel Y. Sanborn, "Brigham Young Genealogy," *Utah Genealogical and Historical Magazine* 11 (1920): 21. William's service in an Indian war is actually a supposition derived from a county history stating that those New Hampshire townships were settled by such rewarded veterans.

[2]Gates and Sanborn, "Brigham Young Genealogy," p. 21.

[3]Mabel Young Sanborn, "The Ancestry of President Brigham Young," *Utah Genealogical and Historical Magazine* 20 (1929): 100.

[4]For an excellent and detailed account of this period of the French and Indian War, see Lawrence H. Gipson, *The Years of Defeat, 1754-1757*, vol. 6 of *The British Empire Before the American Revolution*, 13 vols. (New York: Alfred A. Knopf, 1939-1967).

[5]Gates and Sanborn, "Brigham Young Genealogy," p. 21. See also Susa Young Gates, "Notes on the Young and Howe Families," *Utah Genealogical and Historical*

Magazine 11 (October 1920): 180.

[6]Gates and Sanborn, "Brigham Young Genealogy," p. 22, quotes "Drake's history of [Middlesex] county, on page 492," as follows: "John Young, son of Joseph Young, and born in Hopkinton, March 7, 1763, enlisted at the age of thirteen years and served throughout the war."

[7]*Deseret News*, 7:47.

[8]A Hopkinton war record cited in Sanborn, "Ancestry of President Brigham Young," pp. 99-100, lists John Young as a seventeen-year-old recruit in the summer of 1780, called into duty at Hopkinton for a six-month enlistment in the Continental Army.

[9]Gates and Sanborn, "Brigham Young Genealogy," p. 22. There has arisen some controversy over John Young's war record, particularly whether he was at Saratoga as he claimed. See M. Hamlin Cannon, "A Pension Office Note on Brigham Young's Father," *American Historical Review* 49 (October 1944): 82-90; S. Dilworth Young, *Here Is Brigham: Brigham Young—the Years to 1844* (Salt Lake City: Bookcraft, 1964), pp. 14-16.

[10]For a quick survey of the action at Saratoga, see John Richard Alden, *The American Revolution, 1775-1783* (New York: Harper & Row, 1954), pp. 141-49.

[11]Gates, "Notes," p. 180; Gates and Sanborn, "Brigham Young Genealogy," p. 22.

[12]Gates, "Notes," pp. 180, 185; Susa Young Gates, "Mothers of the Latter-day Prophets: Abigail Howe Young," *Juvenile Instructor* 59 (January 1924): 3-6.

[13]Ibid., p. 180.

[14]Ibid., p. 181. The Church of Jesus Christ of Latter-day Saints became the official title of the restored church in April 1838, by revelation. Prior to that time it was known as the Church of Christ and the Church of the Latter-day Saints. (See D&C 115:3-4.)

[15]Smith, *Essentials in Church History*, p. 126.

[16]Gates, "Notes," p. 181.

[17]Ibid., pp. 181-82.

[18]Smith, *History of the Church*, 4:14-15.

[19]Brigham Young became de facto head of the Twelve prior to March 1839, with the apostasy and excommunication of Thomas B. Marsh, but he was not officially sustained as president of the body until April 4, 1840. Smith, *Essentials in Church History*, p. 570.

[20]Smith, *History of the Church*, 6:322, quoting a conference sermon of Brigham Young in Nauvoo on April 9, 1844. See also Susa Young Gates, "Brigham Young, American Patriot," *Juvenile Instructor* 61 (June 1926): 291-99.

[21]Sermon by Brigham Young, in *Journal of Discourses*, 26 vols. (London, 1854-86; reprint ed., Salt Lake City, 1967), 6:346-47.

[22]Ibid., p. 345.

[23]Sermon by Brigham Young, February 18, 1855, *Journal of Discourses*, 2:176. See also sermon by Brigham Young, July 4, 1854, *Journal of Discourses*, 7:14.

[24]Sermon by Brigham Young, July 4, 1854, *Journal of Discourses*, 7:13.

[25]Ibid., p. 15.

[26]Sermon by Brigham Young, February 18, 1855, *Journal of Discourses*, 2:170.

[27]Sermon by Brigham Young, July 4, 1854, *Journal of Discourses*, 7:14.

[28]Sermon by Brigham Young, February 18, 1855, *Journal of Discourses*, 2:185.

[29]Ibid., p. 345.

[30]For a compassionate treatment of the Utah War affair, see Leonard J. Arrington, *Great Basin Kingdom: An Economic History of the Latter-day Saints, 1830-1900* (Cambridge, Mass.: Harvard University Press, 1958), pp. 161-94.

[31]Sermon by Brigham Young, July 31, 1859, *Journal of Discourses*, 6:344.

[32]Sermon by Brigham Young, March 8, 1863, *Journal of Discourses*, 10:106.

[33]Ibid.

[34]See ibid., pp. 108, 111. For a careful examination of Mormons and the war, see Gustive O. Larson, "Utah and the Civil War," *Utah Historical Quarterly* 33 (Winter 1965): 55-77.

[35]Dean C. Jessee, ed., *Letters of Brigham Young to His Sons* (Salt Lake City: Deseret Book Company, 1974), pp. 161, 189; Leonard J. Arrington, "Willard Young: The Prophet's Son at West Point," *Dialogue: A Journal of Mormon Thought* 4 (Winter 1969): 37-46.

[36]Jessee, *Letters of Brigham Young to His Sons*, pp. 161-63.

[37]Obituary, "Richard Whitehead Young," *West Point Alumni Association Annual Report*, June 14, 1920, pp. 105-08; Smith, *Essentials in Church History*, p. 602.

[38]J. Cecil Alter, *Utah, Storied Domain*, 3 vols. (Chicago: American Historical Society, 1932), 2:201. She was named Susan or Susanne at birth, adopted "Amelia" at the time of her baptism, and became Susa when a clerk omitted the "n" during the reading of Brigham Young's will. Susa Young Gates, "The Editor Presumes to Talk About Herself," *Young Woman's Journal* 7 (January 1896): 203.

[39]Gates, "Editor Presumes," p. 203.

[40]Susa Young Gates Collection, Utah State Historical Society, Salt Lake City. For an interesting analysis of her literary career and works, see Paul Cracroft, "Susa Young Gates: Her Life and Literary Work" (M.A. thesis, University of Utah, 1951).

[41]Susa was particularly active in the suffrage movement and became friends over the course of years with such national leaders as Susan B. Anthony and Elizabeth Cady Stanton.

[42]Susa Young Gates, "What My Faith Means to Me," *Juvenile Instructor* 53 (June 1918): 292.

[43]Ibid., p. 291.

[44]Susa Young Gates, "Woman's Right of Suffrage," *Young Woman's Journal* 11 (March 1900): 135.

[45]Susa Young Gates, "International Council of Women," *Young Woman's Journal* 10 (October 1899): 440.

[46]Russell McFarland to Emma Lucy Gates Bowen, May 1933, quoted in Elsa Talmage Brandley, "Susa Young Gates," *Improvement Era* 36 (July 1933): 545.

[47]Gates, "International Council of Women," p. 450.

[48]*Journal History of the Church*, Ms., Church Archives, December 3, 1897, p. 2.

[49]George Q. Cannon Journal, Ms., Vault of the First Presidency of the Church, Salt Lake City, December 3, 1897.

[50]In the milieu of the Reed Smoot seating controversy in the United States Senate, national conventions of the Daughters of the American Revolution, another patriotic women's society, condemned the Mormon Church and disqualified from membership those who practiced polygamy or who were descendants of polygamists. One delegate dissented because she believed it possible that many members of the society were descended from Abraham. *Salt Lake Herald*, February 23, 1902; *Deseret News*, May 10, 1902, and April 19, 1904.

[51]Susa Young Gates, "With the Editor," *Young Woman's Journal* 10 (May 1899): 288.

CHAPTER 3

[1]William Smith, Jr., quoted in Robert McCluer Calhoon, *The Loyalists in Revolutionary America, 1760-1781* (New York: Harcourt Brace Jovanovich, 1973), p. 506.

[2]See Paul Smith, "The American Loyalists," *William and Mary Quarterly*, 25

(April 1968): 269. William H. Nelson, *The American Tory* (Oxford: Clarendon Press, 1961), p. 92, has suggested that one-third of the "politically active" population was Loyalist.

[3]Leonard W. Larabee, *Conservatism in Early American History* (New York: New York University Press, 1948), p. 166, explained them simply as follows: "They were Loyalists, in short, because they had both the weaknesses and the strength of all true conservatives."

[4]Historical views of the Loyalists include opinions such as that of Donald Barr Chidsey, *The Loyalists: The Story of Those Americans Who Fought Against Independence* (New York: Crown Publishers, 1973), who believes that the Tories "have enough to answer for when arrained before the bar of history" (p. 144), and the more sympathetic considerations pioneered by Lorenzo Sabine, *A Historical Essay on the Loyalists of the American Revolution* (Boston, 1847). Sabine expressed then revolutionary notions that the American struggle for independence was actually a civil war, that most Americans became Patriots only under the pressure of climactic events, and that neither Whigs nor Tories had a monopoly on good or evil. Claude H. Van Tyne, *The Loyalists in the American Revolution* (New York: P. Smith, 1929), further rehabilitated the "men of the lost cause of '76." See also Paul Hubert Smith, *Loyalists and Redcoats: A Study in British Revolutionary Policy* (Chapel Hill, N.C.: University of North Carolina Press, 1964).

[5]Wallace Brown, *The King's Friends: The Composition and Motives of the American Loyalist Claimants* (Providence, R.I.: Brown University Press, 1965), p. 78. "The outstanding fact about the Loyalist movement in New York," wrote Brown, "is not just its great numerical strength, but also its wealth of political, military, and literary talent. . . ." (p. 106.) See also Alexander C. Flick, *Loyalism in New York During the American Revolution* (New York: Columbia University Press, 1901).

[6]Brown, *King's Friends*, p. 282.

[7]Thomas Jones, *History of New York During the Revolutionary War*, ed. by Edward Floyd DeLancey, 2 vols. (New York, 1879), 1:101.

[8]See above, chapter 2.

[9]Calhoon, *Loyalists in Revolutionary America*, p. 502.

[10]Journal History, June 30, 1832.

[11]Daniel Wood Record Book D, pp. 1-2, Ms., Church Archives.

[12]Journal History, March 19, 1833.

[13]Wood Book D, pp. 2-3.

[14]Ibid.; *Deseret News*, 7:385.

[15]George Olin Zabriskie, "The Wood Family" (manuscript in private possession, Evelyn M. Nelson, Salt Lake City), pp. 34-35.

[16]Ibid., pp. 8, 10. Many Loyalists numbered themselves with the resistance to British policy but broke with the Patriots when it came to open rebellion and independence.

[17]Walter S. Herrington, *History of the County of Lennox and Addington* (Adessa, Ont., 1902), pictured the United Empire Loyalists "for many years after [1784] trudging through the State of New York by different routes to join their old comrades on this side of the lake." See also Arthur G. Bradley, *The United Empire Loyalists, Founders of British Canada* (London: T. Butterworth, 1932). In addition, Rebecca Moss, Daniel's oldest daughter, declared in her brief autobiography, "History of Rebecca Wood Moss," *Biographies and Reminiscences from the James Henry Moyle Collection*, ed. by Gene A. Sessions (Salt Lake City: James Moyle Genealogical and Historical Association, 1974), p. 61, that Henry Wood "and his family were called loyalists."

[18]William D. Reid, *The Loyalists in Ontario: The Sons and Daughters of the American Loyalists of Ontario* (Lambertville, N.J.: Unterdon House, 1973), p. 301.

[19]Undated memorandum, box 21, James Henry Moyle Collection, Ms., Church Archives. Moyle, Daniel Wood's grandson, expressed pride in the Sniders and Ameys who "gave up farms, homes and livestock, etc., in that loyalty and appreciation, so that to be a United Empirist in the choicest classes of Canada is quite as great an honor as to be the sons or daughters of the American Revolutionists. Each, like the Northerners and Southerners, are proud of their record for devotion to the right as they saw it."

[20]Wood Book D, p. 2.

[21]Journal History, July 13, 1833.

[22]Wood Book D, pp. 2-3.

[23]Ibid., pp. 3-4; undated memorandum, box 21, Moyle Collection. Several of Daniel's brothers joined the Church, but only he lasted through the persecutions to pioneer in the Great Basin. The rest apostatized and either remained in or returned to the vicinity of Loughborough, where their descendants live today.

[24]Wood Book D, p. 4.

[25]Ibid., pp. 7-8. See Smith, *Essentials in Church History,* pp. 181-93, for a summary of these "difficulties in Missouri."

[26]Smith, *Essentials in Church History,* pp. 187-88.

[27]Wood Book D, pp. 8-10.

[28]Smith, *Essentials in Church History,* pp. 200-1.

[29]Wood Book D, pp. 10-13.

[30]Ibid., pp. 13-14. See also a later exchange of letters between Daniel and Abraham recorded in Book A in which Abraham questioned his brother in Utah concerning polygamy and a rumor that Brigham Young had had "72 children born all in one night." Daniel's predicative response (dated June 6, 1857) chided Abraham for thinking that Mormons "are a bad people because we have so many women." After defending the principle, Daniel added: "This information I freely give and want you to take heed to it . . . for the more you know the more you will have to answer to. . . ."

[31]Wood Book D, p. 15.

[32]James H. Moyle to Joseph C. Wood, June 17, 1937, box 21, Moyle Collection.

[33]Wood Book D, pp. 16-20.

[34]Ibid., pp. 22-24.

[35]Ibid., pp. 24.

[36]Ibid., p. 25.

[37]Ibid., pp. 26-27, 30.

[38]Ibid., pp. 28-30. The carriage was evidently very fancy and became known as "the Queen of the Valley" after its arrival in Utah. Moyle to Wood, June 17, 1937, box 21, Moyle Collection.

[39]Wood Book D, pp. 29-30.

[40]Ibid., pp. 37-55.

[41]Ibid., pp. 56-58. See also William G. Hartley, "Mormons, Crickets, and Gulls: A New Look at an Old Story," *Utah Historical Quarterly* 38 (Summer 1970): 224-39.

[42]A family tradition played humorously upon the name Woods Cross and upon Daniel's quick tongue. According to the story, he was visiting in Canada when the tracks of the Utah Central Railroad were laid across his land without his permission. When he returned home and the conductor called, "Woods Cross," Daniel shouted back, "Yes, damn cross!" Moyle to Wood, June 17, 1937, box 21, Moyle Collection.

[43]Family records indicate a total of eight wives.

[44]See Wood Book D, pp. 58ff. See also James H. Moyle, *Mormon Democrat: The Religious and Political Memoirs of James Henry Moyle,* ed. by Gene A. Sessions (Salt Lake City: James Moyle Genealogical and Historical Association, 1975), pp. 83, 89-91, for the grandson's recollections of visiting at Wood family meetings.

[45]See Moyle, *Mormon Democrat,* pp. vii-x.

[46]"Address Delivered by James H. Moyle, Commissioner of Customs, at the Laying of the Cornerstone of the United States Court House-Custom House at St. Louis, Missouri, April 28, 1934," box 6, Moyle Collection.

[47]*Conference Report*, April 1949, p. 62.

[48]*Conference Report*, October 1950, pp. 96-97.

[49]The monument was the official work of family association president George C. Wood and his predecessor, Albert Mabey. See *Church News*, April 7, 1962, p. 3.

[50]Another Wood descendant, James D. Moyle, was serving as president of the Utah chapter of the Sons of the American Revolution when the society held its national congress in Salt Lake City in 1957.

CHAPTER 4

[1]See Alden, *American Revolution*, pp. 11-24, for an excellent historical understanding of the events that led up to "the shot heard 'round the world."

[2]Sir John W. Fortescue, ed., *The Correspondence of King George the Third from 1760 to December, 1783*, 6 vols. (London: Macmillan and Co., Limited, 1927-1928, 3:153, quoted in Alden, *American Revolution*, p. 16.

[3]For a detailed examination of these events, see Allen French, *Day of Concord and Lexington* (Boston: Little, Brown, and Company, 1925).

[4]See J. R. Alden, "Why the March to Concord?" *American Historical Review*, 49 (1944): 446-54; Alden, *General Gage in America* (Baton Rouge: Louisiana State University Press, 1948), pp. 238-44.

[5]Controversy still exists among historians as to the exact events at Lexington. For a good analysis of the varying views, see Allen French, *General Gage's Informers* (Ann Arbor: University of Michigan Press, 1932), pp. 47-60.

[6]Alden, *American Revolution*, p. 23.

[7]Ibid., pp. 23-24.

[8]John Henry Evans and Minnie Egan Anderson, *Ezra T. Benson, Pioneer, Statesman, Saint* (Salt Lake City: Deseret News Press, 1947), pp. 29-30.

[9]Ibid., p. 30.

[10]Ibid., pp. 37-40. The Evans-Anderson biography of Ezra T. Benson relied heavily upon the apostle's autobiography, "A Brief History of Ezra T. Benson, by Himself," for the details of his life prior to 1847. That document itself has appeared at least twice in print, serialized first in early issues of the *Deseret News*, then in the *Instructor* 80 (February-May 1945): 53-56, 101-103, 111, 162-64, 179, 213-17, 227. An examination of a copy of the handwritten original, Ms., Church Archives, reveals that as it was published, the "History" underwent editing for spelling, punctuation, and grammar. References to the "History" in the present essay, then, cite it as it appears in the Evans-Anderson work because of the latter's ready accessibility.

[11]Evans and Anderson, *Ezra T. Benson*, pp. 7-10.

[12]Ibid., p. 10.

[13]Only Elder Hyde eventually undertook the mission, dedicating Palestine for the return of the Jews on October 24, 1841. See Smith, *History of the Church*, 4:xxxi-xxxiii, 112-13, 128-29, 274.

[14]Evans and Anderson, *Ezra T. Benson*, p. 11.

[15]Ibid., pp. 10-12.

[16]Ibid., pp. 50-57.

[17]Ibid., p. 57.

[18]Ibid., pp. 58-60, 64.

[19]Ibid., pp. 66-91. See also Smith, *History of the Church*, 7:236fn.

[20]Evans and Anderson, *Ezra T. Benson*, pp. 96-98; Smith, *History of the Church*, 7:296, 555.

[21]Evans and Anderson, *Ezra T. Benson*, p. 104.

[22]Ibid., pp. 115-16.

[23]Ibid., p. 125.

[24]Ibid. See also Smith, *Essentials in Church History*, p. 338.

[25]Evans and Anderson, *Ezra T. Benson*, pp. 145ff.

[26]See Journal of Ezra T. Benson, 1857, Ms., Church Archives. Evidently, Evans and Anderson did not include this missionary diary among their sources.

[27]Evans and Anderson, *Ezra T. Benson*, p. 226, quoting Cyrus H. Wheelock.

[28]Ibid., p. 231.

[29]Ibid., pp. 238-320, passim.

[30]Ibid., pp. 340-41.

[31]Ezra Taft Benson, *Cross Fire: The Eight Years with Eisenhower* (New York: Doubleday, 1962), p. 15.

[32]Evans and Anderson, *Ezra T. Benson*, p. 342.

[33]Benson, *Cross Fire*, p. 16.

[34]Ibid., p. 261.

[35]Evans and Anderson, *Ezra T. Benson*, pp. 342-43.

[36]Benson, *Cross Fire*, p. 143.

[37]Ibid., p. 266.

[38]Ibid. See also Smith, *Essentials in Church History*, p. 535. For the full story of the 1947 mission, see Frederick W. Babbel, *On Wings of Faith* (Salt Lake City: Bookcraft, 1972).

[39]Benson, *Cross Fire*, p. 569.

[40]Ibid., p. 12.

[41]Ibid., p. 55. For an extensive analysis of Benson's administration of the Department of Agriculture, see Edward L. Schapsmeier and Frederick H. Schapsmeier, *Ezra Taft Benson and the Politics of Agriculture, the Eisenhower Years, 1953-1961* (Danville, Illinois: Interstate Printers and Publishers, 1975), which is an expansion of the authors' paper, "Eisenhower and Ezra Taft Benson: Farm Policy in the 1950's," originally delivered at a meeting of the American Historical Association, December 30, 1969, in Washington, D.C., and subsequently published in *Agricultural History* 44 (October 1970): 369-78.

[42]"General Statement on Agricultural Policy by Ezra Taft Benson," February 5, 1953, Papers of Ezra Taft Benson, Eisenhower Library, Abilene, Kansas, cited in Schapsmeier and Schapsmeier, "Eisenhower and Ezra Taft Benson," p. 370.

[43]Benson, *Cross Fire*, p. 68. The Secretary uttered this statement at St. Paul, Minnesota, February 11, 1953.

[44]Ibid., p. 70.

[45]Ibid., p. 79.

[46]Ibid., p. 577.

[47]Ibid., p. 115.

[48]Ibid., p. 199.

[49]Ibid., p. 128.

[50]Ibid., p. 413.

CHAPTER 5

[1]S. K. Hall, Ancestor's Service, submitted to the National Society of the Sons of the American Revolution and copied from the Old War Records of the United States Pension Office, Washington, D.C.

[2]Ibid.

[3]Ibid.; Alden, *American Revolution*, p. 208; Carl Van Doren, *Mutiny in January* (New York: Viking Press, 1943), pp. 18-19.

[4]Hall, Ancestor's Service; Richard B. Morris, ed., *Encyclopedia of American History* (New York: Harper & Row, 1953), pp. 106-11.

[5]Junius F. Wells, "The Wells Family Genealogy," *Utah Genealogical and Historical Magazine* 6 (January 1915): 3-4. See also Jenson, *Biographical Encyclopedia,* 1:63.

[6]Heber J. Grant to George Sutherland, June 5, 1941, Heber J. Grant Collection, Church Archives.

[7]For this period of Daniel's life see Wells, "Family Genealogy," p. 4; "Narrative of Daniel H. Wells," pp. 1-2, Utah Manuscripts, Bancroft Library, Berkeley, California; also printed in *Utah Historical Quarterly* 6 (July 1933): 124-32.

[8]Wells, "Family Genealogy," pp. 4-5; Jenson, *Biographical Encyclopedia,* 1:62-63; Smith, *History of the Church,* 3:173-77, 341-55, 4:239-49.

[9]Wells, "Family Genealogy," p. 5; Roberts, *Comprehensive History of the Church,* vol. 2 passim; "Narrative," pp. 2-5.

[10]Smith, *Essentials in Church History,* 344-46; Roberts, *Comprehensive History of the Church,* 3:14-15; "Narrative," p. 5.

[11]Jenson, *Biographical Encyclopedia,* 1:63; "Narrative," pp. 5-8.

[12]Ibid.

[13]Sermon of Daniel H. Wells, October 26, 1862, *Journal of Discourses,* 10:8. For the period of Daniel's life covered in this paragraph, see Jenson, *Biographical Encyclopedia,* 1:63-64; Wells, "Family Genealogy," p. 5; "Narrative," pp. 8-32.

[14]Sermon of Daniel H. Wells, October 26, 1862, *Journal of Discourses,* 10:8.

[15]Ibid.

[16]See Jenson, *Biographical Encyclopedia,* 1:64-66.

[17]Ibid., 1:65.

[18]Ibid.

[19]See "Birthday Celebration of Our Honored President," *Relief Society Magazine* 4 (April 1917): 200-201, in which Emmeline related her memory of her fourth birthday and her grandfather telling her at the party of his Revolutionary War experiences.

[20]See Thomas C. Romney, *The Gospel in Action* (Salt Lake City: Deseret Sunday School Union Board, 1949), p. 250; Jenson, *Biographical Encyclopedia,* 2:731. Inasmuch as it finally decided the issue of American autonomy, the War of 1812 has often been called "the Second War for Independence."

[21]Romney, *Gospel in Action,* p. 251; Jenson, *Biographical Encyclopedia,* 2:731.

[22]Quoted in Romney, *Gospel in Action,* p. 252.

[23]Jenson, *Biographical Encyclopedia,* 2:731.

[24]Romney, *Gospel in Action,* pp. 252-53.

[25]Ibid., pp. 253-55; Jenson, *Biographical Encyclopedia,* 2:731-34.

[26]Ibid. An interesting and recent assessment of Emmeline B. Wells is Phyllis Southwick, "Emmeline B. Wells," paper delivered October 17, 1974, Salt Lake City. Tape on file at the Women's Resource Center, University of Utah.

[27]Heber M. Wells became a member of the Utah Society of the Sons of the American Revolution on the basis of David Chapin's service in the war. On the governor's life, see Orson F. Whitney, *History of Utah,* 4 vols. (Salt Lake City: George Q. Cannon & Sons Co., 1904), 4:619-20; Noble Warrum, *Utah Since Statehood, Historical and Biographical,* 4 vols. (Chicago: S.J. Clarke Publishing Co., 1919), 2:682-83; Edward Leo Lyman, "Heber M. Wells and the Beginnings of Utah's Statehood" (M.S. thesis, University of Utah, 1967).

[28]Obituary, "Briant Harris Wells," *Assembly Magazine,* January 1951, p. 51, quoting General R. P. Hughes. See also Junius F. Wells, "Utah's Brigadier Generals," *Improvement Era* 21 (October 1918): 1076-80.

[29]Obituary, "Wells," pp. 50-51.

³⁰Ibid., pp. 51-52. See also *Deseret News,* February 13, 1926, June 12, 1949; *Salt Lake Tribune,* October 2, 1924, October 1, 1934; *Salt Lake Telegram,* March 15, 1928; *New York Post,* February 22, 1930.

³¹Obituary, "Wells," p. 52.

CHAPTER 6

¹Alden, *The American Revolution,* p. 38. See additionally ibid., pp. 33-41; Charles Francis Adams, "The Battle of Bunker Hill," *American Historical Review* 1 (April 1896): 401-13.

²Alden, *The American Revolution,* p. 39.

³Josephine B. Walker, *The Bunker Family History* (Delta, Utah: Edward Bunker Family Association, 1957), pp. 2-6.

⁴Autobiography of Edward Bunker, 1894, Ms., Church Archives. See also typed, corrected version of Bunker's reminiscence in Walker, *Bunker Family History,* pp. 7-14. Ms. version is cited hereafter.

⁵Autobiography of Edward Bunker.

⁶Literature dealing with the Mormon Battalion is extensive. Perhaps the best chronicle of the march is in Charles S. Peterson, John F. Yurtinus, David E. Atkinson, and A. Kent Powell, *Mormon Battalion Trail Guide* (Salt Lake City: Utah State Historical Society, 1972). Of the items listed in the *Guide's* thorough bibliography (pp. 69-73), Daniel Tyler's history of the Battalion taken from his own diaries and recollections, *A Concise History of the Mormon Battalion in the Mexican War 1846-1847* (Salt Lake City, 1882), is the best and most readily available source for the details of life during the march. Several primary accounts, or extracts from such, have also appeared in print, including Philip St. George Cooke, "Cooke's Journal of the March of the Mormon Battalion," *Exploring Southwestern Trails,* 1846-1854, ed. by Ralph P. Bieber and Averam B. Bender (Glendale, California: Arthur H. Clark, 1938), and numerous journals published in the *Utah Historical Quarterly* and elsewhere. See Peterson, *Guide,* pp. 69-71. Other diaries of Battalion members are extant at the Church Archives and at the Utah Historical Society. See in addition Andrew Jenson, Manuscript History of the Mormon Battalion, Ms., Church Archives; B.H. Roberts, *The Mormon Battalion: Its History and Achievements* (Salt Lake City: Deseret News, 1919); Hamilton Gardner, "The Command and Staff of the Mormon Battalion in the Mexican War," *Utah Historical Quarterly* 20 (October 1952): 331-51; Philip St. George Cooke, *The Conquest of New Mexico and California* (New York: G.P. Putnam's Sons, 1878); Otis E. Young, *The West of Philip St. George Cooke* (Glendale, California: Arthur H. Clark, 1955). For an excellent concise history of the war itself, see Otis A. Singletary, *The Mexican War* (Chicago: University of Chicago Press, 1960).

⁷Peterson, et al., *Guide,* pp. 3-10; Tyler, *Mormon Battalion,* pp. 118-25, 132-47.

⁸Francis Parkman, *Journals,* ed. by Mason Wade (New York: Harper, 1947), p. 479. See also Peterson, et al., *Guide,* pp. 13-14.

⁹See Tyler, *Mormon Battalion,* pp. 157-58.

¹⁰Frank Alfred Golder, Thomas A. Bailey, and J. Lyman Smith, *The March of the Mormon Battalion from Council Bluffs to California Taken from the Journal of Henry Standage* (New York: Century, 1928), p. 166.

¹¹Ibid.

¹²Tyler, *Mormon Battalion,* pp. 148-49.

¹³Peterson, et al., *Guide,* p. 22.

¹⁴Ibid.

¹⁵Ibid., p. 23.

¹⁶Ibid., p. 31.

[17]Tyler, *Mormon Battalion*, pp. 206-7.

[18]Peterson, et al., *Guide*, pp. 42-50.

[19]Cooke, "Journal," p. 143.

[20]Peterson, et al., *Guide*, pp. 42-50.

[21]William Hyde Journal, December 25, 1846, in Peterson, et al., *Guide* p. 50.

[22]Tyler, *Mormon Battalion*, p. 247. See also Peterson, et al., *Guide*, pp. 50-57.

[23]Peterson, et al., *Guide*, pp. 57-59.

[24]Tyler, *Mormon Battalion*, p. 252.

[25]Autobiography of Edward Bunker.

[26]Ibid.; Peterson, et al., *Guide*, pp. 62-63; Jenson, History of the Mormon Battalion, July 18, 1847.

[27]Quoted in Cooke, "Journal," pp. 238-40.

[28]Autobiography of Edward Bunker.

[29]Ibid.

[30]Ibid.; Rose C. Peterson, "The Edward Bunker Company," *Heart Throbs of the West*, ed. by Kate B. Carter, 12 vols. (Salt Lake City: Daughters of Utah Pioneers, 1951-63), 6:354-56. See also LeRoy R. Hafen, "Handcarts to Utah, 1856-1860," *Utah Historical Quarterly*, 24 (Fall 1956): 309-17.

[31]Autobiography of Edward Bunker.

[32]Ibid. For an excellent synopsis of the Utah War and the move south, see Arrington, *Great Basin Kingdom*, pp. 161-94.

[33]Autobiography of Edward Bunker.

[34]Ibid. See also Andrew Karl Larson, *I Was Called to Dixie—The Virgin River Basin: Unique Experiences in Mormon Pioneering* (Salt Lake City: Deseret News Press, 1962), pp. 38-184.

[35]Autobiography of Edward Bunker.

[36]Ibid.

[37]Ibid. See also Juanita Leavitt Brooks, "The History of Bunkerville," Ms., Church Archives.

[38]Walker, *History of the Bunker Family*, p. 14.

CHAPTER 7

[1]See Alden, *American Revolution*, pp. 40-41. For analyses of Howe's role and thinking during the period of his service in America, see Troyer A. Anderson, *The Command of the Howe Brothers During the American Revolution* (New York: Oxford University Press, 1936).

[2]Joseph Hewes, cited in Edmund D. Burnett, ed., *Letters of Members of the Continental Congress*, 8 vols. (Washington, D.C.: Carnegie Institution, 1921-1936), 1:401.

[3]Alden, *American Revolution*, pp. 73-89.

[4]Ibid., p. 90. A trustworthy treatment of Washington's part in the war is James T. Flexner, *George Washington in the American Revolution, 1775-1783* (Boston: Little, Brown, 1968).

[5]For a brief but complete account of the battle, see Willard M. Wallace, *Appeal to Arms: A Military History of the American Revolution* (New York: Harper, 1951), pp. 91-96. Also Charles F. Adams, "The Battle of Long Island," *American Historical Review* 1 (July 1896): 650-70.

[6]Ibid. Also Leonard Lundin, *Cockpit of the Revolution: The War for Independence in New Jersey* (Princeton, New Jersey: Princeton University Press, 1940), pp. 157-217.

[7]Milton Bird, *The Life of Reverend Alexander Chapman* (Nashville, Tenn.,

1872), p. 21, quoted in John Brown, *Autobiography of Pioneer John Brown, 1820-1896,* ed. by John Z. Brown (Salt Lake City: Stevens & Wallis, Inc., 1941), p. 23.

[8]Brown, *Autobiography,* p. 22.
[9]Ibid., p. 25.
[10]Ibid., p. 26.
[11]Ibid., pp. 30-32; quotation on p. 32.
[12]Ibid., p. 32.
[13]Ibid., pp. 32-35.

[14]Ibid., pp. 56-67. John's cousin Betsy and her husband, Robert Crow, had been living in Perry County, Illinois, in the vicinity of John Brown and his mother prior to their conversion to Mormonism.

[15]Ibid., pp. 66-68.
[16]Ibid., p. 70.
[17]Francis Parkman, *The Oregon Trail,* ed. by E. N. Feltskog (Madison: University of Wisconsin Press, 1969), p. 332.
[18]George Frederic Ruxton, *Life in the Far West* (New York, 1849), p. 214.
[19]Ibid.
[20]Ibid.
[21]Brown, *Autobiography,* pp. 70-71.
[22]Ruxton, *Life in the Far West,* p. 214.
[23]Ibid.
[24]LeRoy R. Hafen and Frank M. Young, "The Mormon Settlement at Pueblo, Colorado, During the Mexican War," *Colorado Magazine* 9 (July 1932): 121-36.
[25]Brown, *Autobiography,* pp. 72-73.
[26]Ibid., pp. 73-75.
[27]Ibid., p. 78.
[28]Ibid., pp. 83-102.
[29]"Minutes of the Council of the Twelve, 1849-1871," Ms., Church Archives, p. 15, under February 14, 1849.
[30]Roberta Flake Clayton, ed., *Pioneer Men of Arizona* (Mesa, Ariz., 1975), passim.
[31]Brown, *Autobiography,* pp. 103-19.
[32]Ibid., pp. 120-412 passim.
[33]Ibid., pp. 15-20.
[34]Ibid., p. 20.
[35]Ibid.

[36]Amy Brown Lyman, *In Retrospect* (Salt Lake City: General Board of Relief Society, 1945), pp. 9-26. On Amy Lyman, see also Thomas C. Romney, "Representative Women of the Church: Amy Brown Lyman," *Instructor* 85 (January 1950): 4-5; Alice Reynolds, "Mrs. Amy Brown Lyman," *Relief Society Magazine* 8 (July 1921): 383-85; Mary Connelly Kimball, "Counselor Amy Brown Lyman," *Relief Society Magazine* 16 (January 1929): 9-12; Belle P. Spafford, "Amy Brown Lyman, General President of Relief Society, January 1940-April 1945," *Relief Society Magazine* 32 (May 1945): 269-71; Rose B. Hayes, "Amy Brown Lyman, Life Sketch," in Brown, *Autobiography,* pp. 423-29.

[37]Lyman, *In Retrospect,* pp. 27-142 passim.
[38]Ibid.
[39]Alice L. Reynolds, quoted in Bryant S. Hinckley, "Greatness in Men: Richard R. Lyman," *Improvement Era* 35 (September 1932): 652.
[40]John Brown, "Progression Versus Fogyism," *Millennial Star* 24 (April 1862): 227.

CHAPTER 8

[1]On the effects of the Washington legend, see Curtis P. Nettels, "The Washington Theme in American History," *Proceedings of the Massachusetts Historical Society* 68 (1952): 171-98; Stuart L. Bernath, "George Washington and the Genesis of American Military Discipline," *Mid-America* 49 (April 1967): 83-100. On the 1776-77 campaign in New Jersey, see Lundin, *Cockpit of the Revolution*, p. 157-217. Curtis P. Nettels, *George Washington and American Independence* (Boston: Little, Brown, 1951), emphasizes the strength of the Virginian's image and its important effects upon the sustenance of American will throughout the conflict.

[2]Paine's now famous statement appeared in the first issue of *The Crisis*, a widely circulated Patriot propaganda sheet.

[3]See Alden, *American Revolution*, pp. 107-8.

[4]The story of John Goldy and his sons was a part of the family tradition of which J. Golden Kimball partook a century later while visiting his mother's ancestral home in Mercer County. A check of such sources as E. M. Woodward and John F. Hageman, *History of Burlington and Mercer Counties* (Philadelphia, 1883), however, provides no substantiation for the Goldy legend. See particularly pp. 816-23. But a legend need not be true to be effective in its impact upon the lives of its believers. See Kimball's recounting of the Goldy story in Claude Richards, *J. Golden Kimball: The Story, Sayings, and Sermons of a Unique Personality* (Salt Lake City: Deseret News Press, 1934), p. 16.

[5]Alden, *American Revolution*, pp. 108-11.

[6]Nicholas Cresswell, *The Journal of Nicholas Cresswell, 1774-1777* (New York: Dial Press, 1924), p. 178.

[7]Richards, *J. Golden Kimball*, p. 16.

[8]Ibid.

[9]See William D. Miller, "Myth and New South City Murder Rates," *Mississippi Quarterly* 26 (Spring 1973): 152-53, for ideas on the motivating force of myth and legend.

[10]Kate B. Carter, ed., *Heber C. Kimball, His Wives and Family* (Salt Lake City: Utah Printing, 1967), p. 18.

[11]Existing records do not make clear the connection between Christeen Golden and John Goldy. It is possible that he was the grandfather of Jonathan Golden, her father, and that the surname, as often occurred, changed slightly in form. Mercer County, New Jersey, records extant in various forms in the Genealogical Society Library, Salt Lake City, reveal numerous Goldys and Goldens living in the area during the Revolutionary War years.

[12]Richards, *J. Golden Kimball*, p. 16.

[13]James Linforth, ed., *Route from Liverpool to Great Salt Lake Valley* (Liverpool, 1855), p. 304.

[14]Thomas L. Kane, *The Mormons* (Philadelphia, 1850), p. 87.

[15]Sermon by Heber C. Kimball, August 2, 1857, *Journal of Discourses*, 5:133.

[16]Orson F. Whitney, *Life of Heber C. Kimball, An Apostle* (Salt Lake City: Kimball Family, 1888), p. 19. See also Leonard Allison and Stephen Paschall Sharples, *History of the Kimball Family in America, from 1634-1897, and of Its Ancestors the Kemballs or Kembolds of England*, 2 vols. (Boston, 1897).

[17]Whitney, *Heber C. Kimball*, pp. 18-37.

[18]Ibid., p. 44.

[19]Ibid., pp. 42-46.

[20]Ibid., pp. 47-79. See also Smith, *History of the Church* 2:61-166; D&C 105.

[21]Smith, *Essentials in Church History*, pp. 150-52.

[22]For his own account of this period, see *President Heber C. Kimball's Journal:*

An Account of His Mission to England and the Introduction of the Gospel to that Land (Salt Lake City: Juvenile Instructor Office, 1882), which covers both missions.

[23]Smith, *History of the Church*, 4:9-10n.

[24]Carter, ed., *Kimball, His Wives and Family*, p. 18.

[25]Whitney, *Heber C. Kimball*, p. 429. Another of Heber's wives, Presendia Huntington Kimball, was the niece of Samuel Huntington, a signer of the Declaration of Independence. Both she and her sister Zina were married to Joseph Smith. After his death, she married Heber C. Kimball and Zina married Brigham Young.

[26]See Whitney, *Heber C. Kimball*, pp. 353-99.

[27]Richards, *J. Golden Kimball*, pp. 15-19.

[28]See Whitney, *Heber C. Kimball*, pp. 400-12; *Conference Report*, October 1930, p. 59. Said Golden at that conference: "I claim not to be a prophet, but I am the son of a prophet." For an analysis of Golden's spiritual and intellectual descendance from Heber C. Kimball, see Thomas E. Cheney, *The Golden Legacy: A Folk History of J. Golden Kimball* (Santa Barbara, Cal.: Peregrine Smith, 1974), p. 8-16.

[29]Sermon by Heber C. Kimball, August 23, 1857, *Journal of Discourses*, 5:172.

[30]Sermon by Heber C. Kimball, August 30, 1857, *Journal of Discourses*, 5:159-60.

[31]Richards, *J. Golden Kimball*, p. 19.

[32]Carter, ed., *Kimball, His Wives and Family*, p. 19.

[33]Ibid.

[34]Richards, *J. Golden Kimball*, p. 21.

[35]Ibid., pp. 20-22.

[36]Ibid., pp. 22-28, quotation on p. 28.

[37]Ibid., p. 29-34.

[38]*Conference Report*, April 1921, p. 179.

[39]Ibid., pp. 179-80; Richards, *J. Golden Kimball*, pp. 38-39, 43.

[40]Richards, *J. Golden Kimball*, pp. 40-48, quotation on p. 40.

[41]Carter, ed., *Kimball, His Wives and Family*, p. 19.

[42]Austin Fife and Alta Fife, *Saints of Sage & Saddle* (Bloomington, Ind.: Indiana University Press, 1956), p. 304.

[43]Wallace Stegner, *Mormon Country* (New York: Duell, Sloan & Pearce, 1942), p. 190.

[44]Cheney, *Golden Legacy*, p. 3.

[45]Ibid., p. 143.

[46]Stegner, *Mormon Country*, pp. 193-94.

[47]Cheney, *Golden Legacy*, p. 85.

[48]There have, of course, been many LDS chaplains in the U.S. military since Elias Kimball broke the ground. Prior to World War II thirteen Mormons had served as chaplains in the army and one in the navy. Three of these, including B. H. Roberts of the First Council of the Seventy, served during World War I. After Pearl Harbor, the military placed strict requirements upon the chaplain corps, which made it difficult for Mormons to receive appointments, but in recent years the number of LDS chaplains has grown steadily.

[49]Jenson, *Biographical Encyclopedia*, 2:55-56.

[50]Richards, *J. Golden Kimball*, pp. 297-98.

[51]Augusta Joyce Crocheron, *Representative Women of Deseret, A Book of Biographical Sketches* (Salt Lake City: J.C. Graham & Co., 1884), p. 110. Prior to her marriage to Horace K. Whitney, she was sealed to Joseph Smith. Whitney, *Heber C. Kimball*, p. 339. For examples of her defense of polygamy, see Helen Mar Whitney, *Plural Marriage, as Taught by the Prophet Joseph* (Salt Lake City: Juvenile Instructor Office, 1882), and *Why We Practice Polygamy* (Salt Lake City: Juvenile Instructor Office, 1884).

[52]Crocheron, *Representative Women*, p. 109.

[53]Ibid., p. 114-17; Orson F. Whitney, *Through Memory's Halls: The Life Story of Orson F. Whitney As Told by Himself* (Independence, Mo.: Zion's Printing and Publishing Co., 1930).

[54]Solomon F. Kimball, *Life of David P. Kimball and Other Sketches* (Salt Lake City: Deseret News, 1918), pp. 1-70.

[55]Cheney, *Golden Legacy*, p. 66.

[56]Spencer W. Kimball, *Faith Precedes the Miracle* (Salt Lake City: Deseret Book Company, 1972), pp. xii-xiii; Smith, *Essentials in Church History*, p. 579.

[57]Kimball, *Faith Precedes the Miracle*, pp. xi-xii.

[58]Ibid., p. xii.

[59]*Conference Report*, April 1970, p. 120.

[60]*Webster's Third New International Dictionary of the English Language Unabridged* (Springfield, Mass.: G. & C. Merriam Co., 1971), p. 1291.

CHAPTER 9

[1]Worthington C. Ford, et al., eds., *The Journals of the Continental Congress, 1774-1789*, 34 vols. (Washington, D.C.: Carnegie Institution, 1904-1937), 27:554.

[2]See John Richard Alden's excellent summary of "Savannah to Yorktown" in Alden, *American Revolution*, pp. 227-47.

[3]Christopher L. Ward, *The Delaware Continentals 1776-1783* (Wilmington, Del.: Historical of Delaware, 1941), pp. 332-55, 531-35. See also George W. Kyte, "The British Invasion of South Carolina in 1780," *Historian* 14 (Spring 1952): 149-72.

[4]George W. Kyte, "Victory in the South: An Appraisal of General Greene's Strategy in the Carolinas," *North Carolina Historical Review* 37 (July 1960): 321-47; Kyte, "Strategic Blunder: Lord Cornwallis Abandons the Carolinas, 1781," *Historian* 22 (February 1960): 129-44. See also Robert C. Pugh, "The Revolutionary Militia in the Southern Campaign, 1780-1781," *William and Mary Quarterly* 3rd ser. 14 (April 1957): 154-75; Hugh F. Rankin, "Cowpens: Prelude to Yorktown," *North Carolina Historical Review* 31 (July 1954): 336-69.

[5]George W. Kyte, "General Greene's Plans for the Capture of Charleston," *South Carolina Historical Magazine* 62 (April 1961): 96-106; Alexander R. Stoesen, "The British Occupation of Charleston, 1780-1782," *South Carolina Historical Magazine* 63 (April 1962): 71-82.

[6]Alden, *American Revolution*, pp. 238-39.

[7]Revolutionary War Pension Records, Kentucky 4236, Isaac Garven, microfilm, file 971053, Genealogical Society of The Church of Jesus Christ of Latter-day Saints, Salt Lake City, Utah.

[8]Randolph G. Adams, "A View of Cornwallis's Surrender at Yorktown," *American Historical Review* 37 (October 1931): 25-49; John F. Shafroth, "The Strategy of the Yorktown Campaign, 1781," *Proceedings of the United States Naval Institute* 57 (June 1931): 721-36; Edward M. Riley, "Yorktown During the Revolution," *Virginia Magazine of History and Biography* 57 (January-July 1949): 22-43, 176-88, 274-85; Thomas J. Fleming, *Beat the Last Drum: The Siege of Yorktown, 1781* (New York: St. Martin's Press, 1963). See also William B. Willcox, "The British Road to Yorktown: A Study in Divided Command," *American Historical Review* 52 (October 1946): 1-35; Louis R. Gottschalk, *Lafayette and the Close of the American Revolution* (Chicago: University of Chicago Press, 1942). On the southern campaign as a whole, see M. F. Treacy, *Prelude to Yorktown: The Southern Campaign of Nathanael Greene, 1780-1781* (Chapel Hill: University of North Carolina Press, 1963).

[9]Merrill Jensen, "The Creation of the National Domain, 1781-1784," *Mississippi Valley Historical Review* 26 (December 1939): 323-42; Clarence M. Burton, "The

Boundary Lines of the United States Under the Treaty of 1782," *Magazine of History* 9 (April 1909): 203-12; Paul C. Phillips, *The West in the Diplomacy of the American Revolution* (New York: Russell & Russell, 1913).

[10]Isaac Garven Pension Record.

[11]Revolutionary War Pension Records, Kentucky 3952, Jane Huston Garven, microfilm, file 971053, Genealogical Society.

[12]William Brooks Garven, Family Group Sheet, Genealogical Society.

[13]Seward, who later became Secretary of State in the Lincoln administration, made his famous "Irrepressible Conflict" speech on the floor of the Senate during a heated debate with Senator Jefferson Davis of Mississippi, who served during the Civil War as president of the Confederacy.

[14]U.S. Adjutant General's Office, *Index to the Compiled Service Records of Confederate Soldiers Who Served in Organizations from the State of Missouri (1861-1865)* (Washington, D.C., 1962); U.S. Adjutant General's Office, *Index to the Compiled Service Records of Volunteer Union Soldiers Who Served in Organizations from the State of Missouri (1861-1865)* (Washington, D.C., 1962).

[15]Alexander H. Waller, *History of Randolph County, Missouri* (Topeka, Kansas, 1920), pp. 133-34.

[16]Beard's thesis, as expounded in Charles and Mary Beard, *The Rise of American Civilization*, 2 vols. (New York: Macmillan, 1930), was that the Civil War was "a social revolution" in which "the capitalists, laborers, and farmers of the North and West drove from power in the national government the planting aristocracy of the South." See ibid., 2:54. Recent scholars have contested severely Beard's concept of the war, but his "Second Revolution" epithet is nevertheless stimulating and provocative.

[17]Waller, *History of Randolph County*, pp. 739-40; Hartman Rector, Family Group Sheet, Genealogical Society; interview with Constance Rector by the author, June 3, 1975, Salt Lake City, hereafter cited as Rector Interview. Joel L. Rector was a descendant of John Jacob Rector, an early German colonist among several brought into Virginia by Governor Alexander Spotswood in 1714 to establish the iron industry and to buttress the colony against French and Indian incursions. See Charles Hubert Huffman, ed., "John Jacob Rector, Early Germana Colonist," *Memorial Foundation of the Germana Colonies in Virginia* 4 (April 1963).

[18]Hartman Rector, Jr., "The Land Choice Above All," *Speeches of the Year: BYU Devotional and Ten-Stake Fireside Addresses, 1974* (Provo, Utah: Brigham Young University Press, 1975), p. 411.

[19]Ibid., p. 410.

[20]Hartman Rector and Connie Rector, *No More Strangers* (Salt Lake City: Bookcraft, 1971), pp. 1-3; Rector Interview. See D&C 123:12.

[21]Rector and Rector, *No More Strangers*, p. 4.

[22]Ibid., pp. 4-5.

[23]Ibid., p. 6.

[24]Ibid., pp. 5-6.

[25]Ibid., p. 7.

[26]Ibid., p. 9.

[27]Ibid.

[28]Jay M. Todd, "Four Sustained in New Callings," *Improvement Era* 71 (May 1968): 10-11.

[29]Ibid.

[30]Rector Interview.

[31]Todd, "Four Sustained," p. 11.

[32]Rector, "The Land Choice Above All," pp. 416-17.

[33]Ibid., p. 418.

[34]Ibid., p. 419.
[35]D&C 101:79-80.
[36]Rector, "The Land Choice Above All," p. 419.
[37]Ibid., p. 424.

Index